ADDITIONAL PRAISE FOR
THE GUARANTEE

"*The Guarantee* helps those of us outside the political melee make sense of where we go from here. She's exactly the kind of person I want articulating a bold economic vision for all of us—here in the present, and the future."

—Jane McGonigal, PhD, game designer and *New York Times* bestselling author of *Imaginable, SuperBetter,* and *Reality Is Broken*

"*The Guarantee* shows us the way forward for America. With a bird's eye view, and the unique ability to see into the future, Natalie Foster brings to the fore the ideas we need most right now."

—Dorian Warren, co-president of Community Change

"Like all good ideas, the guarantees need a good hypewoman and you will find none better than Natalie Foster. Her enthusiasm is contagious in the best possible way. Read this book and you'll find yourself believing whole new ways of being and doing are possible for American people and politics."

—Michael Tubbs, author of *The Deeper the Roots* and former mayor of Stockton, California

"Sometimes an idea whose time has come needs an author whose journey illustrates the way for all of us. By shining a light on her own engagement with new thinkers, creative campaigns, narrative shifts, and rigorous experiments,

Natalie Foster is sketching for us the economy we deserve and the economy we can realistically achieve. *The Guarantee* is a timely treatise on policy—and it is a timeless call to action in the name of justice and solidarity."

—Manuel Pastor, director of USC Equity Research
Institute and co-author of *Solidarity Economics*

"Reading *The Guarantee* makes a new economic paradigm feel not only possible, but real."

—Ilyse Hogue, author of *The Lie That Binds* and
former president of NARAL Pro-Choice America

"Pay attention to *The Guarantee*."

—Eli Pariser, co-director, New Public,
and author of *The Filter Bubble*

"Given the grip of free-market fundamentalism, it's easy to believe that a good job, a dependable income, decent housing, high-quality healthcare, the opportunity to graduate from college, and the chance to build wealth will forever be out of reach for all too many Americans. Natalie Foster's *The Guarantee*—written by not only a keen observer of our country's economy, politics, and culture, but a key player in the fight to make things better—has caused me to reassess my own doubts. I've long been inspired by Foster's work. Now her words have given me something else: more hope than I had."

—Rick Wartzman, author of *Still Broke:
Walmart's Remarkable Transformation*

THE GUARANTEE

THE GUARANTEE

INSIDE THE FIGHT FOR AMERICA'S NEXT ECONOMY

NATALIE FOSTER

WITH ARIANE CONRAD

THE
NEW
PRESS

NEW YORK
LONDON

Requests for permission to reproduce selections from this book should be made
through our website: https://thenewpress.com/contact.

Published in the United States by The New Press, New York, 2024
Distributed by Two Rivers Distribution

ISBN 978-1-62097-846-7 (hc)
ISBN 978-1-62097-869-6 (ebook)
CIP data is available

The New Press publishes books that promote and enrich public discussion and
understanding of the issues vital to our democracy and to a more equitable world.
These books are made possible by the enthusiasm of our readers; the support of a
committed group of donors, large and small; the collaboration of our many partners
in the independent media and the not-for-profit sector; booksellers, who often
hand-sell New Press books; librarians; and above all by our authors.

www.thenewpress.com

Book design and composition by Bookbright Media
This book was set in Wolfgang and Interval Next

Printed in the United States of America

10 9 8 7 6 5 4 3 2 1

For Matt, Huck, and Juno.
You ground me in the here and now,
making my long game bolder.

I stood on the border, stood on the edge, and claimed it as central and let the rest of the world come over to where I was.

—Toni Morrison

CONTENTS

FOREWORD

by Angela Garbes

Make no mistake: keeping yourself and your people alive in this country is hard work, even though we are rarely compensated for this labor. People feel unsupported, overwhelmed, and alone. It is time we reimagine America as a country where people's basic needs are guaranteed.

As an author who writes about care work, my job includes traveling the country, doing events, and being interviewed for television, radio, and podcasts. I get to be in conversation with people—including many parents and professional caregivers—about the labor they do, day in and day out. Caring for our bodies—housing, nourishing, comforting, and maintaining them—is the most essential work humans have to do, the work that makes all other work possible.

At every event where I speak about care work—whether it's at a bookstore, a library, an employee resource group meeting, or a community center—I hear the same question: What can we do?

The first time I was asked, I was surprised. I'm a writer, not a policy expert. I have ideas, of course, but no substantive knowledge of how to make paid family leave, health care, or affordable housing available to everyone in America. While I want to change the way we think and talk about deservedness and work, my strengths are not organizing people or crafting policy.

Thankfully, these strengths are Natalie Foster's. And the

book you are holding in your hands or reading on your screen right now—*The Guarantee*—is the book I'll be telling everyone to read. The book I'll be gifting and placing in people's hands because it is that urgent.

The questions I hear from people all over America are variations on a fundamental one: How do we ensure that we all get what we all deserve? Because we are all born deserving of a decent life. How do we guarantee health care, housing, an income floor, dignified work, family care, college, and an inheritance for every single person in America?

The Guarantee holds the answers to the questions that are on everyone's minds. In Natalie's words, "This is the conversation we need: one that asks how we guarantee these things, not if we should."

Sometimes it can feel hard to know what the "right" thing to do is. This book offers us moral clarity: it is always the right thing to work for a good life for ourselves and others. To believe that all people are our people. To know that our fates are tied together and, working together, there is much we can accomplish.

Because I have two young children and two aging parents, I think about the need for family care and health care on a daily basis. Being able to pay for two college educations is not my most pressing concern, but it's coming. And while I am fortunate to own my home and have relatively predictable housing costs, many people I care about—neighbors, family, friends—live in fear of rent hikes and are at the mercy of landlords and financial institutions.

In *The Guarantee*, Natalie elucidates how our private lives are very much public issues, and how policy choices shape all of our lives. And she demonstrates how the change we need doesn't necessarily require inventing complex new solutions. More often than not, we already know what we need to do—

and the people living closest to the problems are closest to the solutions.

Life moves quickly these days, so quickly that we rarely stop to question the structures we live within, how they are designed, whom they benefit. Rather, we assume things will always be the way they've always been.

Natalie's book is a pause—because we could all use a moment to stop, take a breath, zoom out, see things more expansively. It is also an invitation to take up this work.

In the fall of 2022, Cara Rose DeFabio, a colleague of Natalie's at the Economic Security Project, invited me to join them in Atlanta for a conference on guaranteed income. At that conference I met a father from Stockton, California, who said his self-esteem had been completely transformed by guaranteed income, which allowed him to provide for his children in a way he never thought possible. I met mayors and employees from cities around the country determined to end poverty in their communities. I met a woman working to secure affordable child care for families in New York City, another woman changing the lives of Black mothers in Jackson, Mississippi, by giving them $1,000 a month, no strings attached. I befriended a Chicago rapper making an EP about a woman whose life was changing because of guaranteed income. And I met a young woman working to provide artists in New York State with monthly cash payments, no questions asked. A few months later, I discovered one of my friends—a brilliant dancer and movement teacher—was one of the artists benefiting from that program. Being in that space of creativity and power in Atlanta gave me a renewed sense of purpose, a well of hope to draw from, a feeling of abundance. It still does.

The Guarantee is an invitation to join a movement well under way, but one that also needs more of us—not just policymakers and thought leaders and people from think tanks—but parents, artists, neighbors, everyday people with firsthand knowledge of the issues that affect their families and communities.

The work of guaranteeing a decent, dignified life for everyone requires everyone. What a relief to know that there is a place for me—for all of us—in this movement.

THE GUARANTEE

INTRODUCTION

Imagine a veteran who's ended up on the streets. Her PTSD has made living close to others unbearable. Suddenly, our government decides to invest in leasing an empty motel, so now we can hand her the key to a place of her own, quiet and safe, with her own bathroom and kitchenette.

Imagine a thirty-something who's locked into a job with no potential for advancement. Weighed down by debt, they can't take the risk of pursuing their own dream. The loan they took out to get a degree has turned out to be a ball and chain. Suddenly, our government erases their debt, and it's as if their college education was free. The bandwidth and energy freed up enables them to launch their own business.

Imagine a guy who has worked as a mechanic for twenty years. The asbestos in the brake linings took its toll on his lungs—he's at extra risk from the newly raging respiratory virus. Suddenly, our government procures a COVID-19 vaccine and mobilizes the National Guard to administer it in a parking lot near him—for free. All he needs to do is drive through.

Imagine a mother of three who's also caring for her aging mother. Even though she is constantly on her feet and never has a moment to rest, her work doesn't qualify for benefits and supports that come with having a paid job. Suddenly, our government starts sending a check every month. Finally, it's as if her unpaid caregiving is being counted as work.

This isn't science fiction. These things happened, right here in the United States, and very recently. They are evidence of a great shift, a sea change, the first real opportunity we've had in decades to re-think and re-tool America's economic policy. These events were no miracle, a word that implies that they came into existence inexplicably—instead, they were the result of many years of hard work by dedicated activists, working alongside academics, policymakers, technologists, and others. The foundations and the infrastructure for these tectonic shifts were years in the making.

"Chance favors only the prepared mind," the chemist Louis Pasteur once said of his successful inventions. Once in a while, maybe once in a lifetime, an opportunity comes along that opens the possibility for a true breakthrough. Those who have been steadily laying groundwork and readying themselves for just such an opening can succeed in doing something that previously seemed impossible. This is what happened in 2020. The pandemic opened the door for this extraordinary slate of developments.

They were glimmers—hints, seeds, samples, tastes—of "the Guarantee."

Under the Guarantee Framework, our government, the government of the wealthiest country on earth, takes responsibility for ensuring that every American's basic needs are met. We're talking about fundamental needs like housing, health care, a college education, dignified work, care for elders and children, an inheritance, and an income floor below which no one falls.

The idea of a guarantee itself is not radical. *Guarantees are everywhere in America.*

They are at the bedrock of our country. The Constitution guarantees certain rights like free speech and freedom of religion—to say they are inalienable is the same as saying they are guaranteed. Social Security has become a wildly popular guarantee of support after retirement.

Guarantees are also fundamental to how we live our lives. Any serious commitment we enter into, from mortgage to marriage, any time we sign on the dotted line, means we are fundamentally counting on a guarantee.

Some folks will say "guarantees are socialism," but the truth is, guarantees are foundational to capitalism. We as a nation guarantee a number of things to ensure optimal conditions for businesses and the market: a stable currency, property rights, patent rights, contract rights, bankruptcy protection. Investors are guaranteed liability protection so they can't be personally responsible for corporate activity. We have institutions designed to implement and uphold these guarantees, such as the Federal Reserve, which ensures that the capital market won't collapse.

Yet such optimal conditions, while guaranteed for businesses and markets, are not provided for the people who actually build these businesses, who purchase from them and keep them running. For the last few generations, there has been huge resistance to the idea of our government guaranteeing that the basic needs of Americans are met. Why? Because it flies in the face of America's recent infatuation with a winners-take-all system.

THE GUARANTEE VS. THE GAMBLE

Our current system has us believing that every person has the capacity to become an overnight Gates or Kardashian, to succeed wildly (with "success" here equating to wealth and access). More than half of millennials, the generation born between 1981 and 1996, believe that they will one day be millionaires, a sentiment refracted through popular shows like "*Who Wants to Be a Millionaire?*[1] This belief is rooted in the idea that we're all playing on a level field, that we all have equivalent resources, and that we start out with an equal chance at getting ahead.

Yet in reality, the odds of succeeding in America are terrible. A quality education is increasingly inaccessible to a significant portion of the population. Hourly wages have stagnated since the 1970s, despite increased worker productivity.[2] Anti-labor policies have eroded the earning and bargaining power of workers, while jobs have gotten ever more precarious. Four out of ten Americans are unable to comfortably pull together $400 in an emergency, and 25 percent of Americans have zero saved for retirement.[3]

We are facing the greatest inequality we've had since the 1920s.[4] Three multibillionaires own more wealth than 166 million Americans—which is half of our country's population.[5] With so many Americans having to focus all their energy on keeping their heads above water, we have begun to bear witness to a brain drain of our own making. Barred from succeeding by lack of education or opportunity, or both, many potential intellectual and technological innovators never even make it to the starting gate.

Here's the thing: the odds are we will fail. When we gamble on "making it big," we're betting against the house. The whole game is predicated on all the people who don't make it. People who don't count, by the game's logic: Poor people. People of color. People skipping essential medical procedures, people working seventy hours per week who have to choose between putting food on the table and paying the electric bill, people who live in their cars or on the streets, people in jail.

Despite these odds, we believe that we can make it big,

because it's easier to cling to this fantasy than to face the reality that failure is more likely our fate. It is unbearable to acknowledge that the majority of Americans are going to be losers in this system, because we don't believe that another system is possible.

There is no getting around the fact that part of our resistance to the Guarantees is based in racism. Black leaders have long been espousing the philosophical foundations of the Guarantee in calling for the full belonging of Black people, as well as Native Americans and other people of color.[6] Our continuing challenge as a country is to overcome white resistance to true economic and democratic citizenship for all.

THE END OF THE OLD ERA

Whether it's called Reaganomics, trickle-down economics, or neoliberalism, America's economic policy of the past forty-five years can be summed up by three tenets: total faith in the market, zero faith in the government, and each of us as individuals left grasping for our bootstraps. Although a sliver of elite Americans has reaped huge financial and political gains, for most of us, it has been a half century of worsening outcomes. Wages stagnated. Household debt exploded. Life expectancy is falling. Inequality has soared, concentrating wealth and political power among a privileged few, undermining democracy. The planet's natural resources have been decimated while its natural cycles have been disrupted, with climate change the most severe consequence. Even productivity and growth have stalled out.[7]

The free market that was supposed to meet all our needs has failed to provide us dignified work, decent housing, care for our children and elders, reliable health care, and a better tomorrow for our children. On top of that, like an abusive relationship, it has gaslit us. It tells us that *we* are to blame, that our well-being is solely our personal responsibility, and that if we just studied hard, worked harder, leaned in, faked it 'til we made it, spent wisely, saved frugally, and stayed positive, we'd be fine. Yet no bootstraps are strong enough to pull up someone weighed down by decades of a deeply unequal system.

This economic framework dates back to the chaos of the 1970s, when inflation spiraled out of control, leading to widespread doubt in government's effectiveness at creating economic stability. Free market advocates took advantage of this moment and pushed forward their "markets know best" ideology, which would be championed by Ronald Reagan in the U.S. and Margaret Thatcher in the UK throughout the 1980s, leading to a new world order. Government went from being a trusted partner of the market to being its servant. Over the course of more than forty years, neoliberalism became the increasingly dominant and unquestioned framework for economic policy, built and bolstered across both sides of the political aisle, and from within most academic and legal institutions.

It has had such widespread acceptance and is considered so inevitable that most people think of it like they think of the weather: something that just happens, not the result of choices. But the economy is not like the weather. Instead, it's a house that we construct, with choices we make every step of the way.

For example, in the midst of the Depression, we believed in the role and the power of government to provide stability by creating institutions. To restore trust in the stock market, it created the Securities and Exchange Commission; to provide employment, it created the Civilian Conservation Corps. The choices we made led to the New Deal, which lifted millions of Americans out of poverty (despite doing little for Black Americans and other people of color) through programs like Social Security and the Works Progress Administration, and created thriving communities and a growing economy whose benefits are still with us today.[8] For over three decades after World War II, the economic worldview held that the government could influence markets to honor and reward good work, and could build and invest for the future.

Now we stand amid the ashes of the system that reigned until the crash of 2008. In the aftermath of that seismic moment, we entered a period of transition: from the death of the neoliberal order to the birth of whatever comes next. We are in the midst of this transition right now.

During the 2010s this transition was palpable as we witnessed the rise in popularity of two political candidates—Bernie Sanders and Donald Trump—who bore little resemblance to those who came before. The transition was evident in the ascendancy of economic populism in the Republican Party and the election of Trump, who leveraged the anger and pain of white Americans who had been left behind by free market forces. It's also plain to see in the presidency of Joe Biden, who came of age before Reaganomics took hold, and whose policymaking is actively shaping the economy.

The question is not whether neoliberalism failed, but what can replace it. The house we can choose to construct next can center the inherent worth and dignity of every American. It can prioritize stability. It can unleash mass abundance to replace the scarcity caused by hoarding.

Yet, just as easily, the new economic order could take a different shape, built with the aims of Trump-style authoritarianism. It's important we recognize this transition for what it is and the opportunity it holds, and build the multiracial America that the next generations deserve.

Over the past dozen years, I've been tracking the people who have been steadily laying the foundations of a new framework for American economic and social policy that I call the Guarantee.

The Guarantee holds that economic security is a fundamental right, not something for the lucky few. Regardless of the color of your skin, regardless of your gender, regardless of the kind of work you do every day, regardless of the size of your paycheck or your employment status: you are worthy of economic security. It is your right.

MY STORY

I grew up in Kansas, the daughter of a Christian minister. We lived in the parsonage, right down the street from the church, so my sister and I could run up there on a moment's notice. My childhood was one of community and love, and my parents created a home where people stopped by for meals or stayed over when they needed a place to sleep. I was brought up to understand that heaven would be a place of abundance, where the love of God would prevail. The implication of that understanding was that we should spend our lives working to get more people to heaven.

I left home to attend Pepperdine University, a Christian college outside Los Angeles, on a scholarship that was rewarded as a result of my academics and the virtue of being a preacher's kid. In Kansas it had seemed that the gulf between the haves and have-nots was minimal. After arriving in LA, I went from babysitting in beachside mansions in Malibu to volunteering in soup kitchens and shelters on Skid Row. My eyes were opened to just how big the injustice in the world is. I realized I wanted to spend my life realizing God's love here on earth: to build the kind of world that I imagined heaven would be.

Around that time, I also discovered the power of organizing for social good. Organizing was a natural bridge from my upbringing in the church—there is so much crossover between building a congregation and building a community campaign. In fact, the conservative pastor Rick Warren's book *The Purpose Driven Church* is actually a great organizing primer. Being an organizer is more than a job: it's a worldview, it's a stance, a way of showing up in the world. Organizers listen deeply and make people feel heard. Organizers don't fix things for people—we create opportunities for them to develop their leadership and skills. This worldview has influenced everything I've done.

As my relationship to my faith shifted, I put my energy and attention into organizing. I organized events on campus, building the skills for what would become my first job. My senior year of college, I organized a series of lectures and volunteer activities we called the week of Peace and Justice. I invited the philosopher and social critic Cornel West and the theologian Jim Wallis to speak. We packed the chapel with students. Jim Wallis's words would help point me toward a path of social change: "Two of the great hungers in our world today are the hunger for spirituality and the hunger for social change. The connection between the two is the one the world is waiting for, especially the new generation. And the first hunger will empower the second." What I learned from Cornel West was even more formative: policy and public investment could embody love. "Justice is what love looks like in public," he said.

The beginning of my working life coincided with the moment the internet's tremendous potential to engage and mobilize people became apparent. Writer Clay Shirky captured the excitement in his 2008 book *Here Comes Everybody*, making him something like a prophet of the new phenomenon. He described how the then-still-new communications tools made what was formerly impossible—harnessing the "free and ready participation of a large, distributed group with a variety of skills"—into something simple.[9] Simple, and affordable, and powerful.

I spent several formative years at MoveOn.org, founded in 1998 by Joan Blades and Wes Boyd, two software developers in California. Created as an online petition to oppose the impeachment of President Bill Clinton, MoveOn.org was already a game changer when that petition, originally sent to a hundred friends and colleagues, got a hundred thousand signatures within a week, and ultimately reached a half-million—one of the first viral emails ever. By 2008 MoveOn had 4.2 million members actively engaging on a broad range of progressive issues and making small donations that aggregated to millions of dollars. Even more exciting to me than the electoral work was engaging the members on a broad range of issues, on everything from health care reform to protecting social security to protesting of the Iraq war.

The internet had transformed what was possible. Many of us took what we'd learned about technology and organizing and helped other organizations, or launched our own. I built the first digital team for the Sierra Club, bringing this storied organization into the internet era, and then was recruited to Organizing for America, President Obama's 2.2-million-member grassroots army, right after he was elected. In the two years I was there—leaving after the 2010 midterm elections—we got the Affordable Care Act passed, an important step in a century-long effort to reform health care in America.

Not long after that, I made my way to California. I wasn't

the first in my midwestern family to head to California. During the Dust Bowl, my grandfather's family had loaded up and headed west, looking for opportunity when Oklahoma became uninhabitable. My husband, Matt Ewing, and I would do the same—looking for other ways to make change after spending time inside the grinding political machinery of Washington, DC, on the heels of the Great Recession. In search of people who were building an alternative to the neoliberal economy, I eventually found myself in the emerging innovations of the "sharing economy" or the "collaborative economy," or what was later termed the "gig economy."[10]

The collaborative economy was enabled by the spread of GPS-outfitted smartphones and social networks, which built a new kind of mutual aid and created peer-to-peer marketplaces. For example, using the Airbnb platform, someone could offer a spare room to someone else who needed it, bypassing hotels. The collaborative platforms enabled the rental or use of all kinds of things that were underutilized—from cars to parking spaces, from ballgowns to boats—creating a win for both sides, a little extra cash coming in for the person making the offer, less cash out the door for the person renting instead of buying. Soon platforms connected people around services too: a ride (Uber, Lyft), an Ikea cabinet to be assembled (TaskRabbit), an apartment to be cleaned (Handy).

In early 2013 I co-founded Peers, a guild-like community of people earning a living in the new collaborative economy platforms. "Our vision," I wrote in a launch email, "is a world where abundance is created through access—not ownership—and where entrepreneurialism drives economic independence for the many." The Peers community was global; for our members in countries that were seeing double-digit unemployment rates in the aftermath of the Great Recession, gigs put food on the table.

What these new platforms allowed for most of all was flexibility. For example, a parent with free time during their child's school hours, or a photographer who couldn't get enough work to fill the day, could now take on supplemental gigs via Uber or TaskRabbit. Flexibility became the new rallying cry and the ultimate prize among privileged creative class workers as well as the think tank class who charted new trends in employment.

Despite the flexibility, however, these new jobs didn't offer benefits like health care, sick days, or overtime, similar to most part-time and seasonal jobs. The earnings were often low wage. And the decentralized nature of the platforms made it almost impossible for workers to connect, strategize, and fight for better conditions.

Within a few years, it became clear to me that the majority of people participating in the gig economy were and are doing so to craft their own social safety net—to make up for the fact that the American safety net has some big gaping holes. Ours is one of the most meager in the developed world. The people participating in the flexibility-touting gig economy were, ironically, in search of stability.

Stability—having that foundation of just enough to cover the basics—was what people needed first, the necessities identified in the base level of Maslow's famous pyramid. Yet stability is harder to come by the further down the income ladder you go. Low-wage jobs are characterized by employees having no control over their schedules, caught between the rock of not getting enough hours to qualify for benefits, and the hard place of being constantly on call, unable to plan for child care or another part-time job for supplemental income.

The issues arising for platform workers—and all low-wage workers—made me realize that what was needed was nothing less than an overhaul of the social safety net for the twenty-first century. I left Peers and went in pursuit of stability for the American worker. Alongside the Fight for $15 to raise the minimum wage, which I cheered on, a conversation about a universal basic income was growing and getting particularly loud in Silicon Valley. The idea was that people would need regular cash infusions once automation and artificial intelligence changed the labor market.

As I dug in, I realized we need not reach to the future to make the case for an income floor. We need only look at the last fifty years of persistent poverty, of increasingly precarious work and financial instability to argue that we need a guaranteed income. In fact, organizers have been calling for one since the 1960s. Dorian Warren, a brilliant scholar and racial justice advocate, pointed out to me that Dr. King's last book, *Where Do We Go from Here: Chaos or Community?*, made a strong case in 1967 for a guaranteed income to abolish poverty and aim for racial economic justice.

It seemed to me that an income guarantee could provide stability to Americans who were struggling. Monthly cash infusions, with no strings attached, as a supplement to wages. It would foster economic resilience, in the chaotic aftermath of neoliberalism.

When money is tight, people are forced into impossible choices: to keep the lights on or feed the family, to refill their meds or fill the tank to get to work. As countless studies on guaranteed income experiments have proven, with just a little bit of extra cash on hand, people can decide for themselves what they need. Sometimes that means a parent can quit their third job and spend more time with their children. For someone else, they may be just shy of a certification or degree, and that money can pay for the education that will bump them into the next income bracket. Maybe those dollars are just the cushion an entrepreneur needs to launch a small business, or to help an inventor reduce their hours at work so they have more time to develop a brilliant new idea.

Giving people money was an idea whose time had come.

This realization led me in 2016 to co-found Economic Security Project, a network dedicated to advancing a guaranteed income in America and reining in the unprecedented concentration of corporate power, with activist and scholar Dorian Warren and Facebook co-founder Chris Hughes.

THIS BOOK

Today the Guarantee Framework is no longer pie in the sky. Over the last dozen years, I've been tracking progress toward a whole set of Guarantees: for health care, a home, an income floor, dignified work, family care, college, and an endowment at birth held in trust through adulthood.

I've focused on the stories of these seven key Guarantees, but that doesn't mean this is a definitive list. Until very recently, it went without saying that clean air and clean drinking water should be available to anyone living in America, just as we always assumed that infrastructure like our roads and bridges would be maintained. That we now have communities where these basic conditions of habitability are not assured—my heart goes out to Flint, Michigan, and Jackson, Mississippi—means we need to start from the ground up with the Guarantee Framework. Movements toward other Guarantees, such as ensuring a right to banking and public banks, or publicly owned clean energy production, are thrilling to contemplate.

The point of this book is to illustrate the power of the concept of the Guarantee. Every arena I discuss—whether housing, higher education, health care, or something else—has hundreds of policy papers behind it, and hundreds of ideas for how to finance and implement it. The details *really* matter in policymaking, but that is not the focus of this book. This book offers a conceptual framework to understand what we should be pointing our economic policymaking toward. The Guarantee Framework is like a compass; it's an orientation, not a specific policy prescription.

There are different ways to achieve Guarantees. Some involve the creation of a high-quality public *option* that sits alongside the offerings of the private market, the way public golf courses coexist with private golf courses. Some involve understanding that a certain Guarantee is really a public good, the way we conceive of highways and clean air. The role of the government in achieving a Guarantee might be "industrial policy"—what my colleague Chris Hughes calls "marketcrafting"—harnessing the power of the market in pursuit of social and political goals. These details matter, and this is the conversation we need—one that asks *how* we guarantee these things, not *if* we should.

My goal in writing this book is to show that there is already a real and significant movement under construction—and that it's possible to guarantee economic rights. My aim is to chart its growth and share the stories of some of its champions, visionaries, and architects. I've kept my examples based in America, with very few exceptions. While I find examples from elsewhere to be inspiring, they often come up against a sense among Americans that we'll never be able to do that here: a sense that America's problems are bigger, and our politics more entrenched.

People I feature include: Tara, a sociology student at Harvard turned community organizer, whose work with tenants in Kansas City is foundational to a Homes Guarantee—to ensure everyone in America has safe and permanently affordable housing. There's Astra, whose improbable trajectory between 2011 and 2022 took her from the Occupy Wall Street protests to advising the White House on the abolition of student debt—her work is part of the mandate for a College Guarantee. Then there's Ady, a young father with a fatal disease who is using his last years on earth to advocate for a Health Care Guarantee—to ensure that everyone has access to affordable, high-quality health care. And Ai-jen, the visionary leader of a domestic workers' organization, whose understanding of the caregiving crisis in America serves as firm foundation of a Family Care Guarantee—which would ensure that care is affordable and available to families at all stages of life, and that the jobs pay well for those doing the care work. Then there's Michelle, a West Virginia native who started a platform for workers to organize, and has become a key part of the movement for a Good Work Guarantee. There's also Solana, whose lifelong mission to build wealth for communities of color evolves from savings accounts to an Inheritance Guarantee—or "baby bonds"—ensuring that every child has the funds for an enterprise or an education when they become an adult. Finally, there's my work behind the scenes of the Income Guarantee movement that's been brought into the mainstream by champions like Aisha in Jackson, Mississippi, and Michael in Stockton, California.

Every one of them is quick to point out that they don't stand alone. There are ancestors upon whose shoulders they stand; there are colleagues and members and partners. Not one of their accomplishments can be credited to them alone. Meanwhile, there are literally hundreds if not thousands of amazing people I could have chosen to highlight instead of this cast of characters. I just had to draw a line somewhere—despite my extreme discomfort with it.

My thinking has been shaped by a number of people. Darrick Hamilton, professor of economics and urban policy at

The New School in New York City, is an important part of the foundation. When he shared the framework he calls "An Economic Bill of Rights for the 21st Century," an expansion of President Franklin D. Roosevelt's original proposal, it all clicked into place. This book is intended to build on his work, envisioning what a Human Rights Economy could look like in America. Solana Rice and Jeremie Greer, co-founders of the racial justice organization Liberation in a Generation, have developed the "Liberation Guarantees" through dozens of listening sessions and workshops with organizers and advocates across the country. Our conversations have been transformative to the writing of this book. From his base in North Carolina, the mighty, resolutely nonpartisan Reverend William Barber II and his Poor People's Campaign call for a "third Reconstruction." The powerhouse Felicia Wong, CEO of the Roosevelt Institute, is championing and tracking the "new progressivism"—which she describes as "centered on the role and purpose of government in combating the inequality and market concentration that undergird today's economy." Academics Manuel Pastor and Chris Benner passionately advocate for "solidarity economics." Gene Sperling, national economic adviser under Presidents Clinton, Obama, and Biden, has argued for "economic dignity," the title of his 2020 book. Margaret Levi has pushed for a "moral political economy." While the visions can differ in some of the details, there is a beautiful resonance between us.

One of the most exciting aspects of this story is how different the architects of the Guarantee look from the policymakers who have been designing our society since the country's founding. These are not your grandma's wonks. So many are people of color, which is fitting given the way economic policy has failed people of color. And so many of us are women, which is revolutionary all by itself.

There are so many people working across the spectrum of the issues, on every level from the neighborhood to the nation, who may not think of themselves as part of this broader framework. One of my goals with this book is for us to see how we're connected, how we can learn and build off each other's efforts, and expand what's possible. To that end, I don't get into the very real debates occurring across the fights for these Guarantees. Progress is hard and tensions are inevitable as we walk forward. The Guarantee Framework is offering all of us a home, to see our various fights contextualized inside something bigger: nothing less than the next great American century.

PROVOKE, LEGITIMIZE, WIN

After I unpack the myths and broken promises of the economic system we've had in place for the past forty-five years in chapter 1, and before I describe some of the implications of the Guarantee in chapter 5, there are three chapters that chronicle the development of the Guarantee Framework between 2011 and 2022. In each of those chapters I track advances toward the Guarantees to Homes, College, Health Care, Good Work, Family Care, Income, and Inheritance. I found it fascinating to compare the strategies and wins of the different architects across three modern presidential administrations.

The titles of those three chapters—"Provoke," "Legitimize," "Win"—come from our work at Economic Security Project.[11] We developed this three-phase model to conceptualize the different kinds of work we were doing toward advancing the idea of a guaranteed income. Although there's always work that doesn't fall neatly into a single bucket, and although the progression from provocation to winning is never linear and sometimes even cyclical, it still felt like an apt description of the trends in those years.

I decided to start the stories in 2011 because that year really seemed like a turning point, when the implications of 2008 and the Great Recession had finally sunk in for people: the elites were getting bailouts while the rest of us were getting sold out. Occupy Wall Street was just one facet of what felt like a global primal scream, saying *enough already*, calling for an end to neoliberalism's cruel and dehumanizing reign.

The decade between Occupy Wall Street and 2021 saw the largest mobilization since the 1960s, with the Women's Marches and #MeToo, the rallies at airports following Trump's Muslim bans; then the climate rallies, Standing Rock and the opposition to the Keystone XL pipeline, and the Green New Deal actions; the March for our Lives and vigils after Sandy Hook, Parkland, and other mass shootings; and finally, the uprisings in honor of #BlackLivesMatter in the wake of George Floyd's murder. We are in the midst of a great transition—and the protests in the street and the policies being pursued both reflect it.

The stories culminate in the pandemic period, when so many of the Guarantees came to fruition. We had monthly cash infusions, a moratorium on evictions and student debt, and the development and distribution of a free vaccine. In the midst of a pandemic and recession, we defied gravity and reduced poverty. The country saw a glimmer of the Guarantees. I'm writing this book to show it is possible.

HOPEPUNK ECONOMICS

The belief that humans are intrinsically petty, greedy, mean, and lazy, motivated only by self-interest, underlies a lot of economic orthodoxy. That's also the worldview behind a lot of the most popular storylines we consume, bleak and violent dystopias like that found in *Game of Thrones* or *Breaking*

Bad or *The Dark Knight*. "Grimdark," the genre is sometimes called. Grimdark's opposite is "noblebright": stories of heroes in shining armor who save the day because of their superior intelligence, courage, morality. In 2017, a blogger by the name of Alexandra Rowland suggested there was another option. She named it "hopepunk."

Rather than fetishizing the lone hero, "community is a huge part of hopepunk," Rowland says. "We accomplish great things when we form bonds with each other. We're stronger, we can build higher, and we can take better care of each other."[12] Hopepunk doesn't believe in one happy ending, because it knows that the fight for progress just keeps on going. Therefore, we have to pace ourselves and care for ourselves, so another part of hopepunk is about rest and relaxation, and kindness and softness. All of these are political acts, forms of resistance to the oppression and manipulation we're fighting. And finally, hopepunk is messy: "Hopepunk isn't pristine and spotless. Hopepunk is grubby, because that's what happens when you fight. It's hard. It's filthy, sweaty, backbreaking work," says Rowland.[13]

The hopepunk worldview and aesthetic have been spreading in popular culture, but I'm going to carry it over into this space. "Hopepunk economics" perfectly describes the messy work being done by the architects of the Guarantee. Neoliberalism may have started off as a noblebright solution, with the free market being the pristine, perfect hero; but it created this grimdark world in which we currently live. Hopepunk economics is concrete, not theoretical. It is not shrouded in obscure terminology; it doesn't claim elite, exclusive institutions as its birthplace; and it doesn't care about degrees or titles. Hopepunk economics knows there's no silver bullet and that the work is going to be drawn out, and messy, and involve compromises. It might tack backward or sideways for a bit before moving forward. It does not let perfect get in the way of good. It is stubborn, and it is passionate.

To those who say guarantees are impossible in America, we say: *We're already doing it.*

1

BOOTSTRAPS AND DEADBEATS

It's hard to remember how total the refusal was, before 2011, to hold the economic system accountable for the damage it was causing. For decades, wages and the economic well-being of average Americans had stagnated or dwindled, while the pundits—using measures such as housing prices, gross domestic product, and the stock market—boasted of an economy that was doing just fine, was often in fact "booming." Everyone seemed to be enthralled by the success story of financialization, where investment banks and hedge funds profited spectacularly based on rampant speculation.

In 2003, 2004, 2005, our mailboxes and airwaves were filled with offers from banks to expand our credit. It didn't matter if you were financially strapped, you could still qualify for a loan, they told us. You can afford a house beyond your wildest dreams, they insisted. Yes, it seemed too good to be true, but they were so reassuring. Of course they were—they were being paid to make these deals, and they weren't the ones left holding the bag: they were passing the risk on to Wall Street, which repackaged it as a form of high-yield investment. Wall Street even took bets on our likeliness to fail to pay back the loans, and sold those bets to fancy investors. We regular Americans thought we were finally achieving the dream, when, in fact, speculators were just using us as pawns.

In late 2007 the house of cards toppled, a slow-motion

wreck that spread over the ensuing years. Rates of unemployment and home foreclosures reached levels not seen since the Great Depression. Ten million Americans lost their homes.[1] Black and Latino Americans lost *half* their collective wealth.[2]

Rather than taking action to address the majority of people's losses and pain, our government instead invested billions to prop up the system, bailing out the profiteers and speculators. Then politicians used these bailouts as an excuse to cut back further on programs that provided us with essential things like support in old age and higher education, instead letting corporations make more money providing them through privatization.

And even after all of this, to call the economic system into question was to be un-American. The free market made America what it was; it powered the American Dream. It was a foregone conclusion; no alternatives existed; no politicians dared to do anything but serve and bolster it. The free market was untouchable and blameless, because neoliberal ideology, pervasive as the air we breathed, made it unthinkable to blame the free market.

In her 2010 book about consumerism and waste, *The Story of Stuff*, the environmentalist Annie Leonard called capitalism the "Economic-System-That-Must-Not-Be-Named," a riff on the villain Voldemort. (It resonates with me, as my kids are deep into Harry Potter.) As late as 2010, even using the word "capitalism"—let alone talking about inequality or neoliberalism—marked you. Complicit silence was the first rule of the every-man-for-himself Fight Club of our economy: *we don't talk about it.*

On the heels of the Great Recession, the 2010 midterm elections had been brutal for Democrats, who lost state houses and governorships, six seats in the Senate, and sixty-three seats in the House. Much of the credit was given to the Tea

Party—the angry, decentralized group of right-wing populists who showed up all summer at town hall meetings across
the country to undermine Obamacare, shouting about "death
panels," "big government takeover," and communism. Looking back, it's clear there's a direct line from then to today, from
the Tea Party's aggressive antics to the bizarre tantrums and
unapologetic racism of Representative Marjorie Taylor Greene
of Georgia and Donald Trump; there's another line straight
from the "birthers" (who alleged that Obama was ineligible to
be president on account of his birthplace) to QAnon.

Van Jones, then best known as a criminal justice reformer
and environmental and civil rights leader, wrote about that
moment and the Tea Party's success, in his 2012 book:

> As Americans continued to suffer the ongoing
> consequences of the financial crisis, and as the
> nurturing aspects of [Obama's] hope-and-change
> campaign dissolved, the pain in America's heart
> intensified. Everyday people needed their sense of
> loss and fear acknowledged. People needed a sto-
> ry that made sense of that pain. Into the vacuum,
> the Tea Party swooped. But rather than trying to
> restore hope, the Tea Partiers were promoting a
> different emotion . . . fear.[3]

Van had served as President Obama's green jobs adviser in
2009, and we stayed in touch while living in Washington,
DC, and working in the administration. By the end of 2010,
he had a vision for an organization that would offer Americans a different story to make sense of their pain. He wanted to call it Rebuild the Dream (which was also the name of
that 2012 book). Van had teamed up with veteran political
organizer Billy Wimsatt, and he needed someone to run the

organization who understood digital organizing. When he asked, I didn't hesitate.

So, late in 2010, I left my role as head of digital at President Obama's grassroots army, Organizing for America. I remember a friend saying to me that I could literally write my own ticket to anywhere. The Obama brand was the most recognizable in the world at that point, and we'd built something powerful. I decided that teaming up with Van and Billy to build a counterweight to the Tea Party, and lay claim to an economy that works for everyone, was my next mission. We might fail, probably would, but that was a risk worth taking.

We co-organized "Save the Dream" rallies in February 2011 to support the protests against union-busting legislation proposed by Tea Party governors in Wisconsin and Ohio. Fifty thousand people turned out. Then we crowdsourced a new economic agenda for the country called the Contract for the American Dream. More than 131,000 Americans came together online and in their communities to write and rate 25,904 solutions for our economy and our democracy, which led to the creation of a ten-point agenda. Over three hundred thousand people formally endorsed it. By the end of the summer, we had a half a million members across the country, ready to engage around student loans, #jobsnotcuts, higher taxes on the ultra-wealthy, and progressive candidates to challenge the rash of Tea Party wins.

In an email dated June 23, 2011, I wrote to our network:

> The idea [of Rebuild the Dream] is this: The American Dream—the fundamental idea that people who work hard should be able to keep their jobs, stay in their homes, and build a better life for their children—is being stolen from us as the economy gets worse. And for many of us, it never existed.

Movements need support hubs, and they need storytellers. The goal isn't to build the next big thing, but rather, to join all of our allies who've been doing movement building work for a long time and help connect the big things already happening. We want to inspire a swarm, not build an empire. We have some ideas on how to do this, but it's going to take the movement's best thinking to do this right.

Having spent the summer listening to the experiences of Americans across the country, it was clear that we needed to spread a story about how the economy worked that would challenge the prevailing narrative and the claims from Capitol Hill that the country was too broke to invest in its people.

Heather McGhee, one of the most talented economic thinkers of our generation, who was then at the think tank Demos, also knew we needed a new economic story. In 2011, Heather and I teamed up to produce a simple slideshow telling the story of the American economy.[4] The central thesis of the story was that economic policy was something that people had constructed, with choices made along the way. It was critical that folks understood that *the economy is not like the weather—something that just happens to us and is outside of our control—it's more like a house that we build.* The slideshow was designed so that Rebuild the Dream members, meeting in church basements, college lecture halls, and living rooms across the country, could take it and use it to unpack the story of our economy.

The three keys to the prevailing story—total faith in the market, zero faith in the government, and each of us as individuals pulling ourselves up by our bootstraps and responsible for our own success—were billed as inescapable truths, like gravity or algebra. But actually, they weren't like the laws of science; they were the stuff of myths.

Seeing the myths is the essential first step in building something new.

MYTH 1: THE FREE MARKET IS INFALLIBLE

In the neoliberal story, the market provides a fair and level playing field for individuals and companies to compete on, and appropriately awards benefits to those who are superior. Markets identify the value of everything, autonomously and infallibly. Prices are a means of allocating scarce resources efficiently, according to need and utility, as governed by supply and demand. A scarcity of what we want and need is what drives competition among us and among the businesses and markets providing the goods and services. For the price system to function efficiently, markets must be free and competitive.

When those who emerge as the winners of competition are unfettered by taxes and regulations, their wealth will trickle down, providing more jobs, higher wages—lifting all boats. The processes of the market are inherently fairer and more rational than any political decision-making process. Government, and all institutions, even nature, are actually just actors within its play. All interactions are economic, all behavior is economic, every arena is measured and assessed by the market's metrics.

However, contrary to the story's promise of stronger growth and greater efficiency, starting in 1980, the overall growth rate of America's economy slowed. While the economy grew at 3.9 percent a year from 1950 to 1980, since 1980 it has only grown at a rate of 2.6 percent.[5] Wage growth also slowed and stagnated, with wages no longer tracking to increases in pro-

Workers produced much more, but typical workers' pay lagged far behind

Disconnect between productivity and typical worker's compensation, 1948–2013

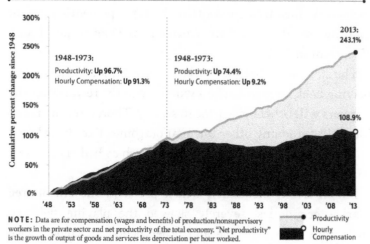

NOTE: Data are for compensation (wages and benefits) of production/nonsupervisory workers in the private sector and net productivity of the total economy. "Net productivity" is the growth of output of goods and services less depreciation per hour worked.

SOURCE: Economic Policy Institute analysis of Bureau of Labor Statistics and Bureau of Economic Analysis data

ductivity for the first time in the postwar era.[6] That means that, even when the factory making the widgets made more of them in less time, perhaps also with fewer components or inputs, this increase—which translates also to a greater profit—was not reflected in how much the workers making the widgets were being paid.

To be clear: there was growth in the financial sector. Financial sector profits grew from constituting less than 10 percent of total corporate profits in 1950 to nearly 30 percent of total corporate profits in 2013.[7] The growth came from increased trading activities full of conflicts of interest and risky bets, unregulated shadow banking (lenders operating outside the rules of traditional banking), and an explosion of household credit: from 48 percent of GDP in 1980 to 99 percent of GDP in 2007.[8] Within a generation, the financial sector exploded out of proportion to the rest of the economy.

Free market policies not only failed to produce more healthy growth overall, they also significantly increased income inequality. Research shows that the top 1 percent's share of total income doubled from 7 percent in 1979 to just under 15 percent in 2021.[9]

The story says that the market is race-blind: it offers a fair playing field, anyone can be a winner, and the rewards for the winners will benefit everyone in society. Therefore, any racial inequality, and any other unequal outcomes like those based on gender, owe to individual failings such as bad choices and lack of effort or skill.

But in truth, inequality, which predated the era of free market economics, severely skewed the playing field, so that many—Black people and other people of color, above all—never stood a chance at winning within the rules of the market. Neoliberalism failed to account for—or simply ignored—the web of historical rules and institutions that led to unequal racialized and gendered economic outcomes. By claiming that unequal outcomes were the result of personal failures, that story hampered our society-wide ability to challenge white supremacy and racism. At every level of education, people of color experience higher rates of unemployment, are paid less than their white counterparts, have fewer assets than their white counterparts, and accrue less wealth. Despite civil rights era rules that were put in place to distribute the fruits of prosperity more equitably, racial disparities in income and wealth have only grown in the decades since then. Between 1983 and 2013, Black and Latino families saw their median wealth drop from $6,800 and $4,000 to just $1,700 and $2,000, respectively.[10] Meanwhile, between 1984 and 2009, the racial wealth gap (between a representative sample of white and Black families) nearly tripled, from $85,000 to $236,500.[11] Race-blind policies don't have race-blind impacts.

In addition to exacerbating inequality, free market policies were also terrible for the majority of workers. Since the early 1980s, most new jobs have been low-wage jobs, and social mobility—the ability to climb the proverbial ladder from one class to the next—declined. In turn, the dream of our children being better off than us has slowly faded.

Relaxed antitrust enforcement, a key pillar of free market economics, was supposed to enable huge companies to benefit from economies of scale, reducing costs for consumers: that didn't pan out. And as fewer and fewer large firms came to dominate the economy, we have seen fewer and fewer small businesses succeed. Our economy is now both top-heavy and less dynamic, with less genuine competition.

MYTH 2: THE GOVERNMENT IS INEPT

We have been taught that government is inherently incompetent, and captive to special interests. In this telling, if government interferes, it will disrupt the natural flow of the market. The market, according to its logic, distributes wealth to those that deserve it; and any actions on the part of government to distribute that wealth differently—to redistribute it in the form of taxes and public benefits, for example—equates to punishing the winners and rewarding the losers. Those social objectives once achieved through public programs are better achieved by harnessing the market—through private enterprise. The smaller the government, the better.

"Government is not the solution to our problem; government is the problem," President Ronald Reagan said in his 1981 inaugural address.[12]

When ordinary people talk about wanting "small government," some mean that they don't want rules imposed
on their individual freedom, such as mandates for vaccines
or mask-wearing, or limits on their ability to buy or carry
guns. Others mean that they don't want to pay (more, or any)
taxes—in this vein, they cite corruption and waste in how
government money is spent; some talk about fiscal restraint
and balancing the budget. Still others mean they believe that
a government that spends too much on a social safety net creates dependence and laziness in its citizens; viewing society
as divided into "makers" and "takers," they believe that "big
government" takes too much from the former to support the
latter.

It wasn't always this way. Once upon a time, polls showed
that the great majority of Americans had faith in the government. During the 1950s and until 1964, nearly 80 percent of
Americans said they could trust the federal government to
do the right thing most of the time. That percentage started
to drop in the mid-1960s, falling to 60 percent in 1968, to
50 percent by 1975, and down to 30 percent by 1979. By 2014,
only 13 percent of Americans believed the federal government could be trusted most of the time.[13]

Those polls almost certainly reflect the opinions of white
America, whose trust began to wane in the second half of
the 1960s, when the civil rights movement and President
Johnson's War on Poverty and Great Society programs began
to distribute America's rights and resources more fairly to
people of color. The cost of those domestic programs, cou-
pled with the cost of the Vietnam War, caused prices to rise,
which was exacerbated by the oil shocks in the early 1970s.
As a result, imported goods cost Americans far less, leading America's own industries to cut shifts and then shutter.
White working-class Americans—who were already resent-

ful of the Great Society programs—were hard hit by the mass layoffs (of course, people of color were hit just as hard if not harder). They were primed for race-baiting.

As Reagan took office in 1981, many conservatives wanted to boost the private sector and cut back government programs. Since Americans of all stripes were attached to the basic social safety net and protection for consumers and workers, conservatives stoked the growing racial resentment in order to win the votes they needed for tax cuts and deregulation. They propagated a myth that hard-working white Christian men were under attack by a government in thrall to lazy minorities and unionized workers. As Heather McGhee describes in her book *The Sum of Us*:

> Conservatives like President Reagan told white voters that government was the enemy, because it favored Black and brown people over them—but their real agenda was to blunt government's ability to challenge concentrated wealth and corporate power. The hurdle conservatives faced was that they needed the white majority to turn against society's two strongest vessels for collective action: the government and labor unions. Racism was the every-ready tool for the job.[14]

The term "welfare state" became synonymous with "big government," based on a theory of dependency: receiving government support is addictive. Cuts to social programs were justified as the way to end poor people's dependency and addiction.

> Even though welfare was a sliver of the federal budget and served at least as many white people

> as Black, the rhetorical weight of the welfare
> stereotype—the idea of a Black person getting for
> free what white people had to work for—helped
> sink white support for all government. . . . Govern-
> ment, it turned out, had become a highly racialized
> character in the white story of our country.[15]

In other words, being "for small government" had racialized implications.

In fact, the "inept government" story is contradicted by the
fundamental role that the government actually must play
in free market ideology: creating the enabling conditions to
privilege markets and enforcing those protections. Examples
of this include the rules for bankruptcy proceedings and the
rules defining property, patents, trademarks, and copyrights.

The question is not whether government is involved in rules
and regulations—because it always is—the question should
really be: for whose benefit are those rules and regulations
written? Our economic policy since the 1980s has clearly prioritized the interests of corporations and the wealthy above
all, pretending that their goals were the common interest.
The truth is, a democratically elected government is the only
entity with the potential to hold the private sector accountable, and we need it to return to the days when it did so.

Economist Mariana Mazzucato, who focuses on the relationship between the public sector and innovation, challenges the prevailing story that government is inefficient
and clunky and the supposedly dynamic, risk-taking private sector—freewheeling entrepreneurs and visionary venture capital—is better suited to drive innovation.[16] Contrary
to common belief, Mazzucato says, public funding has often

taken more risks than privately funded venture capital. In her book *The Entrepreneurial State*, she writes:

> In countries that owe their growth to innovation— and in regions within those countries, like Silicon Valley—the State has historically served not just as an administrator and regulator of the wealth creation process, but a key actor in it, and often a more daring one, willing to take risks that businesses won't. This has been true . . . across the entire innovation chain, from basic research to applied research, commercialization and early-stage financing of companies themselves. Such investments have proved transformative, creating entirely new markets and sectors, including the Internet, nanotechnology, biotechnology and clean energy. . . . In all these cases, the State dared to think—against all odds—about the "impossible": creating a new technological opportunity, making the initial large necessary investments; enabling a decentralized network of actors to carry out the risky research; and then allowing the development and commercialization process to occur in a dynamic way.[17]

Meanwhile the myth of government incompetence has succeeded in concealing or disguising a lot of government programs that Americans actually value. When surveyed, people say they are not using and have never used a "government social program"; but then when the researchers run through a list of specific programs, like student loans or the home-mortgage-interest deduction, it turns out that almost all of the survey respondents have benefited from them. Political science professor Suzanne Mettler calls the phenomenon the "submerged state." Mettler shows how the government's role is made to appear as though played by the private sector. For example, loans that are subsidized and guaranteed by the government but offered through private banks and government-sponsored entities, or benefits that take the form of tax breaks or incentives, or services carried out by nonprofits that are contracted by the government. Industries and upper-income folks often benefit the most from hidden government programs—for example, the home-mortgage-interest deduction, tax benefits for retirement contributions (such as to an IRA), the tax exclusion for employer-sponsored health insurance, and subsidies of industries.[18]

MYTH 3: RESPONSIBILITY LIES WITH THE INDIVIDUAL

Margaret Thatcher famously claimed that there is no such thing as society, there is only the individual.[19] Individualism views people as completely independent and autonomous—it dictates that individuals must compete fiercely in looking out for their own self-interest. To rely on anything or anyone else is a sign of weakness and dependency.

Individualism holds this to be true even though it directly contradicts what we know from the natural laws that govern our species. Individualism contradicts our very biology and ecology—such as the fact that any single human body is actually host to a number of other species (only 43 percent of the body's total cell count are human cells); or that there is a constant interchange between an individual and the environment, with air, water, and food just the most obvious examples.[20] As mammals, and more specifically primates, humans are fundamentally ultrasocial, literally wired to sense and respond to each other. In order to survive, let alone thrive, we need social bonds. Isolated and marginalized individuals are most likely to suffer and be stressed out (or, in more primitive times, to starve or be picked off by predators).[21]

Now, however, we're living amidst a resurgence of collectivism, which, unlike individualism, emphasizes the value of collective wisdom, dialogue, and relationships as determinants of success. As the popular proverb has it: "If you want to go fast, go alone. If you want to go far, go together."

But in the old story, individual outcomes, whether positive or negative, are a result of personal choices and character. The old story says poor people are poor because they are lazy, and the wealthy are rich because they work harder. This idea of deservedness, or meritocracy, goes all the way back to the country's beginnings. In contrast to the old European societies, where status, and even what kind of profession you could pursue, was automatically determined at birth, as a consequence of the family you were born into, part of the founding idea of America was the concept of the proverbial level playing field, where wealth and advantage are the appropriate rewards for skill and talent.

Today, while a majority of the population believes they can "make it big," the data shows that only a tiny percentage of people actually achieve this. When asked to rank the factors that affect this kind of social mobility, Americans regard hard work and ambition most highly. The quality of their education, having access to the right people, growing up in a stable family and in the right neighborhood—people rank these influences next in importance. How wealthy your family is, your gender, and your race, all come at the very bottom, although Black people rank race almost twice in importance compared with how white people rank it.[22]

In the real world, the ability to succeed, and to amass wealth, is actually connected to systemic factors as well as to history. Exclusions and discrimination barring you from jobs, from housing, and from education, historically and into the present day, prove a huge detriment to your ability to succeed. A group of researchers from the U.S Census Bureau and Harvard and Brown Universities (including MacArthur Foundation "genius grant" awardee Raj Chetty) found that your residential zip code—where you grow up—is more predictive of social mobility and economic fate than any other national metric.[23] Disinvestment in communities—which might show up as a lack of grocery stores from which to buy quality food, or overcrowded classrooms, or dangerous housing—has a profoundly negative impact on the ability to succeed of the people growing up and living in those communities. Geographical luck-of-the-draw affects the quality of schools you can attend; the quality of the air you breathe, water you drink, and food you have access to; and the role models accessible to you—as well as the quality of jobs available to your parents and later to you. Policies that intentionally kept benefits from people of color, like the omission of domestic and agricultural workers from the 1930s labor protections and provisions, further work against wealth. Part of the reason why historical events still have such a powerful influence on people's success today is the intergenerational transfer of wealth—families passing down wealth, especially in the form of real estate. White families have eight times more wealth on average than Black families.[24]

Meritocracy is so damaging because it has led to the belief that just as winners deserve rewards, those who struggle and fall behind and fail are also responsible for their fates. They are to blame, rather than the system that we know has long been unfair, exploitative, and oppressive. Jhumpa Bhattacharya and Anne Price of the Maven Collaborative have developed an alternate term for the personal responsibility myth: "toxic individualism." "This narrative rears its ugly head in many iterations across sectors," they write. "In jobs and workforce conversations this often shows up as 'skills gap' or a lack of 'soft skills'—a.k.a. if only 'certain people' had better behavior, or we just need to 'upskill' folks looking for work and all will be well. In racial wealth inequity work it often shows up in our near-obsession with teaching financial literacy or financial coaching as a solution to the problem."[25]

And it's not just that the successful judge and look down on the unsuccessful (with success here equating to wealth and access); the unsuccessful blame themselves and experience much higher rates of anxiety, depression, and even suicide.[26] It's only been exacerbated by social media amplifying the comparisons between "winners" and "losers."

Our bootstraps have failed us. Or actually, they performed as intended. I've seen it said elsewhere, but it bears repeating: the expression "to pull yourself up by your bootstraps" originally referred to an impossible task. You literally cannot even budge the weight of your body by tugging on the little tabs meant to help you get your boots on, let alone go "up"—whatever that's supposed to mean. Up in the air? Up a ladder? It was only over time that the idiom evolved to mean what it does today: that socioeconomic advancement is something that everyone can achieve if they just try hard enough.

The bootstraps ideology has left us anxious, depressed, and with one of the most immoral facts of our time: an astounding racial wealth gap.

IT'S TIME FOR A NEW STORY

The three myths underlying neoliberalism have been hugely influential. The neoliberal story leveraged that most hallowed of American values, freedom, which in this context means "being left alone to do what I want." It promised us more autonomy by diminishing the reach of government. A freer market would translate to more choice, and choice for the consumer was easily conflated with personal freedom. But— as many anti-consumerist critics have pointed out—true freedom is not having a dozen coffees on the menu to choose from, or hundreds of brands of jeans; true freedom is having a voice and a hand in *creating the menus* rather than choosing from their options. As times got tougher, as prosperity became more elusive, freedom in the *real* sense—the sense of having real choices, like about where you can live, what kind of work you can pursue, what kind of education your children can get—that freedom dwindled.

But the story got in our heads, to the point that even those of us who are suffering from its fallout wind up criticizing ourselves for failing. We believe what the story tells us, according to its standards of personal responsibility: it's our fault. The story's logic became total, eclipsing other worldviews until it became, like the air we breathe, invisible. The first order of business after the crash of 2008 was to make the fallacies of the old story visible.

There were many who jumped in to do so. Naomi Klein had just published *The Shock Doctrine*, which argued that politicians exploited crises such as natural disasters and wars to pass cruel and unpopular neoliberal policies while citizens were too overwhelmed to protest them. Documentary filmmaker Michael Moore released *Capitalism: A Love Story*, which exposed the greed behind wealth inequality. French economist Thomas Piketty's heavyweight book *Capital in the Twenty-First Century* surprised everyone by becoming an overnight sensation, with its central thesis that the free market caused wealth concentration and inequality by design, not by accident, and the only solution to it was government intervention. *Capital* pushed another book exposing the underside of financialization off the top of the bestseller list: *Flash Boys* by Michael Lewis. Hollywood joined in the fray, releasing movies like *Margin Call*, *The Wolf of Wall Street*, and *The Big Short*, all of which skewered Wall Street corruption.

Around this time, Felicia Wong took over the helm of the New York–based think tank the Roosevelt Institute. Under her leadership, and employing its rigorous focus on data, the Institute helped tell a different story, advancing a critique of corporate power, challenging the current economic orthodoxy, and thinking through the next viable economic worldview. Roosevelt's research made clear that markets without rules unduly concentrate wealth into the hands of a few, making it too hard for small businesses to compete, crowding out our creativity and entrepreneurship, and capturing political power among the financial elite. And, in the tradition of Franklin and Eleanor, it called for government—public institutions—to play an important role in creating stability in the future. "Inequality is a choice—one that we make with the rules we create to structure our society and economy," the Roosevelt Institute declared in its seminal 2015 report *Rewriting the Rules of the Economy.*[27]

Felicia studied the rise of neoliberalism and shared what she learned with me. She pointed to the Mont Pelerin Society, founded in 1947 by philosopher and economist Friedrich Hayek and still in existence today. Hayek, who was Austrian, was troubled by the rising power of workers, whose strikes and unrest protested the advances in international trade at the expense of their wages. It was democracy that gave those workers power. At Mont Pelerin, the Swiss mountain resort where he gathered together like-minded scholars, the group created a statement of aims for how to place the market beyond the reach of democracy.[28]

To propagate its ideas, the Mont Pelerin Society published books and articles, hosted seminars and conferences, and engaged in public debates. It funded academic centers steeped in its philosophy, most notably the University of Chicago school of economics. One of its key strategies was to build a network of people sympathetic to its cause who would show up in all arenas of society. They insinuated themselves in institutions like the General Agreement on Tariffs and Trade and its successor, the World Trade Organization, and the European Economic Community and its successor, the European Union. In the U.S. they made their voices heard via the American Legislative Exchange Council and the State Policy Network, where they held annual trainings for state legislators and enlisted them as members. They drafted legislation for their political and corporate stakeholders. By the time Margaret Thatcher and Ronald Reagan were elected, Mont Pelerin's thinking had pervaded the policy realm.

My takeaway was that the Mont Pelerin Society had played a very strategic long game in order to get its story of the economy to prevail. That was the level of effort required to introduce a new story of the economy and make it stick.

By the fall of 2011, there was another populist movement brewing, inspired by the recent uprisings during the Arab Spring, that tapped into the same roots of pain and disappointment among the American people that the Tea Party had. The movement's members were mostly young and were living in an economy offering few future prospects. In September of 2011, their tents mushroomed in Manhattan's Zuccotti Park; they marched down to the financial district daily, brandishing their handmade posters: *We Are the 99%! I'm Young, Educated and Angry! They Got a Bailout—We Got Sold Out!* Decentralized and leaderless (or leader-*full*), soon there were Occupy sites across the country, and then the world. With their framing of the 99 percent and the 1 percent, they gave us a simple, powerful way to talk about the broken promises of our system.

Momentum was building around the understanding that the economy wasn't working for anybody but the 1 percent. It was clear that the old economic myth was cracking and crumbling, but what was less clear was what would replace it. During the next decade, we would lay the foundations for the bedrock of a new economic system, one that could usher in an economic future that creates widespread security and resilience, ends the racial wealth gap, and affirms the inherent value and dignity of everyone.

2
PROVOKE (2011–2016)

Between 2011 and 2016, signs of the neoliberal order's weakness became apparent, as people from many different backgrounds challenged it, mounting a resistance. The resistance wasn't centralized and it wasn't always pretty—it was organic, spontaneous, hopepunk. It would involve everyone from Occupy Wall Street to think tanks, from academics to nurses, from traditional unions to tech companies. In these years we started articulating the need for the Guarantees, even if we weren't yet clear on the exact shape or the strategy to enact them. Advocates began to move provocative ideas from the margins to the mainstream. As the popular saying goes, "First they ignore you, then they laugh at you, then they fight you, then you win."

We were challenging and dismantling the old story and the ways—the total reliance on the market, the zero reliance on government, and the way we as individuals were left grasping for our bootstraps. In doing so, we were laying the foundations for what would come.

HOMES

The protests of 2011 were a direct response to the economic hurricane that began in late 2007, and the eye of that hurricane was housing. Millions of Americans lost their homes to foreclosures between 2007 and 2009. Black and Latino borrowers who were targeted by the subprime mortgage practices of the early 2000s lost their houses at twice the rates of their white counterparts.[1]

The fault for the meltdown was attributed not to banks or Wall Street, but to *people who really shouldn't have bought homes—irresponsible people—who bought homes on easy credit.* I was one of them, having scraped together enough from my earnings as a field organizer for the Sierra Club in Atlanta to purchase my first house, in March of 2008. I had bought into the story that becoming a homeowner would be the surest path to stability, in part because we'd always lived in the parsonage growing up. After searching long and hard, I had found a little bungalow that I could just afford—with a $160,000 price tag—thanks to one of those nifty variable-rate mortgages. Just weeks later, the unraveling of subprime mortgages would dominate headlines. By the end of that fateful year my new house was worth less than half that: $60,000. Like most Americans, I had zero safety net. My parents and family were in no position to help me. I was fortunate to just then meet the man who is now my husband, and move in with him. I found a tenant and rented the bungalow for just enough to cover the mortgage. Some eight years later I was finally able to sell the place for exactly what I had paid for it. I feel lucky, when I compare my fate to millions of other Americans who lost their homes to foreclosures and were forced into substandard rental units, or their cars, or shelters, or onto the streets, while their former homes stood empty or were scooped up cheap by financiers waiting to turn real estate into their next cash cow.

Triage

When NYPD swooped in and swept the Occupiers out of Zuccotti Park in the wee hours of November 15, 2011, Occupy's press releases defiantly declared afterward: "You cannot evict an idea whose time has come!"[2] Foreclosures, evictions, and homelessness were on many of the protesters' minds. Housing would become a long-game focus for many of them. But before anyone could focus on solutions, they first had to stem the bleeding. Some of the Occupiers subsequently launched Occupy Our Homes, joining forces with existing community organizations such as ACORN and People's Action, which had been fighting predatory lenders and defending homeowners since the early 2000s.

Early in October 2011, I received an email from longtime activist Stephen Lerner, drawing attention to the story of a Los Angeles resident named Rose Gudiel. Rose was a government employee of the state of California. She lived with her father, who was a warehouse worker, as well as her mother, who used a wheelchair, and her brother. The whole family pitched in to make the mortgage payments for the house that Rose had purchased in a working-class neighborhood called La Puente. When in 2009 the state ordered unpaid furloughs because of California's fiscal crisis, Rose lost a chunk of her income. Then her brother died and, without his income, Rose missed a mortgage payment. Her mortgage servicer, One-West Bank, immediately began foreclosure proceedings. Rose repeatedly asked for a modification of her loan, but the bank told her she didn't qualify for help and gave her an order to vacate the house. At that point, Rose turned to Alliance of Californians for Community Empowerment.

Rose's home defense coincided with the launch of Occupy Los Angeles. Rose spoke at Occupy's general assemblies several times, and Occupy folks pitched tents in front of her house to deter the LA Sheriff's office from enforcing the eviction. On October 4, 2011, hundreds of people turned out for a march up the winding hills of Bel Air to the stately home of

OneWest Bank's chairman, a peaceful pilgrimage that proved an embarrassment for the bank.

The update email I received from Stephen a few days later was thrilling:

> On Wednesday, October 5th they took over the lobby of Fannie Mae (current holder of the loan) in Pasadena, shut down business with songs and chants, and Rose, her mother, and 7 other supporters refused to leave when the police issued their final warning. The group of 9 were arrested as the crowd of 150 outside cheered. On Thursday, October 6th, Rose received a call from OneWest saying that Fannie Mae was willing to rescind the foreclosure and put a loan modification on the table! Now it's time to launch the *"Let a Million Roses Bloom"* campaign. Victims of unjust foreclosures across the country are taking a stand to defend their homes—Re-Occupy their homes.[3]

The response to Rose's story was indicative of the power of the alliances between Occupiers and more experienced community groups including the Service Employees International Union (SEIU), New York Communities for Change, and Take Back the Land—in addition to ACORN and People's Action. Together, this coalition of groups decided to plan a national day of action on December 6, 2011. Protests and direct actions in twenty-five cities around the country disrupted auctions where foreclosed houses were being parceled out to investors (mostly hedge funds and private equity groups), and halted the evictions of homeowners who had fallen behind on their mortgage payments—sometimes even camping in front yards to block eviction orders from being served, as they'd done at Rose's.

Although these actions were still considered the work of radicals, the issues they drew attention to were starting to be taken seriously by the mainstream. Amy Schur of Alliance of Californians for Community Empowerment talked about the significance of the moment:

> It used to be that people felt they got themselves into their own mess [with their mortgages]. To a large degree, they would blame themselves. That meant they were hesitant to come forward. They didn't think of this as an issue you could fight collectively. That has really shifted, for a lot of reasons. We have a narrative now: "Big banks crashed the economy. They got bailed out. They keep paying themselves bonuses. But what have they done for Main Street?" People have become much more comfortable thinking of it that way, instead of just blaming themselves. The right wing had done a pretty effective job of getting people to blame government unions, immigrants or poor people [for our economic problems], as opposed to those who are really to blame. But, at this point, there is a tremendous awareness of the culpability of Wall Street banks.[4]

This was a sea change in the attitudes of average Americans. It meant that the myth of personal responsibility was unraveling. The emergent "We are the 99%" refrain helped people see themselves as in this together.

Renters Enter the Picture

In 2011, Tara Raghuveer was studying sociology at Harvard. Tara's parents, both doctors, had immigrated from India to the U.S. by way of Australia when Tara was in fourth grade. They landed in Kansas City, where she grew up in a middle-class, predominantly white neighborhood. "At college I studied housing," she said, "but the reading I was being assigned was basically neoliberal propaganda, decrying the failures of public housing and calling for solutions from the private market. And then I read Matthew Desmond's dissertation in the *American Journal of Sociology* on eviction in Milwaukee."[5]

Sociologist Matthew Desmond had started his ethnographic research in Milwaukee in 2008. For his Milwaukee Area Renters Study and his Eviction Court Study, he interviewed 1,100 tenants and collected stories and extensive data on housing, residential mobility, eviction, and poverty.[6] The vast amount of data suggested an inversion of the common knowledge: it wasn't so much that poverty caused evictions; but that evictions were causing poverty.

When Tara read his thesis, it clicked for her: "The vast majority of vulnerable people now *had* to rent in the private market. The 'failed' public housing developments weren't even in the picture for the majority of poor and working-class tenants."[7]

The air quotes Tara used in referring to the "failure" of public housing point to the history of disinvestment and outright sabotage of the homes that were intended to be protected in perpetuity from market pressures and rising prices. In the 1940s, fearing competition from well-designed government-sponsored housing, the real estate industry (including developers and banks) campaigned against it and got budgets for public housing slashed.[8] From that point on, drastically underfunded public housing developments were shoddily constructed, using the poorest quality materials, on the worst sites, and barely maintained. Some of the best of public housing, built during the New Deal in partnership with unions, churches, and other nonprofits, would meanwhile be converted to market-rate housing. What remains of America's public housing today are about 1.1 million apartments—many of which are in need of serious renovation—that house about 2.1 million low-income people whose average household income is less than $15,000 per year.[9]

Since the 1970s, the federal government has instead relied on housing vouchers (which lower-income folks use to pay for homes in the private market) and subsidies to developers meant to entice them to build affordable units.

Tara approached Desmond, who had joined the faculty at Harvard in 2012, and asked if she could replicate his study in her hometown of Kansas City. "It struck me that Milwaukee was kind of like Kansas City. It's a river town, midsize, Midwestern, with a similar history of racial segregation." He was thrilled: "No one else is studying eviction," he told her.[10] Tara started doing ethnographic research: observing court cases, collecting data, and doing interviews with tenants and landlords.

One day during her research, she met an elderly couple, Chuck and Ivy, at a McDonald's for a tenant interview. They were about to get evicted from their trailer home and it was the beginning of December. Chuck was eighty-five, Ivy eighty-three. They got coffees in Styrofoam cups and sat in the plastic booths. Chuck did most of the talking.

Both had worked their whole lives. They lived on Social Security and Chuck's veteran's benefits, and they paid over half their income in rent. When Tara met them, they had fallen behind and would be evicted with no place to go and no one, no family or anyone else, to turn to for help.

"The whole thing is lopsided," Tara recalls Chuck telling her. "They keep raising our rent, tacking on extra costs, you know? They just pinned me with $47 for water, trash . . . $25 for Sheila, our dog. We just got notice that the total rent is $725. And we ran out of money yesterday."[11]

Tara remembers Ivy glancing up from her coffee, quietly saying: "But I don't mind living in the truck, honey, it won't bother me." The end of Tara's story was heartbreaking:

> The main thing I remember is that Ivy couldn't look me in the eyes. She was just staring at her coffee, stirring it. And there was a deep sense of hopelessness. And you know, I was a researcher at the time, so there wasn't anything responsibly or ethically I could do or should do, even if I had known what to do, which of course I did not. I have no idea what happened to them and I can only assume that they were gobbled up by the eviction machine that I've seen gobble up so many other people.
>
> It was just one of those things where I was like, I just can't, I can't square this reality. This is a couple that has worked their whole lives. They did everything they were told to do. He's a vet. She was clearly experiencing early stages of dementia. It was the beginning of winter. And I was like, what the . . . ? And there was something about the proximity to where I grew up. . . . It was just like this punch in the gut. This academic exercise was dead. My organizer brain met up with my researcher brain and I was like: *A researcher in a little dress with a PowerPoint is not gonna bring about any change here.*[12]

Soon after, Tara left academia to become a community organizer with People's Action.

* * *

Matthew Desmond's book *Evicted* came out in 2016. As gripping as any great novel, it won a Pulitzer Prize for its riveting accounts of low-income renters and landlords in Milwaukee. It illustrated how profitable it had become to rent to low-income tenants, who are often desperate and have no option but to pay high rents and accept undignified, unsanitary, or dangerous living conditions. The book would have a profound impact, drawing attention to the people whom housing policy has barely acknowledged.

Forty-three million households in the United States rent their homes, and 21 million of them cannot afford their rent.[13] Renters are far more likely than homeowners to be low-income, to be people of color, to have a disability, and to be women.

"Renting is given meaning by its relationship to ownership," writes Shane Phillips, author of *The Affordable City*. "It's how you live if you can't afford, or aren't yet ready, to own. America treats renting as it has treated the minimum wage for the past several decades: unworthy of serious concern, just a phase in young people's lives, and a long-term outcome only for those unwilling to pull themselves up by their bootstraps."[14] Thanks in large part to policies like the mortgage interest deduction, local and state deductions of property tax, and capital gains exemptions, which together amount to some $150 billion per year, homeowners enjoy a median net worth ($255,000) that is forty times that of renters ($6,300).[15] There are definitely affluent renters, many of them clustered in cities like Manhattan, San Francisco, Boston—but renting is non-negotiable for people with lower incomes, many people of color, and most immigrants. With respect to housing, the only more precarious situation than low-income rental is being unhoused, and many people veer from one into the other, thanks to a lack of legal protections for renters, rampant evictions, and the shortage of housing.

In the same way that centering the most vulnerable when addressing issues like poverty or health care leads to improving the situation for everyone, centering the rights of tenants would become a key strategy toward the Homes Guarantee.

The Shortfall

By late 2012, housing prices in many markets had recovered and then started pushing steadily higher thanks to real estate speculation, but also because of a shortage of homes. The decline in housing stock (expressed as a ratio, relative to the population) had started back in the 1990s (with a minimal lift between 2000 and 2005). Fewer homes were built between 2008 and 2018 than had been since the 1960s.[16] By 2018, the shortfall would amount to 2.8 million units, and by 2020, 3.8 million units.[17] Part of the reason was an increase in restrictions on lending for both developers and buyers; another part was a shortage in labor in the home-building industry; and yet another was the increased cost, and decreasing availability, of land and building materials.[18]

And then, probably most significantly, there were the NIMBYs (people with a "Not in My Backyard" stance on development) and restrictive zoning rules that made it almost impossible to build, period, but particularly anything that wasn't a single-family home. Multi-unit buildings like apartment complexes and duplexes are the most efficient way to house more people, but were very hard to impossible to build in places with exclusionary zoning laws. Although NIMBYs often claim their objections are grounded in environmental protection or the preservation of historic buildings, racism is usually in the mix, as Richard Rothstein writes in his book *The Color of Law*:

To prevent lower-income African Americans from living in neighborhoods where middle-class whites resided, local and federal officials began in the 1910s to promote zoning ordinances to reserve middle-class neighborhoods for single-family homes that lower-income families of all races could not afford. Certainly, an important and perhaps primary motivation of zoning rules that kept apartment buildings out of single-family neighborhoods was a social class elitism that was not itself racially biased. But there was also enough open racial intent behind exclusionary zoning that it is integral to the story of de jure segregation.[19]

With demand high and prices rising fast, existing homeowners tended to hold on to their homes, fearing they wouldn't be able to afford a different place, even as the market promised them more equity to use as a deposit on that next property. That they held on to their houses made it even harder for first-time buyers. As people were squeezed out of homeownership, the demand for rental properties went up. Increased demand meant that rents increased. As tenants reached the limits of what they could afford to pay each month, it got harder for them to save anything toward a down payment, especially if they were, like so many, also weighed down by student loans and other debt. Lower-rent places then fetched higher prices, leaving fewer places at lower rents. Lower-income renters were left to compete over the remaining supply—the least safe and least desirable homes. The most economically vulnerable suffered the highest housing precarity. These dynamics would also push more and more people into homelessness.

In fact, these market dynamics, and the overriding sense that homes were synonymous with the real estate market,

was what many housing activists considered the problem.
So this was not about housing in the fundamental way that,
say, a child thinks about houses—as *home*, the place that literally gives you a roof over your head, the cozy place where
you sleep safely. This was housing as property, as an asset to
invest, to buy and sell, to profit: real estate. When Tara Raghuveer articulated the Homes Guarantee years later, she would
call this the "conspiracy of the profiteers that has stifled our
imagination, leaving us to believe that housing is a commodity and not a human right, and that it must only be delivered
by the private market."[20]

Millennials, who came of age around the 2008 financial
crisis, would find buying and even renting amid the skyrocketing prices nearly impossible. Their struggles to afford housing would shape the culture of this period, shining a spotlight
on the lack of tenant protections and housing supply.

Kim-Mai Cutler was raised in the Bay Area. Her mom, a
Vietnamese refugee who had arrived with her family in the
1970s, pooled her income with her five sisters in order to buy a
house in San Jose. In a classic American story of social mobility, the sisters leveraged the equity from that first house to buy
homes of their own when they were ready to start families.

Kim-Mai got her political science degree at UC Berkeley
and was working as a journalist in 2014 when the protests
erupted against the "Google buses"—private transport hired
by Google as well as by Facebook, Apple, Yahoo, and other
tech companies—whose campuses were in Silicon Valley but
whose employees were living an hour away in San Francisco.
The protesters complained that tech workers were further
driving up rents, putting the city out of reach of anyone without a six-figure salary, like the cities' bus drivers, health care
workers, and restaurant workers. The protesters demanded

that the tech companies build housing on their campuses. But the city council of Mountain View, where Google and others are based, had expressly forbidden it (citing, in part, the need to protect a local species, the burrowing owl). While Mountain View was creating close to fifty thousand new jobs, the city's zoning plan allowed for just seven thousand new homes to be built . . . by 2030.[21]

Kim-Mai stood out on the street, watching the protests, and realized that at least one of the answers was to build more housing, so that newcomers didn't have to play musical chairs with the existing tenants. Why was building housing so hard? That query would prompt her to sit and write the definitive think piece on Bay Area housing titled "How Burrowing Owls Lead to Vomiting Anarchists (or SF's Housing Crisis Explained)," in which she wrote:

> I am pretty tired of seeing the city's young and disenfranchised fight each other amid an extreme housing shortage created by 30 to 40 years of NIMBYism from the old wealth of the city *and* down from the peninsula suburbs. . . .
>
> While we have to thank these movements for preserving so much of the land surrounding San Francisco and the city's beautiful Victorians, one side effect is that the city has added an average of 1,500 units per year for the last 20 years. Meanwhile, the U.S. Census estimates that the city's population grew by 32,000 people from 2010 to 2013 alone.[22]

It went viral. Kim-Mai started getting emails, DMs, and phone calls. The piece mobilized people, mostly from the tech world, who were looking for solutions to the housing crisis.[23]

Several like-minded folks started new organizations under the banner of YIMBY—Yes in My Backyard—to advocate for more housing supply. This movement recruited housing activists across the country who believed in increasing housing supply, especially in high-demand urban areas, in order to address housing availability, affordability, and inequality. YIMBYs supported policies that promote denser development, mixed-used neighborhoods, and reduced regulatory barriers to new construction. They asserted that even new market-rate homes would be an important step to alleviating the housing crisis: the theory being that by taking pressure off the top, more units would automatically become available for all. In doing so, they came up against historically disenfranchised groups who kept getting displaced every time new developments were built—the nefarious dynamics of gentrification— and the voices who maintained that the market could not bring solutions for the people most in need.

But one thing was clear: more units were needed. Regardless of whether we were fighting for more public housing, more affordable housing, or more housing on the private market, there was no way to guarantee housing for all without building more housing.

COLLEGE

Not only were families dealing with the rising costs of housing, they also suffered from the skyrocketing price of college. Between 1978 and 2012, average tuition rates for college rose 1,120 percent, a faster and higher increase than *any other product or service.* (For comparison, medical expenses climbed

601 percent and food costs 244 percent during the same period.)[24] Students who were enrolled in public four-year universities in the 2010–2011 year were paying $8,500 on average per year in tuition and fees (as in-state students), a cost that had jumped 15 percent just between 2008 and 2010.[25] A decade later, by the 2021–2022 school year, the cost would rise to just shy of $11,000, a 29 percent increase.[26] And tuition is only one of the costs of attending most colleges: expenses include books, housing, food, transportation, and child care, which together run in the tens of thousands.[27]

The reasons for the tuition hikes were numerous but a key factor was state funding cuts over the previous three decades as well as a massive increase in demand. Colleges and universities competed with each other for students' business since they were increasingly tuition-driven enterprises. Students and their parents had become "customers" who bore responsibility for the costs, using their own funds or student loans or grants. To attract customers, universities offered bells and whistles: cafeterias were replaced with high-end food courts; dorms went upscale; tricked-out wellness centers offered rock-climbing walls and Olympic-size pools. These kinds of campus improvements further drove up costs.

But federal aid for students has done the opposite of keeping pace with rising tuitions. Pell grants, created in the early 1970s to give financial aid that does not have to be repaid to students who wouldn't otherwise be able to afford college, covered more than 75 percent of the cost of attending a four-year public college when the program was launched.[28] Now the grants cover an average of just 28 percent of tuition.[29] It's a reflection of the market-driven mindset, which casts higher education as an investment made by the individual, yielding a return in the form of future earnings, as opposed to a public good, where the whole community benefits from an educated population. This explains why so much financial aid takes the form of loans rather than grants, and why public colleges and universities have been systematically defunded.

Merit-based aid—which rewards higher-scoring and -achieving students—privileges the wealthy, who are more likely to get extra tutoring or attend high schools with advanced classes and other kinds of supports. And low-income students are far more likely to drop out of college than are wealthier students: by the end of their second year, fully one-quarter of them have left without a credential.[30] Nearly 40 percent of student debt holders do not have a degree.[31]

If people miss student loan payments, the consequences can be severe. When they default, they cannot rent or buy homes, or lease a car, or even find jobs with employers that check credit.[32] Professional licenses (in nursing or teaching, for example) can be revoked. Tax refunds and—for the growing population of elders carrying student loan debts—social security can be garnished. And with the fees assigned to defaulted loans that double the amount owed, getting back on one's feet is nearly impossible. Education-related debts slow economic growth, preventing people from starting families or buying homes or saving for retirement. And the debts contribute to anxiety and depression.

Occupy Student Debt

Student debt was another issue shared and shouldered by many of the young people in Zuccotti Park in 2011.

The anthropologist David Graeber had published his script-flipping opus earlier in 2011—*Debt* came out in July—and he was part of the assemblies that led up to Occupy's first actions on Wall Street in September. "If history shows anything," he wrote in *Debt*, "it is that there's no better way to justify relations founded on violence, to make such relations seem moral, than by reframing them in the language of debt—above all, because it immediately makes it seem that it's the victim who's doing something wrong."[33]

David recruited his friend Astra Taylor, and together they and a few others dug in to take action. Occupy Student Debt, they called it.

In her early thirties (an elder by Occupy standards), Astra had an unusual education experience. Her parents, both white countercultural lefties, had "unschooled" Astra and her siblings, who grew up in college towns in Arizona and Georgia during the 1980s and 1990s. Astra did attend public high school, but abandoned it after three years to attend classes at the University of Georgia, and then was accepted into Brown University, the most liberal of the Ivy Leagues. She hated it. Ultimately she got an MA from the New School in New York and started making documentary films. She owed tens of thousands of dollars in student loans for both colleges, and defaulted on her debt during the 2008 financial crisis. "Overnight, they added 19 percent to my principal. Like millions of others, I was caught in a debt trap."[34]

Why doesn't America have free public universities like many other wealthy countries do? Astra delved into the history, uncovering not just profit motives, but racism. There *was* a time in America when public college was basically free, just as high school was. In the nineteenth century, free (or close-to-free) colleges served mostly white students from middle-class backgrounds who studied to be high school teachers, ministers, and community leaders and who, after graduation, would go on to serve public needs and advance the welfare of society. Then, in the first two decades of the twentieth century, private colleges began serving upper-class white kids, and the motivation for a college degree shifted away from social good to personal gain. In the 1960s, just as campuses were getting more populous and racially diverse, free college ended. As Black and brown people gained access to higher education, white supremacist politicians reacted by increasing the cost of college.[35]

During his 1966 campaign to be California's governor, Ronald Reagan targeted the University of California system, especially UC Berkeley, claiming the state needed to save money. At the time, students paid about $300 in annual fees to attend the school, the equivalent of about $2,000 in today's dollars.[36] (At this writing, in-state tuition at UC Berkeley is $15,000, with yearly student costs amounting to nearly $40,000.)[37]

Reagan succeeded in hiking the fees and also firing UC president Clark Kerr, who'd been a key architect of higher education as a public good—not just in California but nationwide.[38] And Reagan's actions inspired conservative politicians across the country to follow suit. This marked the point of no return in terms of higher education's shift from a public good to a private investment.

Occupy Student Debt's first major action took place in April 2012, on the day that outstanding student loan debt hit $1 trillion. (As I write, in 2023, it has topped $1.7 trillion.)[39] "1T Day," they named it, and called publicly for both the cancellation of student debt and the provision of free public college, demands that were ridiculed by the press as a pipe dream.

Next, several of them started pursuing something David Graeber had posited on an Occupy listserv: what if they themselves could buy debt on the sketchy secondary market, where it's sold for pennies on the dollar, and just cancel it? A little over a year after Occupy, they tried crowdfunding to buy up debt. They called the project the Rolling Jubilee, after the biblical tradition of the year in which people forgave one another's debts. They raised $750,000, enough to buy about $32 million worth of medical, tuition, payday loan, and criminal punishment debt belonging to thousands of random people.[40] "Instead of collecting on them," Astra would later write, "we erased them, sending people letters notifying them that their obligations were gone, no strings attached."[41] Imagine the miraculous feeling of receiving one of those letters in the mail.

The Rolling Jubilee was no small achievement, yet, compared with the total $1 trillion owed in student debt—not to mention the rest of household debt—it was just a drop in the bucket. And federal loans, which make up the bulk of student debt, are guaranteed by the government and not sold at deep discounts like other loans, so they remained out of reach of the Rolling Jubilee's strategy.

Interest Rates

By 2014, ten years had passed since Melissa Byrne graduated from college. She'd already paid off tens of thousands in student loans, and still owed more than $100,000. "I don't remember the original principal of my loans. But between deferrals and forbearance, I learned the tragic lesson of compounded interest."[42]

After years of silence and shame about her debt, she finally realized the power of sharing her story as she began to organize to fight student debt bondage. Raised by a single mom, Melissa had gone to college with belief in its promise. "I didn't understand the financial aid process.... I just knew that I had to take out these loans. My mom instilled in me the importance of education. I was told that if I studied hard and went to college, I would be able to move forward in America. I would be able to work hard to expand the American Dream for people who come behind me. I would be able to support my mom for all the support she gave me. Instead, I find that to go to college, I mortgaged my future."[43]

It's not the student debtors who should be ashamed; it's the lawmakers who paved the way for loans to turn "the greatest vehicle of social mobility into a debt machine," in the words of *New York Times* columnist Tressie McMillan Cottom, who commented further:

> You can be forgiven for not knowing that the "go to college" refrain would have a darker side. But we should not forgive those who knew better. Policymakers knew by the 2010s that the train was going off the rails. . . . They knew that Black debtors would likely never earn enough to pay off their college debt. They knew that poor immigrant and first-generation Black and Hispanic students were turning to their elderly parents and grandparents to co-sign for loans. We knew that Social Security checks would end up garnished as a result, throwing thousands of elderly people into the very poverty that the program was designed to prevent. . . .We knew that we had incentivized bad actors in the student loan servicing market. We knew that student loan debt was most expensive for the families who had the most to lose. And we kept offering the loans with the same cheerful promise: It's worth it.
>
> When you are scammed by a friend, it is a shame. When your country scams you, it is a fraud.[44]

Student debt relief and college access and affordability, were becoming hot political topics. In 2014, there were two proposals put forth to give relief to student debtors. One came from

Senator Elizabeth Warren: her "Bank on Students" bill aimed to reduce interest rates on student loans.[45] The other was an executive order from President Obama that capped student loan repayment of federal loans at 10 percent of income—and, if a borrower didn't miss a payment for twenty years, their remaining debt would be canceled. The order would only go into effect in 2015; it didn't address the skyrocketing cost of tuition; and it didn't apply to the student loans from private banks.

Melissa was furious: "An interest rate reduction here, or a cap on payments there, won't make my life better or the lives of the 40 million dramatically better. It's surface-level, message-level actions that don't tackle the real problem of student loans—the principal. We need a broad vision for student loan forgiveness as a form of direct economic investment, and we need a future of free higher education."[46]

Looking to make a significant contribution toward winning justice for student debtors and winning free college, Melissa spent the next years crafting some of the most effective messaging and creative actions around student debt.

A Union of Debtors

In 2014, Astra Taylor co-founded an organization called the Debt Collective, a kind of union of debtors. Their key insight was that alone, each debtor was at the mercy of institutions, but together, they could become too big to fail. "You are not a loan," declared their clever tagline.

A year later the Debt Collective took on for-profit colleges. First rising in popularity in the 1970s, for-profit colleges had soared since the 1990s by filling a niche that public and private nonprofit institutions had left unserved: gearing curricula and schedules toward working adults, including via online learning. In the early 1970s, for-profits enrolled just 0.2 percent of all college students in the United States; by the time of Occupy, that number was 12–13 percent. In the decade between 1998 to 2008, enrollment had more than tripled.[47]

"They are taking advantage of the lack of a guarantee. No one would choose the pricey inferior for-profit option if we had robust college for all," Astra commented.[48]

As publicly traded companies beholden more to their shareholders than to their students or professors, for-profit colleges were and are under pressure to keep growing their profits. Because enrollments, not graduation rates, accomplish that priority, for-profits have engaged in both aggressive marketing and cost-cutting measures. For-profits also charge 30–40 percent more than nonprofit schools do for the same credentials.[49] In 2009, 86 percent of for-profit revenue was from taxpayers: federal funds including Pell Grants, loans, and funding to help military members and veterans pay for school.[50] The percentage was so high because low-income students are eligible for higher amounts of federal grants and loans, and for-profits explicitly targeted low-income students and Black and brown students, for example by spending $200,000 for two weeks of intensive advertising on the BET channel in 2014.

According to a 2015 piece in *New Yorker* magazine:

> Dependence on student loans was not incidental to the for-profit boom—*it was the business model.* The schools may have been meeting a genuine market need, but, in most cases, their profits came not from building a better mousetrap but from gaming the taxpayer-funded financial-aid system. Since the schools weren't lending money themselves, they didn't have to worry about whether it would be paid back. So they had every incentive to encourage students to take out as much financial aid as

possible, often by giving them a distorted picture
of what they could expect in the future. [For-profit
chain] Corinthian, for instance, was found to have
lied about job-placement rates nearly a thousand
times.[51]

By 2015, there had been a number of investigations into
the fraudulent practices of for-profit colleges. In 2012 Iowa
senator Tom Harkin concluded a two-year investigation that
found there was "overwhelming documentation of exorbi-
tant tuition, aggressive recruiting practices, abysmal student
outcomes, taxpayer dollars spent on marketing and pocketed
as profit, and regulatory evasion and manipulation."[52] As
attorney general of California, Kamala Harris in 2013 had
sued Corinthian Colleges, one of the largest of the for-profit
chains, for predatory and exploitative practices.[53]

Corinthian responded by ridding itself first of its California
campuses and then, in spring of 2015, announcing the shutdown of the remainder of its campuses nationwide, a move
that left thousands of students stranded midway through
their programs (another shortcoming of for-profits is that
their credits tend not to be transferable to other schools).[54]

Earlier that year, fifteen former students of Corinthian,
known as the Corinthian 15, launched the nation's first student debt strike. They were supported by the Debt Collective,
which had uncovered a clause in the Higher Education Act
that allowed borrowers to contest repayment of their loans if
the school had lied to students during enrollment. The Debt
Collective engineered an online debt dispute app, and within
a month it had collected hundreds of contestations from for-
profit students. In March the Corinthian 15 and key members
of the Debt Collective traveled to DC to confront education
officials; Corinthian, meanwhile, was declaring bankruptcy.

In June of that year, Secretary of Education Arne Duncan announced his department would offer some forgiveness to some Corinthian students.[55] The Corinthian 15 kept up the strike, refusing to repay what hadn't been forgiven.

Melissa Byrne commented on this moment's shift in the stigma around student debt: "I learned through working with the foreclosure fights that addressing the shame involved is the first step. People facing foreclosure were seen as people who screwed up and deserved what they got. In many ways, there is that same shame and stigma towards people with student loan debt. Yes, we signed on the dotted lines each semester to take on more debt, but it was so much more complicated."[56]

The College Promise

Meanwhile, another wave was rising in the movement toward free college: the College Promise program. Its roots were in an experimental program funded by anonymous donors since 2006 in the city of Kalamazoo, Michigan, who offered to pay tuition for any graduate of public high school to attend one of Michigan's public colleges and universities (and a select number of the private ones). As a result, Kalamazoo's school enrollment numbers jumped; teachers were drawn to the district; new schools were built for the first time since the 1970s; and the area also pulled in new businesses, with workers eager for their children to benefit from the program.[57]

In 2014 Tennessee launched a statewide version of the model, offering high school seniors the opportunity to attend two-year certificate or associate degree programs tuition-free, paid for by the state lottery. Chicago also announced a tuition-free Promise program for community colleges that year. In January 2015, President Obama mentioned the model in his State of the Union address. "Tennessee, a state with Republican leadership, and Chicago, a city with Democratic leadership, are showing that free community college is possible," he said. "I want to spread that idea all across America, so that two years of college becomes as free and universal in America as high school is today."[58] Five years later, there were 350 local and state Promise programs in place.[59]

Their growth, and President Obama's shoutout, resulted in free college becoming a major talking point as the 2016 election season neared. Bernie Sanders announced legislation to make college tuition-free for all in May 2015. Hillary Clinton moved from a stance of "affordable college" to her proposal to eliminate tuition at public colleges for families making less than $125,000 annually, announced shortly before the Democratic National Convention at which she was made the Democratic candidate.[60] Midway through 2016, a poll found that 62 percent of Americans supported making public college tuition-free.[61]

HEALTH CARE

Nearly a year after the election of President Barack Obama, my digital team at Organizing for America (OFA) and I were huddled around a small television in one of our beige cubicles at the Democratic National Committee headquarters, jostling for a view as the House finally voted to pass the Affordable Care Act (ACA), which journalist David Leonhardt of the *New York Times* called "the most sweeping piece of federal legislation since Medicare was passed in 1965."[62] Many of us had tears in our eyes. One of my staff was undoubtedly thinking of his mother, who died suddenly when he was in college. His family couldn't afford medications to treat her lupus. He stood next to her body in the ER and promised her that he'd work on universal health care. Years later, in her memory, he'd indeed worked hours around the clock to see this moment become a reality. "Obamacare" was a far cry from perfect, but it was a win for more than 30 million mothers, fathers, daughters, sons, neighbors, and friends who would finally have access to life-saving, affordable care.

The health reform fight had been much messier and far less glamorous than the election it had followed. In the face of endless waves of disinformation from the Tea Party about non-existent "death panels" and imaginary tax hikes, and an unprecedented barrage of big-money lobbyists that deluged Congress, desperate to kill the bill, we at OFA rolled up our sleeves to fight lies with facts. Not many people realized that the project of health reform actually broadened Obama's grassroots base from the numbers it had hit leading up to the 2008 election. In fact, over 1.2 million new supporters who had not signed up for the election took action with OFA to pass health reform.[63]

We placed over 2.8 million calls to voters to talk about health reform. We gathered research on call-in radio programs and helped launch "On the Air"—a first-of-its-kind radio call-in tool to bring the voices of grassroots health reform supporters onto the airwaves. We submitted 457,720 letters to the editor sharing personal stories with newspapers nationwide, including thousands of letters specifically written from small business owners, Republicans, and independent voters discussing the value of health reform from their perspective. We organized a staggering number of public events—more than 33,000!—during the year-long campaign. From small house parties, to town halls and bake sales, to large rallies, OFA supporters turned out in force to set the record straight, one conversation at a time. And this just covers OFA's work—so many organizations fought hard for this victory.

Our victory was neither complete nor final. The path was marred by painful compromises and the deadly influence of special interests, but I'm still proud I had a hand in it. The Affordable Care Act was significant legislation that expanded Medicaid coverage, created insurance marketplaces where individuals could purchase affordable plans regardless of their employment, and prohibited insurers from denying coverage based on preexisting conditions, among many other things.

One more thing that we didn't see as clearly at the time: the Affordable Care Act was a "future of work" policy. The rise of contingent or gig work outside of traditional employment complicates the ability to obtain health insurance, and the ACA enabled health care access for more of those workers. The ACA also laid the groundwork to ensure that when the COVID-19 pandemic forced millions out of work overnight, it didn't strip them of their health coverage.

The ACA had an immediate impact on my own family. In 2013, my parents decided to move to Colorado to be near my sister when she had the first of her children. They packed up all their earthly belongings in a U-Haul in Kansas and drove across the plains and into the mountains to start a new life. In Kansas my father had been a minister, and my mother a minister's wife—which is a full-time but unpaid job. She also worked as an aid in Head Start and the Kansas public schools, which gave her a small pension. To pay for the move, my mother started drawing her pension: $800 per month.

Once in Colorado, it wasn't easy for two folks in their sixties to find work after the unusual experience of decades in ministry. My dad started driving for Super Shuttle, the graveyard shift, ferrying passengers to the Denver airport into the early morning hours. After that, having always been great at fixing and building things, he hung up his shingle as a handyman. My mom started working at a nonprofit. Her job didn't pay much, and didn't offer health care, but she stayed so they could afford their health insurance costs. They purchased health insurance off the Colorado health insurance marketplace called Connect for Colorado, which was a direct result of the Affordable Care Act. Before the ACA, there was no marketplace where someone like my mom could have gotten affordable health insurance.

A few years later my mom turned sixty-five, which meant she could enroll in Medicare. It was a blessing. Between the relatively generous program of Medicare plus Social Security, which supplemented my dad's earnings as a handyman and Super Shuttle driver, she was able to quit her job and thus be free to play a significant role in her grandkids' lives and volunteer for her church.

The Confusion of Coverage

A quick refresher on the beast that is American health care: If you are employed, your employment package may include health insurance coverage, in which case you generally get to choose your insurer and maybe your health care providers too, with options dependent on the package selected by your employer. Many people—between one in three to one in six—report staying in jobs they really don't like—a situation known as "job lock"—just because of the health care coverage. If health care weren't a factor, 26 percent of Americans say they'd start their own company—the "entrepreneurship lock."[64]

But just because you have a job doesn't mean you're covered. Employees in small firms, and those who work in retail, construction, and service firms, are disproportionately likely to be uninsured. Workers who earn low wages, work part-time, or have short job tenure are also likely to be uninsured. If you perform labor outside the bounds of traditional employment, for example as a caregiver, you're uninsured. Uninsured workers are more likely to be Black or Latino, to be male, to be under age thirty-five, and to be single.[65]

If, like my mom, you are over sixty-five, you are covered by Medicare, a federally funded program that is also available to younger people who qualify for disability benefits. Despite it being a health care program primarily for people over the age of sixty-five, Medicare doesn't cover the cost of most long-term care, such as ongoing support for people with mobility issues or dementia.

If you're a veteran, you have access to a comprehensive, centrally coordinated, government-run health service. The Veterans Health Administration is the closest thing America has to socialized health care in the vein of the UK's National Health Service, where the government owns the hospitals, employs the physicians, and functions as the insurer.

And finally, if you're low-income, you may qualify for Medicaid, which is partially funded by the federal government but run by your state, with eligibility criteria and the types of services covered depending on the particular state. Medicaid does cover long-term care for low-income seniors or people with disabilities; in fact it pays for more than 50 percent of the nation's long-term care. The ACA expanded eligibility and streamlined Medicaid enrollment, although a 2012 Supreme Court ruling made the expansion optional for states. And some states opted out, in a bizarre cutting-off-their-nose-to-spite-their-Republican-face move.

For those without coverage, the ACA reforms created "marketplaces," which provided alternatives that enabled people to avoid atrociously high premiums that had previously been the norm for individually negotiated private insurance. Even so, about 27 million Americans are uninsured.[66]

Many Americans, even those of us with some form of insurance, skip our doctor visits, or procedures we need, or medications essential to our well-being, because the costs are too high. In 2018, the average American household spent $5,000 per person on health care (for the year), with nearly 70 percent of that going toward health insurance.[67] Insurance companies are infamous for refusing to pay up when push comes to shove. We are accustomed to having to spend hours if not weeks on the phone with them, fighting to get entirely legitimate costs reimbursed. Many of us resort to crowdfunding to cover the costs of critical, life-saving health care.

The staggering amounts of money involved in our medical-industrial complex mean that the players who gain the most, such as insurance companies and pharmaceutical companies, will defend the status quo with everything they've got. According to the *New York Times*:

> Eighteen percent of the United States economy, or $3.5 trillion, is tied to health care, up from 5 percent in 1960. The United States spends at least double per capita what other industrialized nations spend on health care. The health sector is among America's most profitable industries. And despite the vast profits and expenditures, the United States has comparatively worse health outcomes than other advanced nations that spend far less on health care: higher overall mortality rates, higher premature deaths and higher preventable deaths—all on top of the fact that two-thirds of all bankruptcies and nearly half of all foreclosures in America today are related to medical costs.[68]

It is, in a word, a mess.

"The fact is, there's no healthcare system in this country. There's only a healthcare industry that profits off of human suffering," pronounced California Nurses Association leader RoseAnn DeMoro back in 2006,[69] fresh off the nurses' win defending staffing cuts from then governor Arnold Schwarzenegger.[70] CNA's tactics in those years were the stuff of legend: there was not only their merciless hounding of the governor until they got their way, but also, for example, the event they threw to mark the two ballot propositions that Big Pharma wrote for California's 2005 special elections, at which the nurses served "roast corporate pork and minced principles." The press loved them.

Nurses don't make a big profit off how care is delivered and are often the fiercest advocates for patients. Around 2011, nurses emerged as the powerhouse force calling for a *real* health care guarantee in America: one that would provide universal affordable coverage and quality care.

Nurses Arrive at Medicare for All

California Nurses Association had launched the National Nurses Organizing Committee in 2005 in response to nurses' requests to build a national movement, and out of that, National Nurses United (NNU) was born in 2009. With 155,000 registered nurses from all fifty states as members, it was a "super union."[71]

In 2011, NNU launched its "Heal America, Tax Wall Street" campaign, calling for single-payer health care.

"Single-payer" was the prevailing, if not very sexy or intuitive, language of that moment. In the case that, like me, you still get confused by the terminology, even after having heard it a gazillion times: "single-payer" refers to a system in which a single entity—most likely a government agency, using tax dollars—collects all health care funding and pays for all health care costs. This would eliminate the need for privately owned, for-profit health insurance companies. One of the compelling reasons for the single-payer model is the phenomenon of "adverse selection": insurers seek to avoid giving coverage to sick people, leaving them to whatever public option exists, and, when all of these sick people get clustered together, it drives up the public costs. The single-payer model, by contrast, must cover everyone regardless of their condition, sharing the costs of the healthy and the sick. Whether the health care services themselves are provided by government-run entities (as in the UK, where the government owns the hospitals and pays the doctors) or by private providers (as in Canada, where many hospitals are privately operated), or a combination of the two, isn't specified. In other words, single-payer is *not* synonymous with "socialized medicine" (the UK model). Advocates of single-payer usually conceive of it as care and services being universal: everyone in the country, or at least every citizen, would be covered. Secondary coverage is usually available in single-payer models for those who can afford to pay for additional or higher-quality services. So there's a level of coverage and care below which nobody can fall—a floor—but there's no upward limit for those who have the means.

In June 2011, a thousand nurses in matching red T-shirts stormed Wall Street to demand single-payer coverage, as well as good jobs, education, a clean environment, and retirement security for all. They coined slogans like "Patient health, not corporate wealth," demanding a 0.5 percent tax on stock trades and credit swaps, which would raise as much as $350 billion a year.[72] They did street theater—for example, chasing people dressed as chipmunks who lugged big acorns to their Wall Street "nests." A few months later, thousands of nurses descended upon sixty congressional offices in

twenty-one states.[73] They intended their actions and spec-
tacles to educate the broader public on how the increasingly
financialized health care model was hurting patients.

Cathy Kennedy had been a registered nurse in California
since the 1980s, working in neonatal care—saving babies and
dealing with parents in the most intense moments of their
lives. The daughter of Japanese and African American parents, Cathy became both co-president of the California Nurses
Association and vice president of the NNU in 2020. A Health
Guarantee, for her, as for thousands of other nurses, is plain
commonsense. "Health care," she said, "is a human right.
It's not for the privileged few. Everyone should have access
to high quality, comprehensive healthcare. What I see as a
registered nurse is people who have to make a decision as to
whether or not they're gonna go to a doctor's visit, or put food
on the table, or pay rent, or pay a healthcare premium. People
shouldn't have to worry about things like that, or be tied to a
bad job because of the healthcare benefits. What we're saying
is that if you're sick, you should be able to go to the hospital
without having to worry about whether or not you can afford
to pay the bill."[74]

Cathy explained the counterintuitive reluctance of the labor
movement to galvanize around the issue: it's because bargaining for better health care costs within the existing system is
one of major benefits that unions can still offer to workers. It's
a central draw for people to join a union, because the health
coverage that unions can win is definitely better (if a far cry
from really good) than what's available to non-union workers. Since unions have been struggling for so long, they don't
want to lose this incentive for membership.

"But what we have been saying is that if you take healthcare off the table, because it is provided for all, that means
you can focus on wages, on providing better employment for
folks. We believe it's a winning situation. We are talking to

our labor partners on getting them to understand that we can do this," Cathy said.[75]

In order for a Health Care Guarantee to become a reality, widespread support from organized labor was (and is) almost certainly going to be necessary, given the size of the corporate interests that need to be fought. Historically, the AFL-CIO's organizing of its retirees had been key to Medicare passing in 1965. Now, after a push from the nurses, the giant labor federation agreed to endorse single-payer health care.[76]

Besides the question of affordability, taking coverage away from private interests and placing it in the hands of a public agency also has the really important benefit of making the whole system more transparent and responsive. Or, as NNU organizer Jasmine Ruddy put it:

> Anytime that we create universal programs that are funded by the government, there's a process that gets built into that. We can elect the people who make decisions about the funding of our health care. We can't make those decisions now— we don't elect the CEOs of Kaiser, right, or of Aetna. I think that it sometimes can get confusing for folks, but what we're talking about is adding a layer of democracy and accountability to the way that we *fund* our healthcare, not the way we provide our healthcare. We're not talking about getting rid of doctors or providers, all that we're talking about is getting rid of the insurance companies and changing the way that we pay for the services.[77]

In 2012 the nurses in California embraced the phrase "Medicare for All" as the new slogan for guaranteed universal health coverage.[78] That was the year they organized a tour of eighteen cities in California in a big red bus, offering free health screenings and holding town hall meetings that reached thousands.[79] They educated health care and community activists nationwide about the shortfalls in the existing system, and explained how what was needed was a single standard of quality care for all, which would be best achieved through improved and expanded Medicare. It would function, essentially, as a Guarantee: to cover all Americans, cover more services, and eliminate most deductibles and co-payments. It would eliminate private insurance—the government would pay for everyone.

When the nurses' candidate, Bernie Sanders—whom NNU was the first national union to endorse in 2015—brought a huge amount of attention to Medicare for All during the 2016 election season, the long-held dream of a Health Care Guarantee was finally part of the mainstream conversation.

FAMILY CARE

There are two sides of the family care equation. One side is the person receiving care—usually an infant, child, elder, or a person who has a disability or is recovering from illness. The other side is the person giving that care—the domestic workers, nannies, paid caregivers, or care workers. Good infrastructure for family care has to support everyone involved in the equation: recipients—*families*—must be able to access and afford it, and, for workers, it has to be dignified, sustainable work that enables them to live well and take care of their own families.

In 2011 there were about two hundred thousand domestic workers—nannies, housekeepers, eldercare providers—

employed in New York City.[80] An "invisible" workforce, hidden away inside homes, almost all of them were women; most of them were immigrant women of color. These facts made even finding them and talking to them, let alone organizing them, incredibly difficult, which meant their 2010 success getting the state of New York to pass the Domestic Workers' Bill of Rights was close to a miracle. It had taken six years, and was the first legislation of its kind nationwide, mandating (at least) minimum wage, overtime pay, and protection from harassment and discrimination. It was a huge victory for the legendary Ai-jen Poo, who had co-founded the New York–based Domestic Workers United (DWU) in 2000, and then a national organization, the National Domestic Workers Alliance (NDWA) in 2007, to champion the rights of the 2.5 million domestic workers nationwide. Ai-jen, the daughter of immigrants from Taiwan, was raised in part by her grandmother so her parents could pursue their careers in medicine. She pursued women's studies at Columbia University in New York, volunteering in domestic violence programs before realizing the plight of the mostly female workforce employed inside homes.

Like farmworkers, domestic workers had been explicitly excluded from the landmark federal labor protections of the 1930s because both were workforces composed almost entirely of African Americans at the time, and racist southern congressmen made the two groups' exclusion a condition of passing the legislation. "The racialized exclusion of domestic workers from labor laws, the gendered devaluation of women's work in the home, the decentralized structure of the industry, and the economic pressures facing immigrants from the global South—[these dynamics make] domestic workers extremely vulnerable to exploitation and abuse," Ai-jen explains, making organizing this workforce "absolutely essential."[81] Despite being legally barred from unionizing, domestic workers, through NDWA, now had a way to learn their rights, exchange information, and gain power.

From Living Rooms to State Capitols

DWU had started out by supporting individual workers who were being mistreated by their employers, were owed wages, or survived trafficking. There was the employer who claimed to have sent a decade's worth of wages back to the domestic worker's home country in the Caribbean but never paid a penny; there was the worker forced to sleep in the family's moldy basement; there was the employer who refused to give up the worker's passport; there was rampant sexual harassment and abuse. DWU soon realized that case-by-case fights weren't going to give workers the conditions or dignity they deserved.

DWU explored the possibility of legislative protections, convening hundreds of workers to hear what they needed and wanted, and formulating proposed legislation based on that. Their earliest visit to the state capitol in Albany in 2004 was sobering: lawmakers just didn't care. "Look, honey, the guy that pumps your gas doesn't get these things by law, why should the babysitter get them?" Ai-jen recalls being told.[82] She realized they needed more powerful allies. It was a major win when John Sweeney, then president of the mighty AFL-CIO, whose mother had been a domestic worker, donned one of DWU's yellow T-shirts and voiced his support. DWU also built ties with SEIU Local 32BJ, a union representing (among others) the doormen in luxury apartment buildings, who already interacted with and had connections to domestic workers. The movement's inspiration to have children speak about their relationships with their beloved nannies, including at the 2009 Children and Families March down Broadway, as well as at the state capitol, was another powerful inflection point.[83]

Ai-jen and her team had an early, catalyzing realization: that *employers* of domestic workers could be allies rather than—as is the case in pretty much every other organized labor scenario—the antagonists. DWU supported employers in educating their fellow employers: "The employer-activists organized 'living room gatherings,' meetings in their homes where they invited friends who employed domestic workers. At these gatherings, they discussed ways in which employers could take responsibility for creating decent working conditions," Ai-jen wrote afterward, in her account of the Bill of Rights fight.[84] This facet of the work became the program Hand in Hand: The Domestic Employers Network; it operates nationwide, partnering with city agencies and other community organizations to conduct education and outreach to domestic employers so that they understand their responsibilities to pay a fair wage, provide benefits, and create clear communication with workers in their homes.[85]

I joined Hand in Hand the year my son was born, in 2012, when I was vaulted into the category of new working parent, and bewildered by the lack of public support. I used the network's resources to create a contract with our caregiver, who quickly became a very important person in the life of my family. Hand in Hand helped me understand that not only was our relationship with the caregiver built on deep trust, but also that my home was an employment site for them— something that isn't obvious to families who are figuring it all out on their own.

All these allies and others joined DWU on subsequent trips to Albany. "Respect for domestic workers is also respect for our children," one of the employer-allies said in her testimony.[86] And so it came to pass that New York adopted the

Domestic Worker Bill of Rights. One state down, forty-nine to go.

Alliances Across Generations

Ai-jen's next major move was built on what DWU had learned from the New York fight about the power of strange bedfellows, together with a keen-eyed observation of a trend it was seeing in its membership: more and more workers who had originally been hired as nannies or housekeepers were being asked (or forced) to serve as caregivers for elders. It was happening because of a monumental demographic shift nationwide. Every eight seconds, another American was turning sixty-five. The 5 million Americans over the age of eighty-five in 2011 were projected to number 11.5 million by 2035, the country's fastest-growing demographic. Seventy percent of people over sixty-five need some form of support, and 90 percent of Americans wanted that care in their own homes, not in institutional facilities.[87] Although others were calling it the "age wave" or even the "silver tsunami," Ai-jen chose to call it "the elder boom."

Where others saw a crisis, Ai-jen saw an opportunity. In 2011 she co-created a campaign called Caring Across Generations, which brought together organizations across the country that were championing the rights of elders, women, immigrants, people with disabilities, and other kinds of workers. The framing of Caring Across Generations appealed not only to those whose own sixty-fifth birthday was approaching or past, but also to the "sandwich generation"—the growing number of people who were providing care for both their children and their elders simultaneously. The year 2012 would find Ai-jen drafting a book that made the case for a "Care Grid"—a set of policies and infrastructure on par with other national infrastructure projects, such as railroads, electrification, and the internet, that would enable Americans to live out their lives with dignity. She wrote:

> We know we need more jobs in home care. We know we need home care to be affordable, easily accessible and delivered at the highest quality. We need these jobs to be well-respected, secure jobs with living wages, benefits, security and opportunities for career advancement. We need the workforce to be prepared, trained and adaptive to the particular needs of the individuals and families they are supporting. And we need for everyone to feel like whole and equal parts of a care team.[88]

It wasn't quite a proposal for a Family Care Guarantee, but it was a good articulation of the need for one.

Caring Across Generations quickly demonstrated its power. In July of 2013, Hawaii passed its own Bill of Rights for Domestic Workers, followed by California in September of that year. In 2014 Massachusetts was brought into the fold, which was followed by Oregon and Connecticut in 2015.[89] Six down, forty-four to go. In 2014, the MacArthur Foundation acknowledged Ai-jen's work with a "genius grant" award, and in 2015, she published her book, *The Age of Dignity: Preparing for the Elder Boom in a Changing America.*

During those same years, dedicated organizing by SEIU, together with NDWA, Caring Across Generations, and several dozen other groups, resulted in a major federal win. In 2014 the Department of Labor ruled to change the federal Fair Labor Standards Act to allow home care workers to qualify for minimum wage and overtime protection, clarifying that caregivers who spend most of their shift helping clients dress, bathe, eat, or clean were no longer excluded from federal labor laws for being mere "companions."[90] It went into effect in late 2015.

These laws were moving protections out of the home and into the policy realm. They were inching us closer to a guarantee of family care—but we were still some years away from fully understanding what would be possible. We'd need a big idea.

GOOD WORK

One aspect of good work involves having a voice and the leverage to advocate for certain standards in wages and working conditions. Beginning in the 1970s, the American workforce shifted away from being largely employed by manufacturing and industry to largely employed by the service sector. With that shift, workers lost the right or the ability to be represented by a union. Sometimes their workplace blocked it; sometimes it was impossible because they worked for a subcontractor, a temp agency, or via a platform for task-based work; sometimes they worked in isolation. At the height of union enrollment in the mid-1950s, more than a third of all workers were enrolled in unions; in recent years just about 10 percent of all workers belong to a union, including only 6 percent of private-sector employees.[91]

Ai-jen was far from being the only leader who was developing innovative strategies to reach and organize workers who were legally, practically, or culturally excluded from traditional unions and collective bargaining, and ultimately win better conditions for them. Starting in the 1990s, worker centers had sprung up in major cities to focus on the rights of immigrant workers, starting with day laborers, taxi drivers, and garment workers. In the 2000s, similar organizations arose in the service sector to support workers in restaurants and retail.[92]

Something all these groups had—and have—in common is an intersectional mindset that understands workers' rights as being inextricably connected to immigration, racial justice, and women's rights and gender equity. It was a stance that was often missing from the majority of traditional unions, which had a history of overwhelmingly white and male memberships, and were often explicitly anti-immigrant n the first half of the twentieth century.

The worker centers developed a number of innovations and workarounds adapted to the challenges of each population of marginalized workers. As with the doormen's union that stepped up to speak on behalf of domestic workers, many groups realized there was power in throwing their weight behind the efforts of other workers, even if they weren't in the same field. Organizations like Jobs With Justice, then under the leadership of Sarita Gupta, facilitated these kinds of mutually supportive campaigns. The previously mentioned Caring Across Generations coalition was one such example, uniting women's rights groups, immigrant rights organizations, and elder rights' groups.

Powerful new strategies to bolster workers' power—and the quality of jobs—were also being developed by old-fashioned labor unions. The inspirational Justice for Janitors campaign of the 1990s—organized by SEIU, the largest union of service workers in the U.S.—succeeded even though many had argued that janitors, like domestic workers, were impossible to organize as largely undocumented, part-time, subcontracted workers of color. The Justice for Janitors campaign targeted the building owners and financiers at the top of the food chain, rather than the cleaning companies that technically employed the janitors.[93] The campaign exposed how, across sectors, subcontracting was being used to separate and isolate workers from the corporations and companies that were actually in control of their wages, benefits, and overall working conditions. This dynamic held true for all kinds of alternative work arrangements for gig workers, independent contractors, on-call workers, online platform workers, and workers for temp agencies. Figuring out how to build power for people working in all these situations was the great challenge of this period—one central to a guarantee of good work.

Raising the Minimum: The Fight for 15

2011 started off with a major loss for workers' rights when Scott Walker, the governor of Wisconsin put into power in 2010 by the Tea Party, stripped the state's public employees of the right to collective bargaining. By March, eighteen states had proposed similar legislation.[94] Employment in the public sector—with its decent pay, strong health care and retirement security, and job stability—is a backbone of Black wealth, accounting for the employment of one in five African Americans.[95] It also employs a greater share of women than the private sector.[96]

Even as states were passing laws that made it much harder to organize a traditional union, there were bright spots elsewhere among the majority of workers who weren't unionized. One such moment took place on Black Friday, the holy day of consumption, in 2012. Organization United for Respect at Walmart (OUR Walmart) organized hundreds of cashiers and stockers in forty-six states, who walked off the job.[97] It was a tiny percent of the company's 1.6 million total workforce, but their courage was inspiring—generating publicity that changed the conversation about the country's largest employer. They repeated the action in 2013 and 2014.[98] Workers also rallied at Walmart's annual shareholders' meetings each of those years, asking for more predictable schedules, hours equating to full-time jobs, and wages and benefits sufficient to ensure that no worker would have to rely on government assistance. In response, dozens of workers were intimidated, disciplined, or fired. Finally, in February 2015, Walmart announced it would raise its wage to $10 per hour starting in early 2016. It was followed almost immediately by Target, T.J. Maxx, and Marshalls. While some of the credit might also have owed to tightening labor markets (Ikea and Gap both had raised their wage to $10 in 2014), the actions had increased power among low-wage workers.

"Walmart could no longer defend being owned by billionaires but paying close to the minimum wage. When workers took action, Walmart suffered reputational damage and had to make changes in how they did business," Andrea Dehlendorf, co-founder of OUR Walmart, told me.[99]

Beginning in 2012, with the support of SEIU and other organizers, fast-food workers began striking, demanding $15 per hour and a union. A few hundred walked off their jobs at various restaurants in New York City in November 2012; then, in the spring of 2013, it happened in Chicago, St. Louis, Kansas City, and Milwaukee. By December of that year, workers in more than a hundred cities had staged one-day walkouts.[100] It was the beginning of the Fight for $15, as the SEIU-led movement for a $15 minimum wage became known. As with the Justice for Janitors fight, organizing fast-food workers had long been stymied by the franchise ownership structure: there wasn't one central employer to bargain with.

In 2013, the Fight for $15 would also take on the town of SeaTac, where Seattle's airport is located, via a ballot proposition that, despite being contested in the courts after winning voter approval, was ultimately instated midway through 2015.[101] The airport battle, led by the founder and president emeritus of Washington State's SEIU 775, David Rolf, affected the 2013 mayoral race in Seattle itself, pushing candidates to clarify their positions on a $15 minimum wage in the face of overwhelming support from voters. In 2014 Seattle became the first city in the nation to pass it. The gridlock on Capitol Hill, where Congress hadn't raised the federal minimum wage since 2009, helped catalyze the growing movement in cities and states. By the end of 2015, fourteen cities, counties, and states had approved a $15 minimum wage though local laws, executive orders, and other means, with dozens more legislative or ballot proposals introduced. In 2016, the governors of California and New York made the $15 wage statewide.[102]

Online Organizing

Meanwhile, in 2013 Michelle Miller, formerly of SEIU, landed on a virtual way to organize outside of traditional union infrastructures: an online platform called Coworker. Michelle is a white woman originally from West Virginia—who, after many years in the field, should count among the country's most incisive labor historians. Michelle's former colleague at SEIU, Jess Kutch, had noticed the "spikes of attention" from the media and the public when retail workers reported shady employers using the Change.org platform. When that occurred, a group would form around the issue for a couple of weeks. There would be some excitement, some media coverage, and then the issue would either be resolved or it wouldn't be, and the energy would ebb back to the status quo.

So the two of them built Coworker as a dedicated platform where workers could create online petitions to raise their issues. Their aim, however, was not just to achieve some outcome on the specific issue workers raised, but also to build connections and community between the employees of companies who worked in different stores. It was a big deal, since these workplaces had until then eluded workplace organizing, preventing workers from building power to push their employers, or the platforms, for better wages, benefits, or conditions. In other words, Coworker supported organizing where there was otherwise no infrastructure or entry point to the labor movement.

"We thought the only way to revitalize the labor movement was to bring as many people into it as possible, and to not be overly obsessed with whether or not they're joining a formal trade union," Michelle says. "But more importantly, to have them have the experience of collective advocacy, to raise the sense of possibility that you could change something in your workplace. We started the experiment with a series of questions: How do we build peer visibility among workers in a digital space? How does that visibility lead to a collective sense of power and ongoing collaboration? How do we thoughtfully apply our staff expertise while maintaining the distance that allows for truly imaginative, worker-led collective building? And how can we mitigate material risk to workers in this process of experimentation?"[103]

One of the first wins was among Starbucks employees, who used Coworker to campaign for the coffee company to change its policy banning visible tattoos. The petition, originally posted in August 2014, racked up more than 25,000 signatures—from the public as well as nearly 14,000 from Starbucks baristas—in more than forty countries.[104] In response, Starbucks changed its policy in October 2014. The win encouraged thousands of baristas to post on other issues and stay in touch with one another across email and social media in the following years; what we didn't yet know was how it was building the foundation for yet more important victories in the years to come.

Another important win came from a petition among Walmart employees for more transparency in scheduling—which had also been one of OUR Walmart's top demands. In 2014, in response to the pressure created by the Coworker petition, Walmart launched the Access to Open Shifts program, which allowed workers to find available slots themselves.[105]

As SEIU president Mary Kay Henry commented (about the fast-food walkouts, but it can be applied to all the developments of this period): "This movement is changing our political debate. The movement is changing what employers think they can get away with, and the movement is making cities and states change minimum wages."[106] A guarantee of good work must include a dignified living wage, but it doesn't stop with wages. There needed to be more to it. And more would come.

INCOME

In 2013, Armin Steuernagel and a crew of activists drove a truck to the parliament building in Bern, Switzerland, and dumped 8 million golden coins outside, one for every Swiss citizen. As Annie Lowrey wrote in the *New York Times*, "It was a publicity stunt for advocates of an audacious social policy that just might become reality in the tiny, rich country."[107] A public referendum had been called to determine whether Switzerland should provide a guaranteed monthly income to everyone, no strings attached, and Swiss voters were about to decide.

I met Armin and the other coin-dumping activists in Switzerland when they invited me to speak about the future of work, specifically exploring how the idea of a guaranteed income could lessen the potentially harmful impacts of artificial intelligence and technological change on the workforce. After a robust discussion about the future of work, Armin looked at us and said, "Why aren't *you* doing this? People in America need a guaranteed income far more than we do here in Switzerland." Armin knew the Swiss referendum wasn't likely to get enough votes to pass, but he wanted to advance a global conversation about the broken connection between work and worth.

The Long History

The idea of a guaranteed income, or an income floor, has been present in America for centuries, going all the way to back to Thomas Paine, who argued for a "national fund" to pay everyone a dividend (along with a lump sum to young people, much like a guaranteed inheritance) in his 1797 pamphlet *Agrarian Justice*.

In the 1930s, a physician in Long Beach, California, named Dr. Francis Townsend wrote a letter to the editor of his local paper. He was appalled, he wrote, by the poverty of the elderly, many of whom had moved to Southern California to retire, only to have their savings wiped away by the Great Depression. Nearly every advanced economy around the world had an old-age pension program in place, like the one that Germany's chancellor Otto von Bismarck had set up in 1889. Townsend proposed that everyone over the age of sixty receive a pension of $150–$200 per month. The response to his letter was swift and massive. By 1934 the idea was being distributed across the country as a pamphlet. More than three thousand "Townsend Clubs" were formed across the country, and they were only one of the popular movements brewing on pension programs.[108] President Roosevelt was forced to take action, and Social Security was born—creating what is essentially a guaranteed income for people over the age of sixty-five.[109]

In his 1967 book *Where Do We Go from Here: Chaos or Community?*, Martin Luther King Jr. issued a visionary call that's often left out of our remembrances of him. "The solution to poverty," King wrote, "is to abolish it directly by a now widely discussed measure: the guaranteed income."[110] In the years before he was assassinated, Dr. King was moved to speak out about economic rights after he was encouraged by the welfare rights organizers, largely Black women, of that era. Among them was Johnnie Tillmon, one of the most influential activists of the time and the executive director of the National Welfare Rights Organization, a multiracial coalition with a membership of 25,000 mothers who were relegated to jobs that didn't pay them enough money to raise their kids and had to suffer the indignities of the welfare system.[111]

Fifty years ago, Tillmon wrote these prophetic words: "The truth is, a job doesn't necessarily mean an adequate income. There are some ten million jobs that now pay less than the minimum wage, and if you're a woman, you've got the best chance of getting one."[112]

These women advocated for a "guaranteed adequate income" that prioritized their dignity and agency—and they succeeded in getting Dr. King to do the same.

"They had the question of economic agenda at the forefront from the very beginning and never saw the question of racial justice as separate from or divorced from economic justice and gender equality," commented Dr. Premilla Nadasen, a professor of history at Barnard College and author of *Rethinking the Welfare Rights Movement*. "So they were practicing what we today would call intersectionality even before it had that name."[113]

In the 1970s, President Richard Nixon proposed a version of guaranteed income called the Family Assistance Plan, but it ultimately failed to gain sufficient support in Congress.[114] Predictably, during the decades of neoliberalism, the idea on the federal level would be swept under the rug like the other bold ideas to guarantee economic security.

Even so, sparks of the idea were kept alive. Starting in 1982, each resident of the state of Alaska began receiving an annual dividend check, with no strings attached, from the oil wealth that they collectively own as Alaskans.[115] The dividend checks from the Alaska Permanent Fund help ease the income volatility of seasonal work in the state. They help people do things like pay for heating through the winter. Studies show that the annual checks also have positive impacts on public health such as higher birth weights and fewer hospital visits.

The Renaissance

In 2011, a student sat in a library in Palo Alto, reading Dr. King's last book. He jotted a note in the margins about guaranteed minimum income—and said to himself, "I'd like to be part of making that happen someday." Michael Tubbs would soon graduate from Stanford and be elected to the city council of his hometown, Stockton, California, making him one of the youngest elected officials in the United States at age twenty-two. The notes in his dog-eared copy of Dr. King's book would travel with him to Stockton City Hall.

In 2014, the social entrepreneur and environmentalist Peter Barnes released a book called *With Liberty and Dividends for All*. That's where I first read about the Alaska Permanent Fund. Peter had come up with a national version he called

Alaska for America, a "cap and dividend" policy in which companies that introduced oil, coal, and natural gas into the economy would be required to obtain auctioned permits to cover each ton of their greenhouse gas emissions. Dividends from the sale of those permits would then be returned directly to all U.S. citizens through equal-size monthly rebates.[116]

Andy Stern's exploration of a guaranteed income would result in his 2016 book *Raising the Floor*. The tenacious labor leader from New Jersey had led SEIU to become the fastest-growing union in the world. When he stepped down as SEIU president, he began researching the idea. Andy would describe a basic income—which would sit alongside wages—as leverage to support workers in fighting for better conditions, something like "empowerment checks." "Workers could refuse unsafe, poorly paid or irregularly scheduled work, or use it as a strike fund."[117]

There was such passionate engagement from different people focused on different arenas. I found it fascinating how this one idea could potentially speak to and impact so many issues: poverty, racial disparities and economic injustice, climate change, innovation, and of course, jobs and employment.

Reasons Beyond Robots

The mainstream universal basic income (UBI) conversation at the time was being framed as an answer to the ongoing loss of jobs to automation and artificial intelligence—and largely bandied about by those in tech. The press covered UBI as if it were crumbs to be handed out from Silicon Valley, quoting only tech billionaires who'd discuss the idea with cool detachment. The conversation ignored gender, race, and even the politics of the day. I wanted to have a different conversation—and I wasn't the only one.

Dorian Warren—scholar, organizer, and media personality

—agreed. He wrote a seminal paper in 2015 developing the concept of "UBI Plus," a universal basic income that included a pro-rated, additional amount for Black Americans who suffered through slavery and continuing economic racism, as a form of reparations.[118] That proposal would be later included in the Movement for Black Lives' policy platform in 2016. Dorian came to UBI from the tradition of Dr. King and the Black Panthers.

Chris Hughes also wanted to push the conversation beyond Silicon Valley. Chris had been roommates with Mark Zuckerberg at Harvard and co-founded Facebook, and then joined the team that first elected President Obama to office, where I met him. After Facebook's initial public offering in 2012, Chris and his husband decided to give away much of the unfathomable wealth which that IPO conferred on them, and in researching causes to support, had discovered the cash-transfer organization GiveDirectly. By 2016, Chris was thinking deeply about economic inequality, and was intrigued by UBI as a potential solution.

We decided to create Economic Security Project (ESP) in 2016 to dig into the research and take these ideas about how to guarantee an income floor in America and put them into action.

Soon we were joined by Taylor Jo Isenberg—a brilliant woman in her mid-twenties who accepted the role of ESP's managing director, after five years with the storied Roosevelt Institute. Her work organizing college campuses around the Roosevelt Institute's principles—the idea of America's social contract, a government committed to providing jobs, security, and opportunity, as articulated by Franklin and Eleanor—was so impressive that it received a major award from the MacArthur Foundation.

Hundreds of people signed onto the launch of ESP, including

academics teaching in fields like economics, sociology, public policy, computer science, philosophy, and law. The list included start-up founders and funders, think tank wonks, labor leaders, and organizers of community groups and campaigns like Black Lives Matter and SEIU. It included writers, artists, activists, public servants, and elected officials. All of them had signed their support for the idea of recurring, unconditional cash infusions; with their signature, they committed to helping ESP explore and experiment, design and test a guaranteed income program for America.

The problems this group came together to solve were poverty and income volatility, which had gotten worse over the past fifty years, as the country had transformed from a manufacturing economy to a service-sector economy, with America's largest employer now Walmart. Those jobs don't have regular hours or regular paychecks that people can count on. With the decline of labor unions and the rise of extreme income inequality, *giving people money* became the idea whose time had come. Once the call for a $15 minimum wage had made it to the national level in 2016, many believed it was time to push for an income guarantee that would function alongside wages, and would come each month with no strings attached. People with money in the stock market have this type of "non-labor" income—their money just makes money. Why shouldn't everyone?

In the context of projections about increasing automation and AI in the future, the tech-based UBI conversation was fascinating, but it wasn't a political imperative. Policy isn't passed based on a future threat; it's hard enough to get policy passed that alleviates current threats. Persistent poverty was a very visceral threat in the here and now, and it was only getting worse.

With a clearer understanding of *why* we needed to do this, it became our work to focus on the *how*. By officially launching Economic Security Project shortly after Donald Trump's election, we set about not only to answer this question, but also to find a match that would light the spark needed in America. We knew it wasn't a dump truck of gold coins in Washington, DC.

The match to light the fire would be leadership—people and organizations. The young city council member in Stockton would run for mayor in 2016 and win with 70 percent of the vote. A visionary nonprofit leader in Jackson, Mississippi, would ask the mothers living in public housing what they most needed, and the resounding answer would be "cash." These two leaders would spark the spread of a guaranteed income in America.

INHERITANCE

In 2011, Solana Rice was the director for financial security initiatives at PolicyLink, leading research on how to advance opportunity and community development for low-income communities and communities of color through wealth building. This followed, she tells me, the single line of inquiry she'd been pursuing since she was a little girl growing up in the Midwest: *Why isn't life fair, and how do we make it fair?* All she saw growing up in her Black family of autoworkers and food and retail workers was hard work and emotional and physical sacrifice, and still the American Dream remained out of their reach.[119]

After pursuing degrees in architecture and city planning, ultimately Solana landed on individual development accounts.

The individual development accounts (IDAs) program had become a bipartisan policy darling during the 1990s, following the influential 1991 book by Michael Sherraden, *Assets and the Poor*, which heralded "asset-based" policy as a new approach to welfare. Rather than the "income maintenance" of old-fashioned welfare, asset-based programs, he posited, would foster individual initiative and self-sufficiency.[120] IDA policies encouraged folks to save, helping them create budgets and set aside money for specific purposes, such as college education, homeownership, self-employment, and retirement security. The asset adherents proposed that in this way, low-income Americans could gain the same opportunities that middle- and upper-income earners had.

Federal policy that reformed welfare in the mid-1990s made federal dollars available to match what low-income people saved through IDAs, ranging from a one-to-one match to as high as six government dollars for every dollar saved.[121] An offshoot of IDAs was the children's savings account, which had an added benefit of being an investment vehicle (with IDAs you just saved your money in a bank account), built on the IRS's tax-advantaged 529 platform.[122] The money was to be used to cover higher education expenses: not just tuition but also fees and room and board.

One of the helpful outcomes of the asset-based welfare movement was an understanding that we needed to be looking at *wealth*, not just income, when grappling with poverty and economic inequality. Income arrives at regular intervals and generally goes to cover survival-level basics. It is almost always just money, while wealth often takes other forms like real estate, investments, a business, or valuable goods. Wealth is often described as "what you own minus what you owe." It powers the major undertakings and life events associated with social mobility, such as attending grad school, starting a business, and buying a home.

"Wealth provides financial agency over one's life," economist Darrick Hamilton explains. "Wealth gives you choice. It provides the economic security to take risks and shield against financial loss."[123] With no wealth, or even worse, with negative wealth, when you have only debt, you are forced to accept anything—any working condition, any wage—because you need to pay for your survival, you need to take care of your family. Without wealth, and especially under the burden of debt, you have almost no choice, no control, no power.

Income can contribute to wealth, but many people don't earn enough to save much, if anything, once the costs of daily life are covered. The majority of wealth is not derived from income, but from inheritance or other gifts. Much of Americans' wealth is held in the form of their homes, which homeowners often pass along to their children. White Americans have had far more assistance in becoming homeowners since the country's founding, while Black Americans were first outright banned and later faced myriad barriers to homeownership. This dynamic, compounded over centuries, is one of the primary reasons for the huge racial wealth gap.

Right around the turn of the millennium, as part of the larger discussion about the solvency of Social Security, and riding on a federal budget surplus and general boomtime vibe (thanks to the dot-com bubble and soaring real estate prices), another handful of wealth-creation policies became popular. One was then President Clinton's Universal Savings Accounts (USAs), funded through annual tax credits and federal matches on savings.[124] Another was Senator Bob Kerrey's KidSave plan, in which the government would have opened tax-deferred savings accounts for every American child, making a $1,000 deposit at birth and $500 deposits in each of the next five years. The money was to be securely invested and could be withdrawn at the age of eighteen, in some versions of the plan, or upon retirement.[125] KidSave had strong

bipartisan support and would be resurrected in 2005 by
Senator Chuck Schumer as the America Saving for Personal
Investment, Retirement, and Education (ASPIRE) Act, which
also found love across the aisle.[126]

However, when presidential candidate Hillary Clinton
floated the idea in late 2007, "of giving every baby born in
America a $5,000 account that will grow over time, so when
that young person turns 18, if they have finished high school,
they will be able to access it to go to college," it went down
like a lead balloon.[127]

As for Solana, she left PolicyLink for the national nonprofit
Prosperity Now in 2014, where she worked on the Prosperity Scorecard, a state-by-state assessment of the racial wealth
divide, how families were faring, and the strength of state policies. The more she learned, the more she realized the limits of
the assets-based model that people were then embracing. For
one thing, there was the way that the model underscored the
individualist narrative and the centrality of the free market.
She recounted to me:

> In this financialized economy, people owning their
> own assets is how people get ahead . . . but they have
> to do it themselves. This conveys a false notion that
> we all self-determine our ability to thrive in this
> free market based on our own effort.
>
> What if I believe this personal responsibility
> myth? If I fail, I feel shitty. If I succeed, I can fall
> prey to feeling like I was exceptional, when really
> I'd be an anomaly to a rule and I even may start
> spreading my gospel of success. Both of which dis-
> tract from the important work of advocating for
> systemic change.

Too many institutions in our movement have spent millions of dollars and countless hours of person-power on misguided "people-fixing" strategies. These include financial literacy, job skill building, remedial education, and housing counseling. These same institutions have designed racialized systems to divert government resources to the "deserving poor" while creating policies and programs to regulate the behavior of the "undeserving," Only programmatic and policy solutions that seek to fix systems, not people, can deliver economic liberation to people of color.[128]

Equally important, Solana realized, individual wealth wasn't correlating to more power for the community as a whole:

What was happening in the communities I was looking at was: you can save a whole bunch of money, and guess what? You're probably going to want to leave your neighborhood. Either because you can afford a little bit more, or you want your kids to have a better school, etcetera. So then what happens to that governance that you just built? What happens to that community of people that you just built around this experience? They're all gone. They've all dissipated.[129]

Solana concluded that building individual wealth couldn't come at the expense of building community power. It would be a couple years before she'd leave and start her own organization, and begin to imagine a guaranteed inheritance—but a change was coming.

CONCLUSION: FROM OCCUPY TO OUTSIDERS

The period between 2011 and 2016 started with an anti-establishment hopepunk protest movement among young people and ended with a presidential race that had anti-establishment populists running on both tickets.

Bernie Sanders had been fighting for the 99 percent long before Occupy, pointing to inequality as a sign that the American Dream was broken. Now he was cool. Trump's MAGA slogan acknowledged the brokenness too, just in another way. He'd be the one, of course, to occupy the White House in the nightmarish years to come. But the frustrations and pain of ordinary Americans fueled both candidates' unexpected success.

That same pain likewise fueled many of the advances made in these years by architects of the Guarantee Framework. Between 2011 and 2016, the idea that the economic system was broken had spread to all corners of the United States. We realized that financialization and corporate control of our democracy needed to be reined in, if not ended. We understood that the free market did not enable 99 percent of us to thrive.

During this same period, key innovations in communications, outreach, and organizing strategies led to power accumulating outside the traditional centers of power. New clarity crystallized in the conversation about the housing and eldercare crises. The president himself talked about universal access to public college, in the form of the College Promise, as a goal for the country. Organized labor was energized in a way it hadn't been for many decades, with much of the new lifeforce coming from workers whom the movement had traditionally left out.

Individual, hyperlocal fights progressed to more collective

action, as when Domestic Workers United moved from supporting individual workers in cases of employer misconduct,
to conducting citywide and statewide campaigns for a set of
employment standards. In a similar vein, the Debt Collective
went from buying and canceling individual debts, to scaling
up to an online debt dispute app that enabled tens of thousands of people to contest their loans.

The challenges to the old economic order had been issued
and the seeds of a new one had been scattered. Now the question was: Would they grow?

3
LEGITIMIZE (2016–2020)

To the surprise of the nearly 66 million people who voted for Hillary Clinton, and possibly to the surprise of the 63 million people who voted for her opponent, Donald Trump was elected president in November of 2016.[1] His "populist" campaign had tapped into the same discontent with the old economic system that fueled many of the architects of the Guarantees. However, while Trump alleged to be a man of the common folks, he presided over tax cuts favoring corporations and wealthy Americans—slashing the corporate tax rate by 40 percent in one fell swoop.[2]

Trump's election emboldened bigots and all those who opposed the progress we'd made which included the following highlights:

- the growing awareness and clarity around the housing crisis that community organizing was addressing, and cultural moments like Matthew Desmond's book *Evicted*;
- a majority of Americans polling in favor of free public college, with philanthropy and politicians supporting tuition-free public college (College Promise) programs in multiple states and cities, and student debtors starting to organize to fight predatory debt;
- a budding recognition of caregiving as key infrastructure that enables people to work outside the

home—and the resulting passage in several states of
a Domestic Workers' Bill of Rights;

- a powerful nurses' union making the case that expanding Medicare to cover all Americans was the
path to a Health Care Guarantee;
- innovations in labor organizing that laid foundations
for workers without the opportunity to unionize to
demand better pay and better conditions;
- the most serious conversation about an income floor
since the 1970s; and
- a growing understanding that the key to widespread
stability, security, and social mobility was *wealth*—
intergenerational wealth, in particular—rather than
income or education alone.

During these years, it would have been understandable if
all forward progress across the Guarantees was halted. No
one would have been surprised if all we did was play defense
and hold the line. In fact, when I look back at the years
2016–2020, it's clear that we did both, against all odds.

Many of the advances in the Guarantee Framework were
informed by a sharpened focus on racism and race equity, given that the White House was occupied by an overtly
white-supremacist president. In January 2017, protesters—my
kids and I among them—descended on airports to show widespread disapproval of President Trump's travel ban on visi-
tors from nine predominantly Muslim countries. In August
2017 the streets of Charlottesville, Virginia, filled with neo-
Confederates and neo-Nazis, Klansmen and far-right mili-
tias, toting their Confederate flags and their guns—and the
president called them "very fine people." Immediately, scores
of advisers resigned from the president's councils;[3] top brass
from across the armed forces denounced the marchers and

the president's reaction;[4] counter-protesters across the country and the world and the internet rallied to condemn racism and reassert that Black Lives Matter—the name of the hashtag that galvanized into a movement in 2014 after police killed Michael Brown in Ferguson, Missouri.[5]

"The political symbolism of Donald Trump along our continued trajectory towards inequality—I don't want to use the term 'silver lining,'" Darrick Hamilton told *Mother Jones* magazine in 2020, "but it might have given us the conditions and platform that allow us to really engage with and work on racial stratification head-on in an explicit way."[6] As Heather McGhee noted, "Donald Trump has perversely given Democrats political permission to talk about race."[7]

In the second half of 2016, the Movement for Black Lives (M4BL) released its policy platform, informed by dozens of established activist and advocacy groups. Frustrated by the inadequacy of both national parties' platforms, M4BL decided to sow its own seeds for the future. Focused on six key areas—political power, community control, economic justice, investment and divestment, reparations, and an end to the war on Black people—the document inspired many architects of Guarantees to make sure that new policy proposals, especially for housing, health care, and income, were targeted to address historical and current racialized inequities.

By 2018, the hopepunk crew of architects was no longer just concerned with challenging the old framework, no longer focused solely on *provocation*. The Guarantee was moving from the margins into the mainstream. The progress entailed a patchwork of efforts; the advances weren't yet landmark federal legislation or Supreme Court decisions. Instead we had local- and state- and company-wide wins, such as changes in zoning restrictions that would address the housing supply problem, and the shift among many employers toward adopting paid family leave. Influential and groundbreaking studies by social scientists and academics ranged from the Education Trust's Dr. Tiffany Jones evolving the College Guarantee, to Darrick Hamilton's work in stratification economics, underscoring the need for an Inheritance Guarantee. New policy ideas imported from overseas, such as Vienna's social housing and Australia's Higher Education Contribution Scheme, helped crystallize equitable ways to provide homes and higher education, respectively. New champions arrived on the scene, like Ady Barkan for a Health Care Guarantee and Dr. Aisha Nyandoro and Mayor Michael Tubbs for the Income Guarantee. The Guarantee Framework entered popular culture and the mainstream news.

We were sailing toward legitimacy. By the time the presidential primaries for the 2020 elections kicked off, candidates were seriously floating nearly the full range of Guarantee-based proposals.

HOMES

More and more community groups and academics were recognizing the state of housing in America for what it was: a full-blown crisis. Homeownership rates were still falling in the wake of the 2008 crash.[8] Demand for rentals was driving up the price of rent, so housing was costing households a bigger chunk of their income even as wages remained stagnant.[9] Four evictions were being filed every minute in 2016.[10] The construction of desperately needed new housing—especially affordable housing—was still stymied by local zoning restrictions and naysayers. Yet in all of this, we were lacking significant leadership on the federal level that might have championed housing as a human right.

"Americans believe that housing is a local issue. And it *is* a local issue. But it is also a regional issue, a state issue, and a national issue. By restricting the debate to the hyperlocal level, we've blocked out our big-picture values," noted Jerusalem Demsas, housing writer for *The Atlantic*.[11]

Between 2016 and 2020, the rise of a tenant power movement that fought to expand protections for renters—as well as a scaling up of the hyperlocal "Yes In My Back Yard" fights to a widespread national focus on the housing shortage—resulted in steady progress toward a Homes Guarantee.

Tenants Strike Back

In 2016, tenants launched rent strikes all across the United States. The rent strike was an old tactic—last seen in the 1960s and '70s, when Black tenants protested the unlivable conditions of neglected housing in disinvested neighborhoods. Now, in the aftermath of recovered prices in the housing market, gentrification was widespread, and landlords responded by pushing longtime tenants out in the pursuit of higher rents. Tenants got organized, however, and revived the rent strike. In 2016, Los Angeles led the way, to be followed by Cleveland, Houston, San Francisco, and Washington, DC.[12]

The Mariachis were one such story:

During the holiday season in late 2016, a landlord named Frank "BJ" Turner delivered a notice to half of his tenants in a building in the Boyle Heights neighborhood of Los Angeles, announcing an 80 percent increase in their rent—not a welcome Christmas gift. Any building in LA built after 1978 was not subject to rent stabilization, meaning landlords could arbitrarily increase rents at any time. The building in question had been built in 1983.[13]

One of the only areas that did not have a racially restricted housing covenant in the early 1900s, Boyle Heights was a historically Japanese, then Jewish and Eastern European, and now mostly Latino neighborhood.[14] Mariachi Plaza, where mariachi players have been gathering since the 1930s to advertise their services, was only a few blocks away. With gentrification looming, the landlord wanted his apartments opened up to higher rents.

Many of the tenants had lived in the building for decades, and had grown up there. None of them—several of whom were mariachi musicians themselves—could afford the increased rent. Rather than move out, the tenants who received the notice decided to stay and fight, despite the risk of eviction. The remaining tenants, realizing they could receive the same notice at any time, decided to join them. With support from La Union de Vecinos (The Union of Neighbors), they launched a rent strike, withholding rent payments until BJ changed his tune. They were inspired by the similarly working-class Latino tenants of a much larger complex in Highland Park, who had started a rent strike earlier in 2016. BJ's tenants put up posters explaining the situation in the windows of their building and held rallies out front, where mariachis played their music in full costume. They got a lot of love on social media. But BJ kept refusing to meet with them.

One year after the original notice, the tenants and their allies showed up at BJ's home, in the wealthy Rancho Park neighborhood on the west side of LA. They shared their story with all of BJ's neighbors who cared to know what was going on. In response, BJ filed a lawsuit to block further protests and force the rent strike to end. The Mariachis (as all the tenants had by now come to be known, including those who weren't musicians) showed up in court with dozens of supporters and a fleet of lawyers to fight it. Finally, in February 2018, BJ agreed to meet.[15]

The two parties negotiated a deal: a three-and-a-half-year contract of stable rents, with a rent increase that topped out at 15 percent, with another guaranteed opportunity to meet after a few years, plus a commitment from BJ to certain necessary repairs around the building. It was a landmark victory for tenants and organizers in LA, was highly publicized, and provided a template for others to follow. Between 2016 and 2018 there were dozens of other building-wide rent strikes. These helped to lay the foundation for a tenants' movement.

The person who told me the mariachis' story was René Christian Moya, a Latino native of northeast LA who had gone to college on the East Coast and gotten his law degree in London. He'd done eviction defense for homeowners in London who lost their homes after the 2008 crash, before returning to LA in 2013 to work on tenants' issues with Alliance of Californians for Community Empowerment (ACCE). He describes his understanding of the situation at that point:

> The 2008 crisis sharpened my focus on housing, when we were seeing in real time the failure of a particular economic narrative about how the world worked, and housing was the earthquake that undid it. Something like 60 percent of global assets are in property, with the vast majority of that in residential real estate. Housing is the place where all these issues came together: wealth inequality, the power of labor vis-à-vis capital, the role of financialization.[16]

Around this time, René pivoted from supporting rent

strikes to developing the Tenant Power Toolkit, a collaboration between ACCE, the LA Tenants Union, and the Debt Collective, among others.

The Tenant Power Toolkit helps tenants to understand their rights and fight their eviction, essentially functioning as legal mutual aid. It also provides them with the means to connect with, and contribute to, collective action to boost tenants' rights, lower rents, and end rent debt—making demands not just of landlords but of government.[17]

The collaboration with the Debt Collective intrigued me. As René explained: tenants' unions really are a form of debtors' union, because the vast majority of evictions nationwide happen because people cannot pay their rent—which then becomes a debt dispute. Unlike other forms of debt, however, when money is owed as rent, the collection process is virtually immediate. The foreclosure process will be launched within about three months, while the eviction process can get started within three *days*.

"And the reason why, ultimately," René told me, "is because land itself doesn't operate in the way that another commodity does. The land is here, remains here; the housing remains here. And so, for landlords or a lot of banks that hold onto this debt, it's much easier for them to just say: 'We're going to just get you out of your home and bring in another tenant who will be able to continue fulfilling that rental obligation.' So eviction becomes this very perverse sort of solution to the debt crisis, a grim resolution to the fallout of neoliberal policies."[18]

After the building-wide rent strikes, tenant groups began demonstrating a greater capacity, aided by the Tenant Power Toolkit and a growing savviness with media and public relations. The tenant movement continued to scale up. Organized tenant power shifted from the level of a single building or complex, with residents focused on their own landlord, to the level of the city, the state, and even the nation.

In 2017, a group of low-income tenants in the South Bronx (Community Action for Safe Apartments, or CASA) finally won the campaign they'd launched in 2013 for the right to legal counsel in eviction court.[19] San Francisco and Newark followed suit in 2018, joined by Cleveland and Philadelphia in 2019. By 2022 ten more cities and three states had safeguarded this right for tenants, resulting in dramatic reductions in the number of evictions.[20]

Tenants also brought attention to rent inflation, and campaigned to keep the cost of renting stable in order to stabilize families and neighborhoods. In 2019, Oregon, New York, and California passed groundbreaking legislation addressing the rising cost of rent.[21]

The Tenant Protection Act, a California statewide measure written by former state assemblymember David Chiu, set limits on rent increases and required landlords to have a "just cause" for evictions.[22] The law was passed in part thanks to the fragile new alliance between tenants' rights groups and housing supply advocates (composed of the emerging YIMBY movement), who were taking steps toward each other.[23] For example, many tenant advocates who didn't trust the financial motives of developers started to advocate for housing production, while YIMBYs who had been wary that rent controls would disincentivize housing development started to believe that abundant housing and strong tenant protection needed to go hand in hand.

"California's law was the biggest expansion in tenant protections in American history, and it came out of the realization that building more housing and protecting tenants aren't mutually exclusive," said Catherine Bracy, the founder of

TechEquity, a group that organizes tech workers to fight for economic justice and whose members came from both the abundant-housing and tenant-protection flanks. "From this era came the understanding that we need to 'protect' renters, 'produce' more housing, *and* 'preserve' existing affordable housing—the 3 P's of housing. People started to see that their fights were linked and we were stronger together."[24]

More cities and states would follow suit with tenant protections, with the city of Kansas City, Missouri, seeing a landmark win in 2019 when it passed a Tenant Bill of Rights.[25] As Matthew Desmond reflected in 2020, "Since the Great Recession, America has witnessed a resurgence of tenant power. . . . In city after city, renters have begun to see themselves as a class, with shared interests and problems, and to organize together."[26]

This rising tenants' movement was accomplishing something important, beyond winning protections for the most precariously housed people: it was reminding the nation that housing is more than a commodity. Even without the ownership stake in the places they live, tenants have been risking everything to keep their homes, because for them, it is about love of place, about family and neighborhood and culture, about continuity—not about housing prices. So the tenant movement shakes the neoliberal concept of housing to its core.

The tenants' movement was advancing the call for housing as a fundamental right and housing as a public good. We don't leave road construction or public schools entirely up to the private market, so why should it be that way for housing?

Zoning Gets Liberated

Several years into its existence, the YIMBY movement began to transcend its original reputation as being solely focused on "trickle-down housing." Ending the zoning restrictions on building multifamily housing became a common goal of both those calling for more housing supply and advocates for affordable housing.

On three-quarters of the residential land in America's cities, it has been illegal to build anything other than a detached single-family home. The percentage is even higher in many suburbs and Sunbelt cities.[27] As California state senator Scott Wiener has observed, "That means that *everything else is banned*. Apartment buildings—banned. Senior housing—banned. Low-income housing, which is only multi-unit—banned. Student housing—banned."[28]

YIMBYs included a wide coalition of people who wanted to fight against restrictive zoning. They encompassed environmentalists who knew that denser housing in cities results in a lower carbon footprint, due to lower car emissions and smaller, more energy-efficient housing units, like apartments and in-law suites. They were joined by race equity advocates who knew that restrictive zoning was actually just a way to ensure housing stayed segregated even after housing discrimination became illegal. Most developers also liked the sound of fewer restrictions on building, and some labor unions looked forward to the new jobs in construction as well as the promise of people being able to live closer to where they work. The coalition for more housing production was bipartisan, homeowners as well as renters, and the big tent was helpful in getting legislation passed.

The first major victory against exclusionary zoning happened in Minneapolis, where in 2018, the city council voted to abolish single-family-home-only zoning and allow duplexes and triplexes to be built anywhere in the city.[29] The city's historic new plan was more racially and economically inclusive, centering on walkability and mass transit. A year later,

Oregon followed, becoming the first state to pass legislation that eliminates single-family-home-only zoning in much of the state. As The Century Foundation noted:

> All of a sudden, however, the seemingly invincible walls that zoning policies have erected are beginning to crumble. Jurisdictions from Massachusetts and Maryland to Oregon and California and the State of Washington are beginning to take action to loosen restrictions. Presidential candidates such as Elizabeth Warren and Cory Booker have proposed federal legislation to reduce exclusionary zoning, and President Trump's secretary of housing and urban development, Ben Carson, is chair of a White House task force that will address exclusionary zoning.[30]

This was a truly tectonic shift—and cities and states were leading the way. As with education policy, the rules on how and where housing is built are determined locally, and each city has different rules, making a one-size-fits-all federal approach difficult. The federal government can, however, use funding to incentivize the move toward less restrictive zoning.

The politics of housing were changing, and the groundwork was being laid to finally build enough housing for all.

A Homes Guarantee Is Born

Tara Raghuveer had joined People's Action, the nationwide federation of grassroots organizations across thirty out of the fifty states that represents millions of poor and working Americans. At People's Action, Tara set out to take those members' disparate aims and weave the threads into a national strategy. "There have always been really powerful local sites of struggle, like the work of tenant organizers, but on the national stage? Housing isn't even a third-rail issue. It's like the ugly stepchild of national politics," Tara told me.[31]

In the middle of 2018, Tara organized a gathering of some fifty housing leaders at a retreat center in upstate New York. They weren't just community organizers like Tara or René; they were also unhoused folks and public housing residents and tenants of terrible landlords, people with immediate proximity to the issues. The goal of the retreat was to decide on the "issue cuts" that People's Action would focus on for its national campaign.

> Examples of the issue cuts were: to make developer money toxic in local elections, or around voter registration in public housing. They were specific, narrow fights. No one thing spoke to enough people in that room for there to be consensus around it. And after hours of discussion debating the merits of different strategies, the leaders in the room just started saying: *It needs to be all of this. It needs to be all of this and more.*
>
> Remember it was summer 2018: energy was starting to build around the 2020 presidential election. These leaders were starting to think that housing should be an issue in national politics.
>
> They said, "We are sick of chanting, 'Housing is a human right.' It's a talking point, but it barely means anything anymore. People can just get away with saying it and then move on with their lives. They can wipe their hands of this issue and therefore all of us."
>
> In health care, the demand is clear. The left's demand is: Medicare for All. On climate now the

demand is clear: it's a Green New Deal. The long-term agenda is clear. On housing, we have no such thing. We need to be the campaign that articulates that.

On the last day of the retreat, I floated the idea of a Housing Guarantee, taking the "Guarantee" framework from one of my mentors. It found resonance. People immediately embraced it. Soon after, it became the Homes Guarantee because "housing" sounds impersonal, inhuman in some ways. It became the "Homes Guarantee" within the next month.

Now all we needed to do was figure out what that meant.[32]

Tara spent the next months getting everyone's input and working through what would become the *Homes Guarantee Briefing Book*.[33] In short, this document calls for stronger renter protections, for investment in existing public housing, and for an end to real estate speculation. It also mandates that the federal government build millions of new units of social housing. Social housing is like a public option for housing, provided at below-market rates and kept permanently off the private market.

The social housing model provided by Austria's capital, Vienna, provided inspiration. Delegations of elected officials from the U.S. began traveling to Vienna to study it. For more than a century, weathering governments of wildly different political persuasions, the social housing of Vienna has offered residents homes built, owned, and managed by the municipal government—some in partnership with nonprofits. Eighty percent of the population is eligible to live in them. Once you have a contract, it never expires, no matter your income. Law dictates that rents can only increase when inflation exceeds 5 percent.

The robust public option for housing helps keep all the housing prices down across Vienna, and most people housed.[34]

The Vienna model—and the Homes Guarantee—were finding resonance. As Tara told me, not only was the Homes Guarantee "not laughed out of the room," it was quickly embraced by progressive lawmakers:

> Finally, on September 5th, 2019, we launched. It was good timing. All these presidential campaigns were particularly ambitious at that point.
>
> Bernie Sanders then adopted most of the Homes Guarantee as his platform. Several progressive elected officials wanted to write housing bills, which we helped them do. Those were introduced in January 2020.[35]

The existence of the *Homes Guarantee Briefing Book*—and the fact that it was co-created with the people in the most precarious housing situations across the country—was monumental. It meant that when the pandemic hit, exacerbating the long-standing housing crisis, we already had a "north star," a comprehensive vision for housing.

This, paired with the changing zoning rules around building new multi-unit housing, was making future potential investments in both social housing and market-rate housing a real possibility.

COLLEGE

Despite the more than 60 percent of Americans in favor of free public college, and the fanfare around the tuition-free

"College Promise" programs popularized by Kalamazoo, Michigan, and the state of Tennessee, between 2016 and 2020 the College Guarantee faced setbacks. "America Wakes Up from Its Dream of Free College," the title of a 2018 article in *The Atlantic* by education writer Adam Harris, captured the vibe after Trump came into power.[36] The subject of free public college did make its way very briefly into the confirmation hearings for the secretary of education in 2017, but was met with Betsy DeVos's trademark smirk, and that was the end of that.[37]

The Broken Promises

In 2017, when Dr. Tiffany Jones, then the director of higher education policy at the Education Trust, a national nonprofit that advocates on behalf of students of color and students from low-income families, analyzed the College Promise programs, she found them lacking. Dr. Jones, originally from Lansing, Michigan, where her parents worked in the auto industry, got her bachelor's at Central Michigan University, her master's in higher education administration from the University of Maryland, and her PhD in in urban education policy from the University of Southern California. Thanks to scholarships, her tuition was covered but, as someone from a low-income Black family, her path was nearly blocked by the price of undergraduate room and board. She worked multiple jobs alongside her classes to make it work.[38]

The Education Trust team developed an equity-driven approach, using eight criteria that asked, for example, whether the Promise programs covered living expenses and fees, whether adult students were eligible, whether repayment of aid would be required under certain circumstances, and whether there were GPA requirements or other requirements to maintain eligibility. The great majority of the Promise programs failed to meet all the criteria, meaning, in Dr. Jones's words: they would "perpetuate, rather than disrupt, systems that favor some and disempower others."[39]

Perversely, her team found, more resources in College Promise programs were going to middle- and upper-middle-class students. That's because most College Promise programs are "last dollar in," meaning that they cover only what's leftover of tuition after all eligible grants have been applied (Pell Grants and any other grants that don't have to be paid back). Poor students get more covered by government funding like Pell, and therefore less from the College Promise coffers.

"For lower- and middle-income students, 'free public college' isn't truly free if only tuition is taken care of," Dr. Jones explained.[40] Tuition only amounts to about one-fifth of the cost of attending college, but College Promise money can't be used to cover the other expenses a student incurs over the course of study (housing, transport, food, books), often exceeding $30,000.[41] Rich parents often pay for those expenses outright. High-scoring students might receive selective merit stipends that cover these cost-of-living expenses, but those stipends skew towards advantaged students too, those who often have had access to tutoring and accelerated schooling such as Advanced Placement classes. "The gap in funding has passively created a disincentive for members of working-class communities, particularly those of color, to enter higher education," according to Dr. Jones.[42]

And because Promise funding is not federally guaranteed, but funded by state or local coffers or philanthropy, it could easily be cut—and it has been. For example, the state of Oregon, after making community colleges tuition-free in 2016, could not fully fund its program in 2017.[43] Some states and cities put restrictions in place, offering free tuition only to high school graduates with a certain GPA or to those who pass a drug test, or they allowed Promise students only to take certain courses.

When the resulting report, *A Promise Fulfilled*, was published by Dr. Jones (now the deputy director of the Bill & Melinda Gates Foundation) and her co-author Katie Berger (now director of education at the Biden White House), it marked an important inflection point in the free college movement. The Promise models came to be known as "tuition-free," as distinct from "debt-free," with the latter referring to programs that cover all costs. It's *debt-free* college that actually benefits the students who most need the support.

The Education Trust report and the conversation it had sparked about the problem with "last dollar in" and "tuition-free" proposals directly influenced policymakers, resulting in several new and improved legislative proposals. Hawaii senator Brian Schatz introduced a bill to provide universal debt-free college. A proposal for a state and federal partnership, it expanded from tuition-only to include living expenses as well.[44] When Bernie Sanders and Representatives Ilhan Omar and Pramila Jayapal introduced the College for All Act in June of 2019, members of the Debt Collective traveled to Washington to endorse the bill, which would have eliminated all $1.6 trillion in student debt and made public college not just tuition-free, but debt-free.[45]

From Debt-Free to Free

Around the same time, Melissa Byrne, the student debtor and organizer, started an organization called We, the 45 Million that would move the conversation further toward a Guarantee. Melissa agreed that the College Promise programs weren't sufficient. Ultimately, she argued, higher education shouldn't be commodified: it must be viewed as a public good.[46]

"The next generation of college students needs an entirely

different framework for talking about college access," Melissa wrote,[47] and the We the 45 Million website elaborates:

> A healthy democracy understands the importance of an educated populace. A society where millions of people cannot reach their full potential and live their lives with agency benefits no one.
>
> Student loans are a poor tax: wealthy families only have to pay for the cost of tuition and fees, but lower-income students will pay all that plus interest and fees on their student loans, all because they were born into the wrong family. We also cannot discount the many people from poor and working-class backgrounds who wanted to go to college or would have tried it out but the thought of taking out student loans terrified them. They did not make a free choice to pursue other options—they were coerced by the economic situation they were born into.[48]

Inspired by the Australian Higher Education Contribution Scheme, Melissa and her organization suggested a different model for how we could achieve free college. She explained:

> Everyone who goes to college should pay for it when they start working. Straight-up free college for everyone would be ideal, but let's talk about what's more feasible. Everyone who goes to college should have to pay a 5 to 10 percent higher education fee for ten to fifteen years after they complete college. This will cover both academic and housing fees.

We need to go all in to support a vision of America where anyone who's willing to spend time studying will have access to the best school for them.[49]

Introduced in 1989, the Higher Education Contribution Scheme has allowed for people to attend college without up-front costs. Then, once graduates start working and earning above a certain threshold, they pay a tax that is dependent on the level of their income, between 1 percent and a maximum of 10 percent of their annual personal income. The tax is collected through employers and remitted to Australia's equivalent of the IRS, just as income taxes are collected. Since the early 1990s, a number of other countries have adopted the same model (like New Zealand in 1991), or part of it (like Brazil, Japan, and Canada).[50]

Melissa's articulation of a bold vision would set the stage for the groundbreaking developments around student debt in the years to come.

HEALTH CARE

With Trump determined to undo "the disaster known as Obamacare," the movement toward a Health Care Guarantee redirected its energy toward defending what we already had in place. Progressives launched a counteroffensive—ultimately thwarting the naysayers' relentless efforts to repeal the ACA—which was particularly impressive, since anti-Obamacare voices held control of the House, the Senate, and the executive branch. "It's a testament to the importance of health care to Americans of all political stripes that the attempts to thwart the Affordable Care Act failed," said Jamila Headley, the co-executive director of Be a Hero.[51]

A New Champion

The vision for the Health Care Guarantee seemed so clear, and yet so out of reach. The nation was plagued with monumental and still mounting expenses, bad health outcomes, a lack of necessary care, and early, unnecessary death. Accustomed to this needless loss of life, but without the political will to address it, we were stuck.

What would it take to bring America closer to a new way of caring for its people? Maybe it would take the voice of a dying man.

In the final weeks of 2016, the Yale-educated thirty-something lawyer and progressive organizer, Ady Barkan, the son of two academics who immigrated to the U.S. from Israel, had received a terrible diagnosis. He had amyotrophic lateral sclerosis (ALS), the fatal neurodegenerative disease also known as Lou Gehrig's. "I knew our health care system was broken before my diagnosis, but having a serious illness clarified just how cruel our system really is," Ady said.[52]

In 2017, already partially paralyzed, Ady was flying home to California after meetings in DC when he saw Republican senator Jeff Flake of Arizona on the plane. He confronted the senator about the pending Republican tax bill, which would gut part of the Affordable Care Act. Ady begged Flake to not support it. "What will you tell my son if you pass this bill and it cuts funding for disability and I can't get a ventilator? . . . Why not take a stand now? You can be an American hero!" Ady pleaded. "You can save my life."[53]

Although the senator voted in favor of the bill, the video of their conversation went viral on social media. Ady built on its popularity and launched the organization Be a Hero, named for his plea to Senator Flake.

As his disease quickly progressed, Ady lost the ability to walk within two years. After pursuing the few medical options available, Ady decided to use his story—and his body—as a campaign tool. "If there's something good that can come out of it, I want to use it to do that good." Implicit in this was a powerful message to lawmakers and politicians: *If a dying man could make this kind of commitment, why can't you?*

In 2018 Ady set off across the country in his motorized wheelchair, in a wheelchair-accessible van purchased with help from the California Nurses/NNU and a GoFundMe campaign. He and his support crew—"Ady's Roadies"—stopped in thirty congressional districts to advocate for health care.[54] The trip was publicized online, sharing the stories of people he met alongside his own, and trainings on how to approach political leaders. Ady's words on the necessity of government-guaranteed health care were never clearer or more powerful:

> To fully achieve health care justice in America, we need to overturn the patchwork, for-profit health care system that we have today. The cruelty of our for-profit health care system is by design. And it has succeeded in failing all of us, except of course the CEOs it is set up to enrich. Only a single-payer system would possess the scale and resources necessary to guarantee home- and community-based services for all.
>
> Let's be honest. If we were creating a health care system from scratch, we would not create a confusing, piecemeal, for-profit approach to healthcare. We keep nibbling at the edges of what is possible.

We already have a Medicare system that is delivering healthcare to 60 million Americans. Why not
expand it to include everyone? No more confusion.
No more fighting with insurance companies, no
more medical bankruptcies. What we would get is
predictable health care coverage for all.[55]

Echoing what the nurses' union had previously demanded
in calling for the expansion of Medicare to cover everyone
(Medicare for All), Ady was describing a Guarantee.

Ady also spoke frequently on the importance of home care
services, and the mandate to cover them:

I now rely on a team of caregivers for 24-hour
homecare. My team of caregivers enables me to
live at home, where I get to be an active participant
in my family's lives. Homecare allows me to work
with my team at Be a Hero, fighting for health care
justice. Without in-home care, I probably would
need to be in a nursing home to stay alive. And, to
be honest, I don't know if that would be a quality
of life that I would be willing to tolerate. So, homecare is literally keeping me alive.

But across the country, almost 1 million disabled
children, adults and seniors sit on waiting lists for
Medicaid's home- and community-based care,
in danger of being ripped away from their homes
and forced to live in unsafe institutions. We need
the full, proposed funding so that we can clear the
820,000-person waiting list for Medicaid's home
care services and bolster the caregiving workforce
by creating nearly a million new jobs.[56]

Ady's fight for the care he needed was long and exhausting: "We eventually secured 24-hour home care after suing my health insurance company in federal court. But it shouldn't take a seasoned activist, a team of lawyers, and the generosity of strangers and friends to get the health care you need to survive."[57]

By January 2019, Ady had lost the use of his vocal cords. Since then he has relied on an eye gaze technology that follows the movements of his eyes and uses a computerized voice to speak. In the months before his voice disappeared, Ady recorded himself singing songs to his son Carl, who had been born shortly before Ady's diagnosis, so that Carl would remember his dad's voice.

Medicare for All in Primary Season

As primary season for the 2020 presidential election unfolded, Medicare for All took center stage among the Democrats. In Bernie Sanders's Medicare for All plan, the $30 trillion price tag would be offset through savings in administrative overhead, pharmaceutical costs, and physician salaries; a combination of payroll, sales, capital gains, and income taxes would pay for the rest. At one of the key primary debates, all ten candidates on stage discussed Medicare for All for twenty minutes. As a piece in the *New York Times* put it, "In a party that three short years ago kept single-payer advocates at Skyping distance, Medicare for All now sits at the head of the table, pulling the Democrats decisively leftward."[58]

Ady decided to have a conversation with every Democratic candidate about health care, to tease out exactly what their position and commitment would be. But one morning he woke, struggling to breathe, and had to cancel his plans. He had to undergo a tracheostomy, which meant he required a ventilator to breathe. "My insurance denied me a ventilator, stating that it was experimental, and then two weeks after that, they rejected access to an FDA-approved ALS drug. Even good health insurance, which I have, does not cover the cost of the care I need to survive. Paying out of pocket would have left us bankrupt."[59]

Undeterred, Ady managed to speak with most of the candidates: Liz. Cory. Bernie. Kamala. Julián. Mayor Pete. Eventually, even Uncle Joe.[60]

"When you're asked by a dying person about health care, giving the standard messaging [and] talking points is probably the most hollow and empty a politician could look," commented Be a Hero co-executive director Jamila Headley. "Getting in there and asking questions about everything from prescription drug pricing, to their stances on Medicare for All, and their own personal health care connections, allowed Ady and Be a Hero to produce some of the most personal and candid content on the issue of health care that we saw during the presidential primary."[61]

When Ady talked to Biden, they started by sharing their stories of loss. Finally, a little more than ten minutes into their conversation, Ady popped the question: "Will America ever have a health care plan that guarantees health care as a human right?" Biden answered by offering a public option that would compete with private plans, subsidies for anyone who wanted in on a gold plan, and home care and eldercare paid for as a basic right. However, he said he didn't support a single-payer plan.

"I hope you understand that this is personal," Ady responded. "When I say I support single-payer, it's because I have spent hours on hold with my health insurance provider when they won't cover the cost. It's because I've had to sue insurance companies when they tell me I have to pay out of pocket for the cost of care."[62]

"The crux of the matter is that no one else can do this. They can't," said Liz Jaff, co-founder of Be a Hero with Ady. "He can legitimately just say to Joe Biden, 'You're wrong on Medicare for All. I'll still endorse you, but you're wrong.' And that is what we need. Politicians get away with a lot. They don't have that kind of accountability. And Ady can do that because of his story, because he is dying. It's hard but it's true."[63]

In his speech at the Democratic National Convention in August 2020, Ady said: "Like so many of you, I have experienced the ways our health care system is fundamentally broken. . . . Enormous costs, denied claims, dehumanizing treatment when we are most in need. . . . We live in the richest country in history and yet we do not guarantee this most basic human right. Everyone living in America should get the health care they need regardless of their employment status or ability to pay."[64]

Ady's influence could be seen across the conversations about health care during the primaries and the surge in popularity of Medicare for All: 69 percent of registered voters were now in favor of the policy, and fifty cities and towns across America had passed resolutions endorsing it.[65]

What happened next, of course, brought the failures of the health care system into even starker relief—and that was the Covid pandemic.

FAMILY CARE

Paid family leave is an essential facet of a Family Care Guarantee. Families need paid leave to welcome a new child, care for a loved one, or take care of themselves during a personal medical emergency.

In 2012 and in 2017, I took paid family leave to welcome my kids, Huck and Juno, into the world. Those sleepless nights, tired mornings, and afternoons spent doing loads of laundry and gazing at the baby with hormone-fueled wonder are how my husband and I learned to be parents. Despite America's great wealth, only a minority of parents and caregivers can afford this privilege. The United States is the only industrialized nation in the world without a national paid leave policy.[66] In 2017, only 15 percent of working people had access to paid leave, and that access was entirely dependent on where they lived and who they worked for.[67] Among low-income workers, just 7 percent of people had access to paid leave.[68]

In 2016, the campaign Paid Leave for the U.S. (PL+US) was created by the public policy advocate and campaign director Katie Bethell. PL+US set an ambitious goal of winning federal paid family and medical leave for every working person in the U.S. by 2022.[69] Its strategy included corporate engagement—first pushing individual companies to introduce or expand their paid leave policies, then later organizing those corporate leaders to be advocates for federal policy. PL+US and other allied organizations also mobilized voters and cultivated champions among elected officials by spreading stories about diverse experiences of parents, caregivers, and families.

By 2018, paid leave advocates won improved policies at Walmart, Starbucks, CVS, and many other large employers, prompting a tectonic shift in the private sector as dozens of others followed suit.[70] Companies like Netflix, Spotify, and Etsy, already leaders in providing high-quality benefits, expanded their policies to be more equitable and to include adoptive parents and same-sex couples.[71]

These campaigns also helped to extend paid leave to low-wage working people, highlighting that paid leave shouldn't be a policy just for the C-suite or Silicon Valley executives.

Toyota updated its policy to include paid parental leave for dads and adoptive parents in their 130,000-person workforce. Lyft expanded its paid leave policy to provide a gender-neutral, sixteen-week parental leave plan for full-time employees. Nearly a hundred other companies including Postmates, Thumbtack, Sun Life, and Once Upon a Farm joined in. In total, PL+US helped *more than 8 million* U.S. workers gain access to employer-provided paid leave.[72]

Paid leave campaigns succeeded because they showed that paid family leave makes business and economic sense and is crucial for employee recruitment, retention, and morale. Companies didn't want to be left behind and increasingly saw the return on investment. Reputation was another factor—Walmart, in particular, is fighting the perception that it's a bad place to work, as it battles Amazon for both consumer dollars and millennial talent. As the single largest employer in America, Walmart is usually a bellwether: by extending paid leave to full-time workers—not just reserving this benefit for those in white-collar positions—it promoted internal equity and helped to lessen societal inequality.

While the embrace and expansion of paid family leave by select employers is progress, a guarantee for family care must include *federal* paid leave policy. The optimal policy would support the choice for a family caregiver to drop out of the paid workforce and provide the care should they wish to, and also would work in tandem with sustainable caregiving jobs providing dignified labor.

Shifting Perceptions of Care Work

During the Trump presidency, the list of states with bills of rights for domestic workers got longer: Illinois in 2016,

Nevada in 2017, New Mexico in 2019. In 2018 Seattle passed a law ensuring minimum wage and breaks (meal breaks for every five hours worked, and rest breaks every four hours); and one day of rest per week for workers living in their employers' home. These wins were hugely significant, no doubt, yet something was becoming clear: enforcing the new protections was challenging. Even the landmark ruling that finally included home care workers in the Fair Labor Standards Act still left some space for employers to argue that their caregivers weren't covered by the FLSA, depending on the specific activities they did during a shift.

"We are in a transition phase now," Ai-jen noted, "where we are moving from this whole economy existing in the shadows to trying to figure out how it becomes more formalized in the marketplace."[73]

An ongoing problem that domestic workers faced was the society-wide perception that domestic work wasn't "real work." It was just "help"; employers of domestic workers weren't real employers, and homes weren't really workplaces. As Ai-jen wrote in the *Hollywood Reporter*:

> At the heart of our troubling reality and what enables it to continue is a cultural narrative that fails to see the women who do this work as fully human; they are less than women, less than mothers, less than fully human. From the historic and pervasive mammy trope and images of whitewashed nannies to more recent representations of Latina house cleaners in film and television, on a spectrum of demeaning to exoticizing, all have failed to represent a fully human experience.[74]

The National Domestic Workers Alliance (NDWA) knew

that data and rational arguments, and even legislation, could only achieve so much. Changing perceptions was key.

NDWA had first experimented with this kind of work back in 2011, in conjunction with the release of the movie *The Help*—the story of two Black domestic workers in the South in the 1950s. The brilliant strategist Bridgit Antoinette Evans crafted an approach to use the film and the Golden Globe and Oscar awards as an opportunity to have a conversation about domestic workers, engaging stars like Viola Davis, Cicely Tyson, and Octavia Spencer (who won a Golden Globe and the Oscar for Best Supporting Role for her performance in the film).[75]

Another major opportunity to shift popular perceptions came at the 2018 Golden Globes Awards, when several actors brought activists as their guests to the event to support the launch of the #TimesUp movement against harassment and assault in the workplace.[76] During red carpet interviews, the actors passed the microphone to their activist-guests. Ai-jen attended as Meryl Streep's guest.

Around this time, award-winning director Alfonso Cuarón was working on *Roma*, which centers on the story of Cleo, an indigenous woman who works as a live-in domestic worker for a middle-class family in Mexico City during the sociopolitical upheaval of the 1970s. Cuarón, who called the film "a love letter to the women who raised him," connected with Ai-jen and Rosa Sanluis, a former domestic worker from Mexico, now an organizer living in the Rio Grande Valley, at the film's world premiere in September 2018 at the Venice Film Festival.[77] From there, NDWA, Cuarón, and the socially engaged production company Participant Media collaborated on a campaign to increase the visibility and value of domestic work, and to accelerate the adoption of solutions that concretely support economic security and dignity for domestic workers.

In January 2019, Cuarón and Ai-jen attended the Golden Globes together, where *Roma* won Best Motion Picture for a Foreign Language Film and Best Director. *Roma* was also nominated for ten Academy Awards and, in February 2019, took home three of them, including Best Director. When Cuarón received his award, in front of an audience of 25 million viewers, he thanked the Academy for recognizing "a film centered around an indigenous woman—one of the 70 million domestic workers in the world without work rights, a character who had been historically relegated to the background in cinema."[78]

GOOD WORK

In prior years, organizers had developed so many powerful alternative ways of connecting and empowering the workers whom unions weren't serving. The Coworker petitions and campaigns like the fast-food walkouts and Fight for $15 had energized the movement to improve jobs and working conditions. Because of those successes, advocates could now expand from wages to include other aspects of good jobs. How did respect and dignity get expressed in workplaces? How much were workers included when their employers made important decisions about the future of that organization?

Workers' aims now expanded from wages and benefits to include other expressions of worthiness, dignity, and power.

Severance and Seats on the Board

The years following 2016 were hard for brick-and-mortar stores. In what became known as the "retail apocalypse," 2017 saw more than eight thousand store closures.[79] The women's clothing company The Limited kicked things off in January 2017, filing for bankruptcy and closing all 250 of its locations. In April, Payless shoes announced it was doing the same, shuttering its four hundred stores. JCPenney, RadioShack, Macy's, and Sears each announced more than a hundred store closures.[80] The entire mall in my hometown in Kansas, the stomping ground of my youth, all but vanished. And 2018 and 2019 were even worse. Toys 'R' Us, which filed in September 2017, decided early in 2018, after one last disappointing holiday season, to close or sell all 735 of its stores, leaving some 33,000 employees without jobs or severance pay. Many of those workers had been with the venerable toy merchant for decades.[81]

Blame for the stores' failures to thrive was usually pinned on Amazon and other online retailers. But almost every retailer that went down had turned to private equity buyouts in the early 2000s. When a company sells itself to a private equity fund, it takes on a high-interest loan, hoping for enough growth in profit to pay off the debt. It's similar to a person taking on a payday loan. Toys 'R' Us, having struggled to compete with Walmart and Target for years, had agreed to a $6.6 billion buyout deal in 2005. It planned to raise its profits by lowering its costs—closing underperforming stores, selling off real estate, and, of course, skimping on staffing.[82] The plan failed—for workers and stores. The company's executives, however, got millions of dollars in bonuses as late as a week before the bankruptcy filing, while the private equity vultures got hundreds of millions in fees.[83]

The Toys 'R' Us workers went on the warpath to hold the private equity firms accountable, spreading the word via social media, with support from the same Organization United for Respect (OUR) organizers who previously crafted the

OUR Walmart campaigns. "Wall Street is at the core of the crisis in retail," workers insisted, demanding $75 million in severance.[84] They protested outside the offices of the private equity culprits, setting up a mock graveyard to mourn the toy store killed by Wall Street greed. It helped that Toys 'R' Us was a beloved brand. The combination of public shaming and support from political figures like Cory Booker and Bernie Sanders succeeded: the Toys 'R' Us workers eventually won a $20 million severance fund.[85]

Rise Up Retail—a campaign by OUR and the Center for Popular Democracy, was about more than wages, or even fair severance. It was about power, voice, and respect. (In fact, OUR would change its name to United for Respect in 2019.) The strategy wasn't just to push individual employers to change their policies, but also, as with NDWA, to push lawmakers to raise the standards for the 16 million people working in retail.

In early February 2019, New Jersey state senator Joseph Cryan introduced legislation—the first of its kind— mandating that laid-off employees of large companies in the state be paid a severance equal to one week of wages for each full year of employment; that employees be given more notice before layoffs, including at least fifteen days' warning ahead of a bankruptcy filing or change in ownership, and that mass firings be prohibited for 180 days after such an upheaval. Additionally, it made Wall Street firms responsible for severance claims by classifying them as joint employers alongside the executives running the companies, and classified severance as wages, so that such payments would get top preference in the bankruptcy process alongside creditor claims. The landmark legislation was signed into law in New Jersey in January 2020.[86]

United for Respect also focused on making companies

give workers seats on the board—"codetermination," as the wonks call it. This idea was also making its way into legislative proposals. In 2018, Senator Elizabeth Warren introduced the Accountable Capitalism Act, which would require companies with more than $1 billion in annual revenue to allow workers to elect at least 40 percent of board members.[87] In 2019, Bernie Sanders's campaign announced a plan to require corporations to give workers a share of corporate board seats, as well as a proposal that would require large businesses to direct a portion of their stocks into a worker-controlled fund.[88]

Tools for Dignity

New technology has so often been part of the problem in the twenty-first century workplace, from straight surveillance, to productivity trackers or "games," to scheduling software oriented toward squeezing out every last drop of profit at the expense of employees' humanity. Or there was the behavioral analytics software that promised to help bosses find what were called "hidden influencers," ostensibly for the purpose of promoting top performers on staff but which actually functioned to help bosses identify organizers. "It was basically insider-threat-detection software, painted with a worker-friendly brush," commented Michelle Miller.[89] Coworker, the petition-based platform modeled off Change.org that Michelle had co-founded in 2013, was a refreshing turn of events: technology developed for worker empowerment.

When we last saw Coworker, the platform was helping low-wage workers in places like Starbucks and Walmart. Coworker was enabling them not only to file grievances but, more importantly, to build solidarity across the widely dispersed locations of their fellow employees—and get support from outside their company too. All of this served as leverage that actually helped them get traction on whatever workplace issue they were tackling.

A funny thing happened around 2016, though: workers at tech companies like IBM and Google started approaching Coworker, needing help to advocate for themselves and organize more respectful workplaces. So, Coworker expanded its offerings to serve their needs, including Know Your Rights and media trainings.[90] It also created the Solidarity Fund, a mutual aid fund for workers in the tech industry.[91]

In what could only be a sign of Coworker's success, in 2020 Tesla blocked employees' access to the Coworker website. The electric vehicle company had recently cut its commissions for sales employees, forcing them to find additional work to make ends meet, or sign up for public benefits. One Tesla employee used Coworker to create a petition asking for a 15 percent increase in base pay to make up for the lost compensation in commissions. The company not only blocked the petition but also made it impossible for employees to send mass messages on the internal email server.[92]

Teachers Demand More Than Wages

In February 2018, nearly twenty thousand teachers across West Virginia went on strike. Their salaries were 20 percent less than the national average, and the state ranked forty-eighth in average teacher salary.[93] They hadn't had a raise since 2014.[94] When the governor's promised salary increase failed to materialize, they walked out, closing the schools for nine days. Non-unionized teachers and other school employees including administrators, bus drivers, and cooks joined them in solidarity, and students and their parents also turned out in support of the strikers. Churches, community centers, and community members helped out by offering places for students to go during the day and by offering meals to students who depended on school meals.[95]

Teachers' strikes are particularly fraught politically, owing to the central role that teachers play in the lives of families. As labor journalist Sarah Jaffe commented: "Like the welfare mothers of Reagan's racist narrative, teachers who made any demands for themselves were seen . . . as bad people." This is a reflection of the complexity of the teaching profession itself, which Jaffe describes well:

> They exist on the edge of a class boundary, not quite granted the respect given to doctors or lawyers, but not quite perceived as the working masses, either. Teaching has been the professional occupation most accessible to immigrants and to Black people, a fact that has also contributed to its complicated status both as a path to upward mobility and as an easy place to lay blame. . . . Overwhelmingly female, teachers' labor is considered similar to mothering—an essential job nevertheless to be done out of sheer love. . . . Expected to do more with less every time budgets need tightening, and yet to take the blame every time those budget cuts do harm. . . . If they demand better conditions for themselves, they're called selfish. . . .
>
> Like the home care workers who filled in the gaps of social care, teachers were expected to solve problems created by homelessness, hunger, and a lack of health care in their communities.[96]

Ultimately, the government of West Virginia gave in to one of the teachers' demands: a pay raise of 5 percent. In solidarity with the rest of the state's public employees, the teachers prolonged their strike until the legislature agreed to give the 5 percent raise to every public worker.

And West Virginia was only the first. #RedforEd, as the wave of protests came to be known—so-called because the teachers wore red, and the majority of strikes were in Republican strongholds—grabbed headlines for four months straight, and continued into 2019. Oklahoma, Arizona, Colorado, Kentucky, and both Carolinas saw statewide walkouts.[97] In Oklahoma, where per-pupil funding had been cut 28 percent during the previous decade (the highest cuts in the nation), teachers forced the state to raise taxes for the first time in twenty-eight years.[98]

Across the country, teachers expressed feeling less alone and overwhelmed as a result of their collective actions. They were more connected, powerful, and hopeful. New teachers flooded into the revitalized unions.

The new movement was especially significant in light of the Supreme Court's June 2018 decision on *Janus v. AFSCME*, which ruled that government employees could not be required to pay union dues or fees.[99] This ruling by the court's conservative majority came just weeks after a related decision, in *Epic Systems Corp. v. Lewis*, that curtailed employees' ability to band together in class-action lawsuits, forcing workers to go it alone if they experience discrimination or abuse. *Janus v. AFSCME* was a major blow, intended to diminish the power of public sector unions by eviscerating their funding streams.

The teachers' unions proved that their power was derived not just from dues, but also from empowering and engaging their members.

What happened next with the #RedforEd wave of 2018 was even more exciting. Teachers got political. They challenged candidates to support public education funding, by canvassing, writing postcards, and phone-banking for local and national candidates who championed schools. For example, by the end of the summer, only four of the nineteen Republicans running for office in the Oklahoma primaries who had voted against the tax increase for teacher pay raises were headed to the general election.[100] In West Virginia, teachers helped defeat Robert Karnes, one of its main antagonists in the state senate, and voted in Republican challenger Bill Hamilton, a moderate more sympathetic to the union's cause.[101]

Teachers started running for office themselves, too. One of them was my cousin, Shannan Coale Tucker. She was one of over 790 candidates in Oklahoma who filed their paperwork to run amid the teacher walkouts.[102] Shannan filed to run in District 8, which includes Woody Guthrie's birthplace, Okemah, where my family is from. She pitted herself against the Republican incumbent who wasn't supporting the teachers' asks, and who also happened to be my family's longtime preacher turned politician. It was a long shot, and she didn't win, but her candidacy was significant to the community nonetheless.

Nearly 1,800 current and former educators ran for state legislative seats in the 2018 midterms.[103] Tony Evers, a former science teacher and principal and superintendent, became governor of Wisconsin. Minnesota's gubernatorial election was also won by a teacher, Tim Walz. In Connecticut, former social studies teacher Jahana Hayes became the state's first Black congresswoman. At least forty other teachers and educators who ran won seats in state offices.[104]

It was a taste of the solidarity we need in order to raise standards for jobs in the public sector.

The Green New Deal

In 2017, the Sunrise Movement launched an ambitious, explicitly multiracial climate organization. Sunrise united the young people who had previously been involved in protesting the Dakota Access Pipeline and those calling for divestment from fossil fuels, and it set out to get proponents of renewable energy elected in the 2018 midterm elections. After the elections, they organized a sit-in, occupying the office of Nancy Pelosi (then Speaker of the House) and demanding action on climate change. Representative Alexandria Ocasio-Cortez joined them, and the action thrust the Green New Deal framework into the public eye.[105]

The Green New Deal has a three-part goal: decarbonization, jobs, and justice. Alongside the calls for renewable energy, expanded public transportation, and other green infrastructure, there's also a focus on employment, which was the core of the original New Deal. The Green New Deal's massive investment in green infrastructure would create a vast number of jobs with quality standards like good pay and benefits, as well as environmental, health, and nondiscrimination standards. That, in turn, would pressure employers across the board, in every sector, to compete for workers and match those standards.

Writing about it for *Vox*, political reporter David Roberts described it as

> an almost outlandishly ambitious undertaking: to coordinate and develop a coherent policy platform that can guide a transformation of the economy, decarbonize every economic sector, guarantee every American a well-paying job with good benefits, strengthen the resilience of the country's most vulnerable communities, command the support of politicians from every region of the country, and inspire enthusiasm and action among activists.[106]

Spray-painted on walls in every American city and embroidered on patches decorating backpacks across America's campuses, the Green New Deal quickly became a household phrase. This hopepunk policy framework was a bold promise to the youngest members of our society—a promise about the climate as well as about good quality jobs—and now that it was out there, they weren't about to let it go.

Policy analyst Rhiana Gunn-Wright helped write the Green New Deal framework, never losing sight of the program's intended impacts on vulnerable and low-income people. From her current perch at the Roosevelt Institute, spurred by her conviction in the role that government should play in shaping markets and directing innovation, she would go on to push green industrial policy and clean energy investments, with an emphasis on geographic and race equity. Much of this became enshrined later in President Biden's energy policy, while advocates like Gunn-Wright kept pushing for even more public investment in the new green economy.[107]

The Green New Deal opened up political space and imagination for legislation like the Inflation Reduction Act to pass. While its name is an homage to inflation—the great political concern of the year it passed—the bill was also one of the biggest climate investments in history, offering funding, programs and incentives to accelerate the transition to a clean energy economy.

INCOME

In late 2017, supporters of the idea of a guaranteed income came together to take stock of their progress—and make a roadmap for the way forward—at a gathering called CashCon.

Cash was the common denominator in policies like a child allowance, a carbon dividend, and a negative income tax; as diverse as they are, all create versions of an Income Guarantee. *Cash. With no strings attached.* Hundreds of people turned out for the daylong event about our economic future, co-convened by Chris Hughes, Dorian Warren, and myself, and hosted by writer/comedian/media personality Baratunde Thurston. I was very, very pregnant with my second child, my daughter Juno Ruth, who was born just a few weeks after the event. I wore the only dress I had that still fit, which was black and stretchy, with comfortable sandals. I was exhausted, but thrilled to see all these people coming together.

Nonprofit leader Aisha Nyandoro flew in from Mississippi; Hawaii state senator Chris Lee joined us; Congressman Ro Khanna came from Silicon Valley; Michael Tubbs, mayor of Stockton, California, was there too. Also joining us was Saket Soni—the visionary labor leader and founder of the National Guestworker Alliance, whose book *The Great Escape* later became a runaway hit. Elizabeth Rhodes from the start-up incubator Y Combinator, which had recently launched a guaranteed income pilot with entrepreneur Sam Altman, came to tell us about it. Vinitha Watson, founder of Zoo Labs, an Oakland-based incubator for bands, joined us to talk about how cash infusions impact artists. Anna Sale, host of WNYC's *Death, Sex & Money* podcast, interviewed Chris Hughes about why he chose to dig into guaranteed income. His book *A Fair Shot* would come out soon, in February 2018. Anna asked him some pointed personal questions about the psychology of wealth and how it felt to be the recipient of a windfall of cash so young. Sitting quietly at Andy Stern's table near the back of the room was a man who would soon become the name most widely associated with UBI in America: Andrew Yang, future presidential candidate. He had tagged along with Andy, whose book *Raising the Floor* had deeply influenced him.

The gathering was held at the Old Mint, a building that once housed a third of our nation's wealth, so impenetrable with its concrete and granite foundations (designed to prevent tunneling) and its iron doors and shutters that it withstood the 1906 earthquake. In the basement, at the end of a long corridor, was the furnace where they once melted down the spoils of the California Gold Rush to make coins.

Several important inflection points occurred during Cash-Con. One was the decision regarding languaging. People had long debated between the terms "UBI" and "basic income" and "guaranteed income." It was something that Saket Soni said that brought clarity: "There's a need for a narrative that ties us together. We need to build trust with people. In order for people to belong and deeply feel part of society, they must be included in fundamental social guarantees. The word 'guarantee' is powerful there. . . . At the same time, people's lives are volatile, and they need grounding. Guaranteeing an income to everyone would offer that. It would give them resilience. And resilience is a twenty-first-century human right."

Saket was right. The guarantee was the most powerful part of the idea: regular, dependable, assured money that would show up regardless of circumstances. In calling for a "guaranteed income," we were also aligning ourselves with those who had used the same term during the 1960s racial and social justice movements.

During one final key moment at CashCon, there was a conversation between Thurston and Mayor Tubbs. Tubbs, the visionary young man who'd been elected Stockton's mayor in the same election that made Trump president—announced that Stockton was going to host the country's first city-led guaranteed income demonstration in modern times. You could feel excitement ripple through the crowd at the news.

Stockton Leads the Way

It was back in the previous spring that I first met Tubbs. I was presenting to a group of city officials from around the country on how to build a twenty-first-century safety net, including the idea of a guaranteed income. When I sat back down, the man sitting next to me, who looked somehow familiar, leaned over and said he was really interested in guaranteed income, and gave me his card. "We should talk," he said.

Michael Tubbs—of course, *that* was why he looked familiar. Stockton's first Black mayor, and, at twenty-six, the youngest mayor ever of a city of that size, who'd grown up in poverty, with his father imprisoned under the Three Strikes law, and gone on to attend Stanford, to intern at the White House. He'd become a City Council member at the age of twenty-two with support from none other than Oprah Winfrey, and then, with an endorsement from President Obama, he'd go on to be elected mayor.[108] His story had been a bright light in the darkness that followed Election Day 2016.

So the next day I wrote him, and we set up a meeting. He was already thinking about guaranteed income. He had gone to his team and asked them for big ideas to abolish poverty, and they had turned up guaranteed income, which he remembered from reading Dr. King. I told him we were talking to a bunch of cities, and we really wanted a heartland city, not a coastal one, and certainly not a Californian city, because the rest of the country just rolls their eyes at California, especially at LA and the Bay Area (my home). We wanted a *relatable* city.

But Stockton is not the Bay Area, as Tubbs would remind me. This was also abundantly clear on my first visit down there with my ESP colleague Cara Rose DeFabio. The drive from the Bay Area took us nearly two hours, through the fertile Central Valley, which produces half of the fruits and vegetables grown in America. In that way, it is more like the heartland.

That day Cara and I pulled up in front of Stockton City Hall, a majestic building of pale stone fronted with columns that's a vestige of the city's more prosperous past. Situated halfway between the ocean and the gold in the foothills of the Sierra Nevada, Stockton had been a Gold Rush boomtown, with the state's fourth largest population in those days. Agriculture and wartime industry kept the wealth flowing and attracted a steady influx of immigrants from several regions of the world: first, Chinese, Italians, Japanese, Filipinos, and Indian Sikhs, who built America's first Sikh temple in Stockton; and later, bracero guest workers from Mexico and refugees from Vietnam, Laos, and Cambodia. Today it's the most racially and ethnically diverse city of its size in the United States.

We found a parking spot directly in front of City Hall, because nothing much was going on. Stockton had fallen on hard times thanks to decades of disinvestment, redlining, and the destruction of vibrant city neighborhoods to make way for highways serving the white suburbs, where most of the businesses and services also fled to; that was followed by drug trade, gangs, and gun violence. Especially in the wake of the 2008 crisis.

A lone employee inside City Hall took us up to the creaky second floor to meet with the mayor.

Mayor Tubbs greeted us warmly and we sat down with him and two of his bright advisers, both young men who had also worked on his mayoral campaign. The team looked like they had stayed up all night working on the concept paper they shared with us: a guaranteed income funded by marijuana tax revenues, which ought to be able to keep the program going not just through a pilot phase, but in perpetuity. We'd agree later that, given that guaranteed income was new and controversial on its own, launching with the still-young cannabis laws might be complicated. But I was impressed by their intention to create something that would last, not just be a flashy showpiece. I left the meeting feeling really excited about Tubbs, his team, and the city.

Soon afterward, a new funding opportunity arose: to pitch Stockton's nascent guaranteed income program as a moonshot project at The Audacious Project. Run by the TED conference's Chris Anderson, the event was held on an island owned by Richard Branson, attended by the likes of Google co-founder Sergey Brin. The winner of the competition—via video presentation; riffraff like us weren't allowed on the island itself—would get $100 million. So we put together a TED talk about a demonstration project in which we would just give people money in an American city. I rehearsed the heck out of it, rose above my nerves to do my spiel, and Tubbs logged on and we talked about what it would accomplish.

We didn't win, which should have come as no surprise, given our proposal's underlying critique of wealth inequality and the exploitative system that had enabled the judges to make their fortunes.

Tubbs wasn't ready to give up. "We could still do a lot with a couple million."

Dorian, Chris, Taylor Jo, and I put our heads together and did some calculations. We had planned to grow the staff at ESP over the next year, but we decided we could allocate that money to the Stockton demonstration project instead. We scraped together $1 million from our organizational budget. In the grand scheme of how large other guaranteed income demonstrations would become, it wasn't that much. But it was significant for us, and we anticipated that we could use it as a match fund to raise a few million more dollars.

This was shortly before CashCon. And even though we didn't have all the money we needed, or all the details hashed out, Mayor Tubbs decided to just announce it to the world. And we were off.

After CashCon, Sukhi Samra was named director of the Stockton Economic Empowerment Demonstration (SEED), as the pilot would be formally known.[109] She and Taylor Jo sequestered themselves in a conference room in Stockton and entered the design phase: conceptualizing, finding the researchers, designing the program, and raising the money. Tubbs was adamant that Stockton residents had to drive the initiative. A community advisory group was created. A listening tour was organized asking, "What would $500 per month mean to you?"

One mother had a surprising answer: "$500 would help me more in the summer than the winter."

"Why?" the team asked her.

"Because in the summer my kids come home from college. So my utilities bills go up, my food bills goes up. I get stressed and anxious. The money would let me be relaxed while they're home."

A lot of people talked about the distrust in this too-good-to-be-true idea, the doubts that they themselves were feeling or hearing about from friends. The listening tour helped overcome that. The community ambassadors kept telling people: *No, if you get the letter, this is real.* It became known as the "$500 project" across Stockton.

The team chose zip codes of people at or below the median income of the city, and letters were mailed to everyone in those zip codes, inviting them to participate. There were 125 families chosen randomly from that pool. This meant that there would be folks in the program who make more than the median income and folks who make less; folks who were working and folks who were not. For the majority of families, $500 represented a 30 percent increase in their monthly income.

Beginning in February 2019, 125 families began receiving $500 a month on debit cards. (It arrived on debit cards, because part of the project involved tracking how people spent the money.) There was a lot of mistrust at the beginning: people would just go to the bank and take out the cash, not believing that it would remain on the card for them to spend as they needed it. But trust did gradually build, as the money kept coming. People started believing that there were really no strings attached. We trusted them to know what to do with the money.

The launch resulted in a ton of media attention. Reporters came from all over to tell the story of a young mayor changing history, the families who were participating in the guaranteed income demonstration, and the city of Stockton rewriting the social contract. The pressure was mounting to see the results.

Cash for Mississippi Mothers

Across the country, another important pilot was taking shape. In April of 2019 I flew to Jackson to visit Aisha Nyandoro and the Magnolia Mother's Trust, which had begun delivering $1,000 per month to a group of very low-income Black mothers in December of 2018.[110]

Aisha describes her work as carrying on the legacy of her grandmother, Lula Clara Dorsey, who was born in 1938 and grew up sharecropping in the Mississippi Delta. "My granny had my mom, dropped out of high school, and was married at the age of seventeen," she explained. "In the late sixties, she went to New York City and participated in an experimental program where she received her GED, bachelor's, and master's degrees simultaneously. Upon completing her degrees, she moved back to her beloved Mississippi, where she led fights for Head Start, prison reform, and health care. Because of her, I truly understand that society as a whole flourishes when we invest in our most vulnerable."[111]

I arrived in Jackson on an unseasonably warm evening, and headed to a dinner Aisha had organized with a few movers and shakers in Jackson. We ate great southern food and heard what it was like to try to move a progressive agenda in the most staunchly conservative and racist state in the union, which regularly ranks last in the nation on various measures of well-being or success.

Over breakfast the next morning I met with the senior economist in the Office of the State Economist for Mississippi, Dr. Sondra Collins. She described what it was like to be poor in Mississippi, how expensive it was, how far the $7.25 per hour minimum wage went after taxes—which was not far enough, not by any measure. Our conversation lingered on the "benefits cliff" and how working more hours doesn't always pencil out. It's the type of thing that someone who has never been on public assistance can't really fathom. At the Formica table, Dr. Collins did math on the back of a napkin to show me how, oftentimes, trying to get ahead by working more hours is not as easy as you think.

If a single mom is working twenty hours a week at minimum wage, and her employer offers her ten more hours per week, she will take home no additional money at the end of the month after her benefits—such as SNAP (food assistance), a housing voucher, WIC (the assistance program for women and children), and Medicaid—have been adjusted.[112] Each benefit has its own cliff, its own rules, and they're incredibly hard to parse, even for an economist.

She looked up at me over our empty breakfast plates and said, "They make it very, very hard to be poor."

One benefit rule that makes it especially difficult to be poor relates to savings. Usually, about $2,000 is the most someone receiving benefits is allowed to hold in assets. Imagine someone living in public housing is trying to save up to move. In many places, $2,000 isn't enough for the deposit and first and last month's rent, so if a person wants to make this move, they lose their benefits. Or take the cruel case of the family whose uncle had saved up for decades for the end-of-life send-off he wanted: a plot in the family cemetery. The amount he had paid for his burial plot exceeded the $2,000 threshold for assets allowable by the food assistance program. His food stamps were cut in the last years of his life.

After breakfast Aisha drove me to the housing development where the recipients of Magnolia Mothers Trust live. We visited several of them, everyone greeting "Mrs. Aisha" with big familiar smiles. One mother gave us a tour of her house, the walls filled with drawings by her kids. Her home was incredibly clean: no dirty dishes, no toys lying out, the bright fresh smell of soap. (This is in stark contrast to my own house, where dishes are usually left out until the evening, the kids' half-finished art projects fill tables or floors, and my clothes linger in piles until the weekend.) We sat at the mother's kitchen table and talked about what the checks meant to her. I was struck by how she knew her bills and expenses down to the cent. She had calculated exactly what the Magnolia Mother's checks would offset, what the gas to and from her job cost, and what she made. The complexity lived in her head with ease.

After we said goodbye, I mentioned to Aisha how I couldn't get over how clean the place had been. She gave me a sad, knowing look and told me that no, the woman hadn't cleaned up just for us; it's a requirement that people living in public housing keep an immaculate house at all times since there could be a surprise inspection at any point. If the property manager sees dirty dishes out, or any other infraction, the family could be kicked out. It's cleanliness out of fear and survival. I'd think of this many times after returning home, as I straightened up my house when I felt like it, only as much as I felt like it, at my own pace.

The last woman we met told me about the day she found out that she'd been selected. She didn't tell anyone else in her life, because she didn't want to be resented, or for relatives to ask her for money. She knew exactly what she would do with the first $1,000. A few years prior, she'd enrolled in a local community college in a phlebotomy program. Phlebotomy—drawing blood—is an entry-level job in the medical field, paid a bit above minimum wage, and considered a steady job with plenty of opportunity, given the aging population. The woman had completed a semester when her car broke down and she had to put her tuition money into fixing the car. If you can't pay, you can't take classes. And you can't re-enroll until you pay. So, she spent a year and a half working at her minimum-wage job, trying to scrape together the $300 to continue her phlebotomy degree.

When she got the first check from Magnolia Mother's Trust, she walked proudly down to the community college, paid off the outstanding $300 debt, and picked back up with her classes. Then she bought a present for her kid and got some fresh fruit at the market.

Something as humble as a $1,000 check allowed her to restart her dream.

It was Aisha who introduced me to the principle of "Black Women Best" as articulated by Janelle Jones, formerly the chief economist of the U.S. Department of Labor. Black women are among the last to recover from economic recessions and the last to reap economic benefits during periods of recovery or growth—a result of deliberate policy choices made by those in power. Policymakers, therefore, should shift their focus. Rather than focusing on helping *the average worker* find a job and the *average family* get out of poverty, they should reorient their thinking to center Black women, and prioritize policies that focus on pulling them out of the recession and into prosperity. Then, they will necessarily be lifting *everyone* up in the process.

Aisha's decision to center Black moms encouraged the guaranteed income movement to develop a deeper relationship to racial and gender justice.

Using the Tax Code

Adam Ruben, MoveOn.org's original political director, who helped the Fight for $15 achieve national prominence, was leading a team of people to figure out the policy mechanics of how to guarantee an income. Could advocates use the tax code, working with existing policies like the Child Tax Credit and Earned Income Tax Credit so they function more like a guaranteed income? He teamed up with experts in Mayor Tubbs's home state at the California Budget and Policy Center to work out the policy details of such a solution. The goal was fewer strings, paid regularly, with broader eligibility.[113]

The governor's office tracked that work. Ann O'Leary, California governor Gavin Newsom's first chief of staff and brilliant policy wonk and lawyer, led the charge on one of the first things Newsom did as governor: a tax credit for low-income families with young kids that put $1,000 a year into their pocket.[114] No strings attached.

That first win in California started an avalanche of expansions of state-level tax credit policy. Over the next few years,

Adam Ruben and his team worked with more than a dozen states to modernize the tax code, with crucial wins in Maine and New Jersey. They ran polling, crunched the numbers, and popularized the idea with leading thinkers.

A sophisticated political operation was underway to do what had previously been unthinkable: give people money. A blueprint now existed for using the tax code to guarantee an income, and that blueprint would be picked up and used when the pandemic hit.

A program of monthly infusions of cash wasn't going to fix income insecurity or solve all of America's problems on its own—it needed to be part of a larger reimagining of our social contract that would include high-quality jobs and high-quality health care, education, and housing. But it was a vital foundation.

INHERITANCE

The data about racialized wealth inequality had been racking up over the years. The most dramatic finding of all was a projection based on the current trajectory of wealth accumulation, which calculated that in twenty-five years, the median wealth of Black Americans will dwindle to zero, with Latino wealth hitting zero twenty years after that, even as people of color comprise more than half of the U.S. population.[115] Twenty-five years is just about the span of one generation.

In response to the data, Solana Rice left behind the world of "asset-based welfare" and co-founded an organization called Liberation in a Generation. She had seen enough. "I can finally stop asking why things aren't fair," she told me. "It's because *racism is profitable*, and that's actually what's driving this entire economy. It drives all of our economic decisions, especially at a policy level. Now I can focus on the work of actually undoing that."[116]

Many other studies and reports corroborated Solana's position with additional statistics. *Beyond Broke: Why Closing the Racial Wealth Gap Is a Priority for National Economic Security* found that for every dollar in wealth held by white people, Black and Latino people held only five and six cents, respectively.[117] Another study found that older Black women with a college degree who were single had an average of $11,000 saved for retirement, while similarly educated older white single women had $394,400.[118] In 2019 the Federal Reserve reported that median white families had eight times more wealth than median Black families.[119] A study of the wealth inequality specifically in the nation's capital found that white families living there had eighty-one times more wealth than Black families.[120]

The DC study—among many other investigations on the issue—was co-authored by the economist Darrick Hamilton.

The Intellectual Father of Baby Bonds

Now a decorated professor and the founder of the Institute on Race, Power and Political Economy at The New School, as well as a key adviser to presidential candidates, Darrick Hamilton had grown up in the 1970s and 1980s in the Bedford-Stuyvesant neighborhood of Brooklyn, which was a mostly Black and mostly poor area that experienced high rates of crime in those years. His parents scrimped and sacrificed to send him and his sister to a private school run by Quakers in well-heeled downtown Brooklyn. The contrast between the two neighborhoods, just three miles apart, was stark; but people of different backgrounds, Hamilton observed, were inherently the same, which contradicted the explanations popular among the politicians and pundits of the time.

Hamilton was still in high school when his parents died—two lives cut short prematurely by the toxic stress of trying to make it as a Black family in America. During their brief lives they had worked around the clock to raise their kids and buy a home. Shortly after his parents passed away, the family home went into foreclosure. If the baby bond programs that Hamilton went on to design had been in place when he was a grieving teen, he would have had the nest egg—the guaranteed inheritance—needed to save his family home.

It was only as late as 1983 that the federal government began to systematically track wealth in America. In 1995, Melvin Oliver and Tom Shapiro published their seminal book *Black Wealth, White Wealth*, an early exploration of wealth and inequality.

A decade later, the field of stratification economics formally came into existence. The term was coined by William Darity Jr., now a professor at Duke University, who had been studying the racial wealth gap. Stratification economics looks at how group identities based on race or shade of skin (as well as other markers like gender or caste) maintain social and economic hierarchy and determine how resources are distributed. Darity became Hamilton's academic adviser at the University of North Carolina, where Hamilton received his PhD.

Back in 2010, Hamilton and Darity developed the "baby bonds" proposal. The idea is to give each baby born in the U.S. a trust fund established and guaranteed by the federal government. Every child would have funds set aside that they could use to start a business or pursue education when they reached eighteen. Unlike the individual development accounts or child savings accounts of previous decades, baby bonds would automatically enroll children and provide the seed funds, not relying on family contributions; they also would expand the allowable uses of the funds beyond education. Baby bonds would provide them financial agency over their life, give them choices, provide the economic security to take risks, and shield them against financial losses, to paraphrase Hamilton's 2017 speech to the National Economic Association.[121]

Although the fund would be universal, those born into affluent families would receive something like $500, while babies of the lowest-income families might receive as much as $50,000. The policy could be officially race-neutral and still give a substantial boost to Black Americans. Hamilton has made the case that capping the mortgage-interest deduction would be more than sufficient to cover the cost of the program.

Despite how provocative the idea of guaranteed inheritance might sound, the idea of baby bonds is popular. The "baby" in "baby bonds" undoubtedly broadens its political appeal. "The idea of granting a birthright to each child avoids the typical and often racially loaded debates about who's deserving and undeserving of help. It's hard to attack a baby for being lazy," Darrick Hamilton points out.[122] You can also conceptualize baby bonds as an extension of social security—just one that is focused on the opposite end of life. Baby bonds start young people off with financial security.

By the time the Democratic primaries for the 2020 presidential election rolled around, baby bonds started gaining real traction and became part of the public conversation. In 2019, New Jersey senator Cory Booker, advised by Hamilton, made baby bonds a centerpiece of his presidential campaign. Booker's proposal featured a $1,000 savings account for every child born, plus up to $2,000 more each year, depending on family income, financed through tweaks to taxes on capital gains and the estate tax.[123] A study found that with the implementation of a baby bonds policy similar to his, the median net worth of young Black Americans (aged eighteen to twenty-five) would increase from $2,900 to $57,845—meaning it would amount to a trust fund, or an inheritance, in the ballpark of $50,000.[124] It's worth noting that for young white people, the increase would be from $46,000 to $79,159.[125] Universal baby bonds would narrow the racial wealth gap from a factor of 16 to a factor of 1.4.[126]

To paraphrase Senator Booker, the idea of baby bonds was "capturing the country's moral imagination." It felt like the idea was finally having its moment.

Terms of Inheritance

Within his "Economic Bill of Rights for the 21st Century" framework, Darrick Hamilton has termed the inheritance guarantee variously as "the right to a meaningful *endowment* of resources as a birthright," and "the right to *seed capital* to build a lifetime of asset economic security."[127] In Solana Rice's formulation, it's called the "wealth guarantee."[128]

The use of the word 'inheritance' in this context comes from Thomas Piketty, the French economist whose book *Capital in the Twenty-First Century* became such a phenomenon after its 2013 release. In Piketty's 2021 follow-up book, *A Brief History of Inequality*, he proposes a "guaranteed minimum inheritance." "That's not *instead of* Social Security, basic income, a free education, free health. It comes on top of all of this," Piketty clarifies.[129]

Piketty proposes a funding stream that is as simple as it is provocative: a redistribution of existing inheritance. "If you look at the distribution, the bottom 50 percent of children actually receive close to zero. And the top 10 percent of top 1 percent receive millions."[130] He proposes to redistribute 60 percent of all inheritance to everyone, resulting in an inheritance of about $150,000 per person, with the very wealthy still receiving more. "This kind of wealth redistribution," Piketty contends, "would give people a lot more bargaining power to participate in society on more equal ground, to chase opportunities, to follow passions and ambitions."[131]

CONCLUSION: THE PRIMARY OF GUARANTEES

The vision and persistence of so many different architects of the Guarantees—among them organizers, community leaders, academics, journalists, debtors, domestic workers, teachers, policy analysts, and policymakers—bucked the political odds during the Trump era and made concrete progress toward the Guarantee Framework. That so much was accomplished under an administration that opposed every aspect of the Guarantee revealed just how fundamental the underlying shift was.

This was most evident when the 2020 presidential election season brought the most exciting Democratic primary race in memory: the "Primary of Guarantees," as I came to think of it, with twenty-eight candidates, among them seven candidates of color and a record number of women (six), as well as an openly gay candidate. If I'd been excited by how tuition-free college had shown up in 2016 as part of Hillary's and Bernie's campaigns, now there was a wide swath of Guarantees informing the national political debates.

Elizabeth Warren and Bernie Sanders both ran on versions of the Homes Guarantee. Hers allocated billions in federal funds for Native American homes, rural homes, and public housing, and for states to build or rehab affordable housing—with tenant protections a condition of the funding. Sander's Housing for All plan allocated trillions to build nearly 10 million homes and to increase Section 8 rental assistance. It also imposed national rent control, a significant "house flipping tax" to disincentivize speculators, and an "empty homes tax" to discourage vacant properties that could be used as homes. Kamala Harris also included fair market rent caps and financial assistance for people renting or living in historically redlined neighborhoods.[132]

Warren, Sanders, Julián Castro, Tulsi Gabbard, Tim Ryan, and Marianne Williamson included free public college in their platforms, while Warren, Castro, and Pete Buttigieg all proposed cancellation of some student debt. Senators Cory Booker, Kirsten Gillibrand, and Harris signed onto legislation that would have covered costs beyond tuition.[133]

On health insurance, a handful of candidates including Booker, Castro, and Gabbard embraced at least partial Medicare for All (requiring patients to pay for some costs), with Warren and Sanders taking an "all or nothing" stance. Sander's platform guaranteed coverage at no cost to individuals for a wide range of benefits, paid for by the government, effectively eliminating the private health insurance sector.[134] Multiple mainstream media outlets noted the sea change, here expressed by *Politico*: "The idea of shifting everyone in the United States into a single government-run health insurance plan with generous benefits has rocketed from the leftist fringes to the political mainstream in just a few years."[135]

As for family care, nearly every candidate was on board with providing paid family leave ranging from twelve weeks to several months.[136] In July of 2020, then-candidate Biden released a groundbreaking proposal to address the issue of care, specifically addressing the need to improve pay and respect for caregivers, calling them "underpaid, unseen and undervalued" in a speech announcing the plan.[137] It leveraged the moment, when the Covid virus outbreaks in nursing homes were amplifying the desire for home-based care, and parents were several months into their loss of the caregiving that schools had provided before the pandemic shutdowns. It was also a direct result of the advocacy of Ai-jen and her collaborators in Caring Across Generations.

Warren also had a plan for universal child care, building on existing Head Start infrastructure to provide public child care centers, making sure that "child care deserts" were served. This addressed care of children in the age gap that existed between parental leave, which serves newborns, and universal pre-K, which starts around four years of age. Critically, a key element of the concept was paying workers in these public child care centers the same as teachers—on average, elementary school teachers make more than twice what child care workers make.[138] Sanders, Harris, Beto O'Rourke, and Senator Amy Klobuchar also came out in favor of some version of universal child care programs.[139]

On the Income Guarantee front, candidate Andrew Yang made universal basic income a centerpiece of his campaign: $1,000 per month to everyone. More politically feasible and exciting, in my estimation, was Kamala Harris's LIFT the Middle Class Act, a monthly check for middle- and low-income families.[140]

Toward a Good Work Guarantee, there was, for starters, agreement from almost every Democratic candidate on doubling the hourly minimum wage, from $7.25 to $15, truly an unthinkable development before the Fight for $15.[141] Booker also proposed a pilot version of a federal jobs guarantee, based on the work of Darrick Hamilton, ensuring that all adults who want employment can get it. In the pilot, fifteen local areas would receive funds to ensure that every adult living there would be guaranteed a job paying at least $15 an hour (or the prevailing wage for the job in question, whichever's higher), and would be offered paid family/sick leave and health benefits.[142] Sanders adopted a jobs guarantee—not just as a pilot—as part of his platform, and Gillibrand endorsed the idea as well.[143]

Finally, the Inheritance Guarantee in the form of baby bonds got a huge boost when Booker made it a centerpiece of his campaign: a $1,000 savings account for every child born, plus up to $2,000 more each year, depending on family income, financed through tweaks to taxes on capital gains and the estate tax.

Although the presidency was going to be clinched by one of the most moderate of the bunch, there's no question that this "big-idea arms race" indicated a significant turn. Hopepunk economics had made it into the presidential primaries. The Guarantees were legit.

In the coming years, further progress on the Guarantees would have to survive a global pandemic, an attempted coup on our democracy, and the overturning of *Roe v. Wade*. Despite it all—or maybe because of it—the calls for the Guarantees would grow even louder.

4

WIN (2020–2022)

Three months into 2020, everything changed. We landed in the unprecedented phenomenon of a modern global pandemic, with still uncalculated social, psychological, and economic consequences. The political aperture at the federal level for the Guarantee Framework opened beyond anything that had been previously possible. Ideas that had been laughed out of the room when I lived in DC and worked for President Obama in his first term were suddenly being embraced.

As economist Milton Friedman noted: "Only a crisis—actual or perceived—produces real change. When that crisis occurs, the actions that are taken depend on the ideas that are lying around."[1] Friedman was talking about the last such opening, when neoliberal capitalism came on the scene in the tumultuous 1970s. He likely wouldn't be thrilled about being quoted in the context of the Guarantee Framework, but it does hold true. Thanks to the work of people described in these pages—and countless others, over decades—many of the ideas that were now "lying around" pointed to a new framework for the economy: the Guarantee. We agreed that government should be shouldering the responsibility of meeting the basic needs of its people.

It's true that many of these instances of the Guarantees were temporary, programs created as relief during an emergency, but they proved what could happen if we put our minds and our hearts and our policy to it. They proved the Guarantee Framework is possible in America.

THE PRE- AND POST-NEOLIBERAL PRESIDENT

"There's those moments in American history where you go from Coolidge to Roosevelt, in that era, where government was the problem and the government was the answer. And then you go from, you know, Reagan to me."[2] Here President Biden was talking to historian Heather Cox Richardson in February of 2022, over a year into a presidency that truly seemed to be a historic sea change. As one tweet quipped: "The era of 'the era of big government is over'" was finally over.[3]

The lion's share of the credit shouldn't go to Biden—and in the interview with Richardson, Biden himself acknowledged that "there are certain periods in world history where you reach inflection points, where things change, not necessarily because of the individuals that are involved, but because of the circumstance and how the world has changed."[4] Still, when and where Biden came from seems significant. Biden came of age before Reaganomics. He was shaped by economic policy that favored strong trade unions and strong government that invested in American industry and our middle class, even if at the time that largely meant white men. Biden understands—at the deepest level—what government is capable of.

Just a few months into the new administration, commentator Ezra Klein wrote in the *New York Times* about Biden's "radicalism": "He's moved away from work requirements and complex targeting in policy design. He's emphasizing the irresponsibility of allowing social and economic problems to fester, as opposed to the irresponsibility of spending money on social and economic problems. His administration is defined by the fear that the government isn't doing enough, not that it's doing too much."[5]

With the Democrats' governing trifecta in the White House, Senate, and House, in March 2021 the $1.9 trillion American Rescue Plan sailed past Republican objections. It funded a range of Guarantee-like provisions under the auspices of the pandemic, from the free vaccine and expanded health care, to rental assistance, to $1,400 stimulus checks and the new monthly and expanded Child Tax Credit, which amounted to a guaranteed income for most American families with children.

By February 2023, in a State of the Union that many applauded as masterful, Biden was outright challenging key tenets of the neoliberal narrative and underscoring the Guarantees:

> We're beginning to restore the dignity of work. For example, 30 million workers had to sign non-compete agreements when they took a job. So a cashier at a burger place can't cross the street to take the same job at another burger place to make a couple bucks more. Not anymore. We're banning those agreements so companies have to compete for workers and pay them what they're worth. I'm so sick and tired of companies breaking the law by preventing workers from organizing. Pass the PRO Act because workers have a right to form a union. And let's guarantee all workers a living wage.
>
> Let's also make sure working parents can afford to raise a family with sick days, paid family and medical leave, and affordable child care that will enable millions more people to go to work. Let's

also restore the full Child Tax Credit, which gave tens of millions of parents some breathing room and cut child poverty in half, to the lowest level in history. And by the way, when we do all of these things, we increase productivity. We increase economic growth.

Let's also finish the job and get more families access to affordable and quality housing.

Let's get seniors who want to stay in their homes the care they need to do so. And give a little more breathing room to millions of family caregivers looking after their loved ones.

Pass my plan so we get seniors and people with disabilities the home care services they need and support the workers who are doing God's work. . . .

Restoring the dignity of work also means making education an affordable ticket to the middle class. When we made 12 years of public education universal in the last century, it made us the best-educated, best-prepared nation in the world. . . . [Let's] provide two years of community college, some of the best career training in America, in addition to being a pathway to a four-year degree.[6]

This was a president clearly articulating that our government had a responsibility to create and expand policies to ensure economic rights for all Americans. He wasn't passing the buck to the market, to the private sector. He was essentially stating that America needed Guarantees.

And it wasn't just talk. Biden's policies were going to get us closer to the Guarantees than any other administration in my lifetime.

HOMES

In the context of the still mysterious and life-threatening pandemic, when quarantine was the only prescription we had, we were told that in order to keep ourselves safe and healthy and our neighbors safe and healthy, we were to Shelter in Place, to Stay Home. But for so many people that was not an option. Some half a million people were unhoused, and the places that gave a good many of them shelter were not safe anymore—the beds or cots were close to each other in dormitories, not to mention the crowded shared bathrooms and dining rooms.[7] When Covid first hit, shelters had some of the highest rates of spread.

The pandemic also meant that hotels and motels across the country were just standing there, empty, with travel and tourism at a total standstill.

All across the country, communities—urban and rural, small towns and big cities—took funds from FEMA and turned them over to local service providers for the unhoused. And those organizations leased the hotels that were standing empty and provided private rooms for the people who had tested positive, were symptomatic, or were at highest risk from the virus.

In March 2020, California launched Project Roomkey, which provided cities and counties with $150 million in FEMA-reimbursed state funding to house high-risk Californians experiencing homelessness.[8] In January 2020, Amy Turk, had just become the CEO of the Downtown Women's Center in LA, which serves the unhoused women in the city's Skid Row community. In college she and I were roommates, and we had volunteered there together, but Amy had never left. Two months into leading the Downtown Women's Center, the pandemic descended, and Amy went into full crisis-management mode. But what could have been a nightmare felt more like a miracle, she told me:

> One day I got a call on my cell phone from the head of the Los Angeles Homeless Services Authority, who said: "We have a hotel. We want you to run it. Can you start tomorrow?" It was a standard courtyard motel, like a Days Inn style, which was perfect. You could stand in the courtyard in the center, and convene everyone when needed. There were no hallways or corridors where we couldn't see what was going on; we could see everyone going in or out, so it was quite safe. The women loved it.
>
> The city mobilized enormous resources to help the unhoused. The fire department, medical directors, and nurses were on site. We doubled the amount of meals we were able to prepare. We hired forty-five new staff members. If I said, "We need transportation for people," we got it. I could say, "We don't have enough food," and it would be delivered the next day. We had three meetings per week with everyone, all the various city commissions, who were involved. It was a massive coordinated effort.
>
> It was like the case study, the proof positive, that if you have dedicated resources you can change people's lives for the better, not just temporarily, but for the long run.
>
> We like to say *housing is health care*. It was never more true.[9]

Project Roomkey pivoted to Project Homekey, with the goal of leveraging federal and state funds to turn those temporary hotel units into permanent housing solutions statewide. Orange County in the LA area and several counties in the Bay Area purchased hotels to convert them into permanent homes. Just down the street from my house in Oakland, a hotel was bought and converted in order to permanently house veterans who previously lived on the street. Similar efforts were undertaken in Oregon, Vermont, and Minnesota—on the state or county level—and in cities like Fort Worth, Austin, and Washington, DC.[10]

It felt like the American "we can put a man on the moon" spirit of the 1960s was being applied to the housing crisis: big shifts seemed possible, finally, on what had felt like such an intractable problem.

An Eviction Moratorium and Rent Relief

Housing advocates have repeatedly pointed out the huge number of Americans who are one paycheck away from losing their homes and landing on the streets. Suddenly, in March 2020, people started losing those paychecks. After large sections of the retail, food service, hospitality, and transportation industries shut down, more than 3.3 million Americans filed for unemployment. A week after that, the number of unemployment claims had doubled, and then, over that first year, would exceed a mind-boggling 20 million. Before the pandemic, 7 million renter households were already struggling to make rent. Now, with the economy all but frozen in place, how could people manage their rent, or their mortgage payments? Housing advocates predicted a tsunami of evictions that would leave as many as 30 million Americans unhoused. Writing for *The Atlantic*, journalist Annie Lowrey commented: "This is not just a sudden housing crisis. This is a sudden housing crisis that has collided with a slow-boiling, structural housing crisis."[11]

An eviction during the raging months of the pandemic felt like a death sentence. Some of the options that prior to Covid would have been available to people after an eviction, such as moving in with family or friends, were now often off the table because of the virus. By the first week of April 2020, a third of the nation's 13.4 million renters were not able to pay their rent.[12]

Congress proved how fast it could move: forty-eight hours after the Senate unanimously voted in favor of a $2 trillion emergency package, the House of Representatives passed it, and President Trump signed it into law hours later, on March 27, 2020. The CARES Act established a temporary moratorium on evictions and mortgage foreclosures, and when it expired at the end of August, the Centers for Disease Control and Prevention imposed a further moratorium on evictions that kept getting extended until October 2021.[13] Not only could people not be turned out on the street if they didn't pay rent, landlords were also prohibited from charging penalties for unpaid rent. The CARES Act also provided emergency rental assistance to households that were not able to make rent payments or related fees, such as security deposits, apartment applications, and late fees.

A year later, in March 2021, under President Biden's administration, Congress passed the American Rescue Plan, which offered more emergency rental assistance, housing vouchers, homelessness assistance programs, homeowner assistance, utilities assistance, housing counseling, and fair housing activities. According to the Treasury, more than 80 percent of the Emergency Rental Assistance funds reached vulnerable communities, helping very low-income households remain in their homes.[14] Advocates like Tara Raghuveer, however, worried that the moment that the rent relief funds ran out, there would be a surge in evictions.

Tara and the Homes Guarantee organizers kept up their pressure on Washington. They had meetings with Housing and Urban Development secretary Marcia Fudge, Federal Housing Finance Agency director Sandra Thompson, and Consumer Financial Protection Bureau director Rohit Chopra. They brought more than a hundred tenant-delegates to demand President Biden sign an executive order guaranteeing rental protections.[15] By January 2023, the White House announced a set of studies and rules to improve fairness in rental housing, as well as its "Blueprint for a Renters Bill of Rights."[16]

And the predicted tsunami of evictions did not come to pass, because, taken together, the eviction moratorium, the stimulus checks, the expanded Child Tax Credit, and other emergency measures provided something like a Guarantee Framework, a net that caught the most vulnerable, and held them safe.

A Housing Supply Action Plan

Despite the success of local campaigns to open up zoning to allow for the construction of more homes, the housing shortage overall was still dire. Even in flush economic times, and assuming adequate political will, building millions of new houses—the shortage is estimated to be between 1.5 and 5.5 million new units—would be a major, multi-year challenge. But the pandemic's disruption of supply chains, and the resulting high cost of lumber and other building materials, made *any* new construction an uphill and costly battle.

Moreover, new zoning rules were going to take some time to enact in some places; in other places, the NIMBYs pushed back and managed to overturn the rules. For example, after pro-housing advocates had succeeded in 2022 in making Gainesville the first city in Florida to eliminate single-family-home-only policies, in early 2023 the newly sworn-in city commissioners voted to reverse it, after "residents loudly expressed concerns about threats to property values, influxes of students into family neighborhoods, a dearth of true affordability and accelerating gentrification in some of Gainesville's predominantly Black neighborhoods."[17]

The YIMBYs and other pro-housing advocates needed to keep up the pressure if they were going to succeed in addressing the shortage. One strategy was to win prominent new allies who would help overcome resistance to new construction.

In 2022, a headline in *New York* magazine blared "AOC Is a YIMBY Now." The article explained how Representative Alexandria Ocasio-Cortez (AOC) was asking candidates for local offices who were seeking her endorsement to tackle the housing crisis:

> Specifically, AOC is asking prospective candidates to rewrite the rules on zoning—the weedy and arguably most consequential city policies to housing—so cities can build more of the kind of housing that actually relieves the housing crisis, namely multifamily, mixed-income buildings. This might include ending single-family zoning, reducing the minimum lot size for development, and enabling affordable housing in affluent neighborhoods. Crucially, AOC is asking those who sign the pledge to vow to carry out these pro-housing policies "even if the local official representing that neighborhood was opposed."[18]

Not long after, the revered environmental leader Bill

McKibben joined in with a long piece in *Mother Jones* about how he arrived at saying, *Yes in our backyards, yes to building more homes*, convinced by the argument that "new affordable housing that will make cities denser and more efficient while cutting the ruinous price of housing."[19] Both endorsements helped unite many different factions in the movement around building homes.

The growing consensus around the need to build more housing finally broke decades-old logjams of inaction. California, my home state and an epicenter of the housing crisis, passed critical legislation in 2022 that could generate up to 2 million housing units statewide—hundreds of thousands of them dedicated as affordable housing—with their construction creating thousands of good jobs. Written and championed by Assemblymember Buffy Wicks, AB 2011 put its focus on converting commercial real estate, such as abandoned big box stores and office buildings, into residential housing, so as to not contribute to urban sprawl. In doing so, it forged a previously unlikely alliance between some housing advocates, real estate developers, and some unions, including the local carpenter's union and SEIU California, one of the most powerful unions in the state.[20]

More and more states also made advances toward social housing—along the lines of the Vienna model of housing maintained off the speculative market. Colorado created a new state office to develop thousands of publicly owned housing units targeted to middle-class families, led by State Senator Jeff Bridges.[21] The Rhode Island legislature approved $10 million for a new pilot program to build mixed-income public housing, and Hawaii passed several bills that make it easier for the state to build mixed-income condos with 99-year leases, similar to how public housing works in Singapore.[22] Montgomery County, Maryland, a suburb near

Washington, DC, made significant progress in constructing nine thousand new, publicly owned apartments. Montgomery County councilmember Andrew Friedson commented, "The status quo and even marginal improvements are not going to come anywhere close to meeting the need. . . . There is now much broader recognition and understanding that governments have to be more aggressive."[23]

We were seeing widespread recognition that government has an important role to play in providing housing. In May 2022, the Biden-Harris administration released the Housing Supply Action Plan, with the aim of creating incentives for local governments to build and preserve thousands of new units for low- and moderate-income families within three years.[24] In the omnibus spending package passed in December of the same year, Congress included the first ever competitive grant program aimed at zoning reform, dubbed a "YIMBY" grant. With a budget of $85 million, it was significantly less than what President Biden had asked for (a $10 billion grant program to reward states and localities that remove barriers to housing development), but it was a start.[25]

COLLEGE

Another way the government helped people survive the sudden economic shutdown during the pandemic was by pressing "pause" on student loan collection, beginning in March 2020. Under the auspices of the HEROES Act of 2003, which gives the secretary of education the power to grant federal-loan relief during a national emergency (the law was originally passed by Congress to abolish debts owed by military service members), the Trump administration waived the interest on federal student loans and permitted student loan debtors to suspend their payments without penalties.[26]

Something shifted in America when student loans were paused, the press secretary of the Debt Collective, Braxton Brewington, told me when we chatted in 2022. A native of Wake County, whose seat is Raleigh, North Carolina, Braxton had his own story of student debt. He'd chosen North Carolina Agricultural and Technical State University, the public historically Black university that his dad had attended, where Braxton double-majored in political science and journalism. Financing college was a struggle. "I wasn't good enough in any sport to get an athletics scholarship," he said. "I had family members who wanted me to enlist, but there was just no way I was going into the military. My parents were still paying off their own student loans. So I cut a deal with my parents, who took out loans on my behalf for my first year, with the agreement I would pay for the next three years."[27]

To diminish the debt load, Braxton had not only worked while taking the challenging classes required for his double major, but also volunteered on local political campaigns. He toiled more than sixty hours per week: "Night shifts, five or six to midnight, on Sunday, Monday, Tuesday, and Wednesday at the grocery store. And then Thursday night, Friday double, Saturday double, Sunday brunch at a restaurant." He did reduce his student loans by tens of thousands of dollars, but he now regrets how little time he had to really be present with his studies. Not to mention the restrictions on time spent with his family; or singing in his beloved award-winning gospel choir—one of many extra-curriculars he had to cut— or the professional opportunities he was offered but just didn't have the bandwidth to pursue; or the fact that he struggled just to get a solid night's sleep.[28]

The student loan moratorium lasted over two years. After it hit the two-year mark in March of 2022, Braxton told me, people started believing that it would be possible to abolish student loan debt and have debt-free college. "It proved we can win cancellation. It's just a matter of when."[29]

Melissa Byrne agreed with Braxton: "What's great about the pause is it gives us the opportunity to win cancellation of student loans—pitching something as temporary is way easier than getting something permanent. We knew that once we got a pause on student loan repayment, no one would want to be the one to turn them back on. Whoever turns them back on—whoever says you all have to start paying again—is going to get all the anger directed toward them. No one wants ballots and bills crossing in the mail. That's why Trump re-extended the pause in September of 2020—because the election was right around the corner. And from there, we can use the energy around cancellation to be able to get to free college."[30]

Student Debt Canceled

Melissa launched her organization We, the 45 Million in June 2021. That same year, she and her crew started showing up at the White House with huge banners saying, "CANCEL STU-DENT DEBT." Beginning in December, she brought an entire brass band along, once a month. They'd assemble before office hours, starting at seven or eight a.m., in front of the staff entrance, so the senior staff of the White House would have to walk past them on their way to work. Once the president even peeked his head out the window. "What's that noise?" he reportedly asked his staff. "It's the student debt people, sir," they replied.[31]

After ten years of advocacy on this front, both Melissa and the Debt Collective had their talking points down. As the debate heated up around canceling student debt, they responded to those who grumbled about the financial burden: *Think about the people who have to pay $500 or $800 or $1,000 every month toward those loans. Instead, they can take that money and go buy their first home. They can start a business. They probably won't start saving it, at least for a few years, because of what they've been losing out on, and so we'll see this ripple effect in the economy.*

In June 2020, the Debt Collective published its timely book *Can't Pay, Won't Pay*, with an incisive analysis of the state of debt:

> For decades, taking on debt has been the only solution to the impossible bind of low wages and a lack of social services. As inequality has skyrocketed and as public budgets have been slashed, millions of people have been forced to fill the gap by borrowing. Over the years our society has moved from a welfare state to a "debtfare" state, with what should be publicly financed goods (universal healthcare, higher education) treated as individual debt obligations. We have to borrow for basic necessities including housing, transportation, schooling, and medical treatment. . . . Today, more than 40% of indebted households use credit cards to cover basic living costs, including rent, food, utilities.[32]

The moral of the story: "We are not in debt because we live beyond our means. We are in debt because we are denied the means to live."[33] It isn't irresponsible, extravagant lifestyles that have so many Americans in debt; it's an irresponsible, extravagant financial system that enriches a few at the cost of the rest and has decimated public spending.

Between the start of the pandemic and the end of 2022, Americans added $2 trillion to their existing debt loads.[34] In the late summer of 2022, I called Astra Taylor to check in. That very morning, she told me incredulously, she had been on a call with the White House deputy chief of staff to discuss an administrative action canceling student loans. We laughed together at her improbable trajectory, from anarchist Occupier to White House adviser, within the space of a decade.

Astra was still celebrating the recent victory of June 2022, when the seven-year-long debt strike by former students of the predatory for-profit chain Corinthian Colleges had finally come to fruition. The Department of Education had enacted the largest student loan cancellation in U.S. history: $5.8 million in debt, affecting 560,000 former students.[35] In the blink of an eye, the debt strikers' demands, first articulated in 2015, were granted.

Astra offered her thoughts about everything that had been happening:

> What we have seen is that actually things can change overnight for the better. It's possible. I mean, we saw people being released from jail. We saw evictions being halted, we saw debt collection halted, not just of student debt—some states halted other forms of debt collection. We saw people keeping their utilities on when they would have otherwise been cut off. The child tax credit. All of this is totally possible.
>
> As for the student loans: The government doesn't need our money. They don't need those billions of dollars every year from 45 million debtors. During the pause, $5 billion a month has gone to rent, therapy, saving for a down payment on a house. It's

gone to dentures—yeah, literally dentures. It's been incredibly transformative for people's daily lives and their stress levels.[36]

Of course, I had to know more about the dentures, and that's how I found myself a few hours later in the inaugural meeting (via Zoom) of elder student loan debtors. I hadn't even heard about this phenomenon—though of course it makes sense—that given the state of wages and other debt loads, Americans are left carrying student loans until the end of their lives. Some had added their kids' or grandkids' student loans to their own along the way. One in five student loan debtors is now over the age of fifty. The fastest-growing demographic of student loan debtors is sixty-two and over, and those over the age of sixty-five default at the highest rates. When they default, the Department of Education can garnish not just their wages and tax refunds (if applicable) but also their Social Security. More than two hundred thousand student loan debtors had their Social Security garnished in 2015.[37]

An article by one of Astra's collaborators, Eleni Schirmer, had just come out in the *New Yorker*, drawing attention to this issue. In it, Schirmer writes: "Credit supposes that which we cannot afford today will be able to be paid back by tomorrow's wealthier self—a self who is wealthier because of riches leveraged by these debts. Perhaps no form of credit better embodies the myth of a future, richer self than student loans. . . . But the surge of aging debtors calls into question the premise of education for human capital."[38]

Thanks to the years of work by the Debt Collective, We the 45 Million, The Education Trust and many others—their organizing and advocacy succeeding in moving public opinion, major media, and prominent political figures to support student debt abolition—in August of 2022 the Biden administration announced cancellation of $10,000 to $20,000 of student debt for millions of Americans. Among the canceled debts was the almost $330,000 owed by a ninety-one-year-old woman named Betty Ann.[39] Using TikTok and other social media, excited student debtors spread the word about the application for debt cancellation. The morning of the announcement, Melissa Byrne showed up outside the White House with her brass band and posters saying, THANK YOU FOR CANCELING STUDENT DEBT.

In response to the initial announcement, Astra tweeted:

> This is a stepping stone, not the destination. . . .
> If Biden can cancel this much debt, he can cancel
> it all. And one day, a president will. And yes, we
> are coming for medical debt, rent, and carceral
> debt too.[40]

HEALTH CARE

COVID-19 exposed the long-standing problems of our medical-industrial complex: the barriers to access, marginalization of public health, high costs and low quality of care, and the disparities and inequities. Over a million Americans had died from Covid by 2023, almost twice as many total deaths as the countries with the next highest losses of life, Brazil and India.[41]

In 2020, hospitals descended into chaos, setting up makeshift clinics and morgues for the overflow. Patients who didn't have the virus but needed other kinds of procedures or treatments were forced to wait and suffer. People of color died at much higher rates—one study midway through the first year of the pandemic found that Black people ages thirty-five to forty-four were dying at *nine times* the rate of white people the same age.[42] The gap narrowed as the pandemic went on but still persisted, and people at the intersection of being poor, of color, and living with disabilities continued to be hit hardest. "COVID-19 is the virus and racism is the public health crisis" became the slogan among advocates for equitable health care.

"It's quite evident," said Cathy Kennedy, the NNU (nurses' union) leader. "As nurses we see it day in, day out . . . we see the injustices and the institutional and structural racism within health care. When you look at what has happened over the last year, how police, the brutality, the deaths of so many of our young Black men and women and other people of color, and now COVID-19, the access to care, how Black and brown folks are dying at higher rates than our white counterparts. It is something that we have been fighting constantly, for a long time, and Covid has just kind of really peeled back that onion so we can see it for what it is."[43]

Beleaguered nurses and other health care professionals worked around the clock, without being provided with sufficient protective gear, or even clear guidance. Three months in, NNU conducted a survey of more than eight thousand nurses and found that less than half said they had received information from their employer on how to handle the crisis.[44] Health care workers suffered from insomnia, anxiety, depression, PTSD, and burnout. By late 2021, nearly half a million of them had quit—about one in five, since the start of the pandemic.[45]

"How much more is necessary to shock our legislators into action?" asked Ady Barkan. "When we lost 3,000 lives on

9/11, we responded by reorganizing our national security system, launching a global war on terror, and conducting two massive invasions and occupations. Three hundred times more people have died in this pandemic, but we have not marshaled our national energy to build a better health care system. It is a scandal and it is a shame."[46]

Distributed Care

Delivering care in the places where people are—whether in parking lots after they've done their shopping, or online, or other places like churches, barbershops, grocery stores, and homes—is referred to as "distributed care" or "person-centered health care." This kind of care is not only more convenient for people than having to go to clinics and hospitals, it also costs less because of the lack of overhead costs in a hospital or clinic. It can serve those who don't trust hospitals.

Distributed care also serves communities where hospitals have closed. Public hospitals have always been particularly important for rural and lower-income communities, offering vital services free or at very low cost to uninsured and poor people, but these facilities have been steadily underfunded and shuttered. More than two hundred rural hospitals closed between 1990 and 2000; over one hundred more closed between 2010 and 2020.[47]

Because Covid mandated physical distancing and sometimes isolation, one of its side effects was that the health care system was forced to develop mechanisms and technologies offering more distributed care. While the virus was raging, we gave out tests in pharmacies and schools and community centers; the Postal Service delivered them directly to our homes. Parks and parking lots became field hospitals, testing centers, and, later, vaccination sites.

Physicians' offices also expanded the availability of

telemedicine, helping deliver care to people without subject-ing them to the risk of in-person visits. Before March 2020, only certain licensed providers and only providers who had a preexisting relationship with the patient had been permit-ted to perform telemedicine. It could only be offered to the patient at designated facilities and other pre-specified sites, and it couldn't be offered across state lines. After the passage of the CARES Act, no preexisting relationship was required and any clinician could perform and bill for telemedicine; and it could now originate and be conducted from any site, including the patient's home. As a report from the National Institutes of Health described it: "The 'house call' from doc-tors is surging in the United States, and instead of ringing the doorbell, your doctor is pinging your smartphone."[48]

Telemedicine is controversial. No one wants a future in which all face-to-face contact is eliminated. Obviously, not every condition can be treated from a distance, but, especially for regular check-ins on chronic diseases, telemedicine has proved to be an effective and less costly option. In building these technologies out during the pandemic, health care pro-viders also had to grapple with the important issues of how to gain and maintain patients' trust—around the accuracy of diagnoses as well as around the security of sensitive health data—and how to express "digital empathy." In surveys of patients who received telemedicine, however, most reported a high level of satisfaction, as good as or exceeding the feedback on in-person visits.[49]

In the past, part of the industry's unwillingness to embrace telemedicine was because of restrictions on reimbursements from insurers. Now, during the pandemic, the Centers for Medicare & Medicaid Services increased its coverage of these services, with the result that many private insurers followed their lead. State and federal governments also relaxed the requirement that physicians have a separate license for each state in which they practice, in order to get more people the care they needed.[50]

When the pandemic forced us to provide certain health care services in alternative spaces, we had a glimpse of how this kind of flexibility and the "twenty-first-century house call" could play a larger role in the future.

A Taste of Free Health Care

During the height of the pandemic, we as a nation decided to keep money from being a barrier to the (Covid-related) care that patients needed the most. Health insurance companies, large employers, and state and federal governments rapidly pivoted to make Covid tests, treatments, and the vaccines—once available—free of charge. Co-pays and deductibles previously required by insurance plans were no longer necessary for clinician visits related to a possible coronavirus infection, or emergency or hospital care for Covid. For many, removing the up-front cost burden meant that people got care earlier, when it is far more cost-effective than at the critical stage.

Then we decided as a nation that we needed a vaccine for Covid—first and foremost to stop the deaths and suffering, but also to take pressure off the entire health care system, which was further strained with every subsequent new variant of the virus and the resulting spike of hospitalizations. The fastest vaccine the world had ever developed (for the mumps, in the 1960s) had taken four years.[51] When then president Trump announced in May of 2020 that a vaccine would be delivered by the end of the year, he boasted: "It's called Operation Warp Speed. That means big, and it means fast."[52]

Such a feat could only be made possible with two key elements: preexisting scientific breakthroughs and unprecedented funding. The science was enabled through decades of

National Institutes of Health initiatives such as the Human Genome Project and studies of other viruses including HIV, Zika, and other coronaviruses—making visible the value of government investments in innovation in the field of health.[53] The massive funds were committed by the government, which not only paid for research, but also bought doses and invested in the pharmaceutical companies to gear up their manufacturing—well before a vaccine had been proven to work. The plan was that by the time the Food and Drug Administration (FDA) approved any vaccines, there would be plenty of doses ready and waiting. The government had already awarded $483 million to the company Moderna in April, before the official launch of Operation Warp Speed, for research and development; now it gave Moderna a further $472 million, and over $1 billion each to the other main vaccine developers AstraZeneca and Novavax. In late July the government's agreement with Pfizer entailed a further $1.95 billion (a purchase of 100 million doses).[54] Billions had also been allocated for human trials, which also happened on a hugely accelerated timeline—a matter of weeks rather than months, which the FDA said was possible because the vaccines were so highly effective.[55]

By the fall of 2020, the Trump administration was invoking the Defense Production Act, to allow the vaccine makers to be at the front of the line when they needed certain ingredients, supplies, or equipment. The law, which dates back to the Korean War, gives the president authority to allocate "materials, services, and facilities" and award contracts that take priority over any other contract in order to "promote the national defense."[56]

At the time, the fact that the promised doses of the vaccines were delayed by a few months—from late 2020, as per Trump's Warp Speed claim, into the first months of 2021—

was a disappointment (especially to a president who hoped to leverage the successful delivery for his re-election). Looking back, it's clear how incredible an accomplishment it still was. To go from the discovery of a deadly new virus to the creation of a tested vaccine that could block its effects in less than one year's time was unprecedented, setting new standards for what focus and resources can do around critical health issues.

Once the vaccine was developed, the government stepped up again. President Biden leveraged the Defense Production Act again to speed vaccination efforts. Public entities were mobilized to get people immunized free of charge. For example, in New York, the Army National Guard, Air National Guard, Naval Militia, State Guard, and the Army Corps of Engineers all pitched in. More than seven thousand service members at two hundred sites administered over 4 million vaccines. They had already produced over 35 million testing kits, delivered over 54 million meals, and administered over 1.5 million tests. They also served as data scientists, working alongside public health officers to collect and process data about the pandemic. It was the largest domestic mobilization in U.S. history.[57]

As a result, cases declined rapidly, and death rates plummeted. People still got sick, especially when new variants developed, but the vaccine succeeded in preventing most severe cases and alleviating the pressure on hospitals and the whole of the health care system.

"Despite a thousand challenges, the public health system at the federal, state, and local level—with taxpayer dollars—came together and got 600 million doses out in 18 months," said Brent Ewig, a public health official who co-authored a book on the vaccine's development called *Vaccinating America*. "Those were your taxpayer dollars at work. And that's what public health does with public funding; it's probably one of the greatest bipartisan investments in American history."[58]

Americans got to experience what it would be like to be able to access health care without worrying about the out-of-pocket costs that keep so many people from getting essential treatments—treatments that can often prevent worsened outcomes with higher costs in the future. The almost overnight transformation of health care delivery begged the question: if we could do this for Covid treatment, why couldn't we do it for diabetes, high blood pressure, or maternity care?

Expanded Access

The pandemic underscored the importance of universal, non-discriminatory health insurance coverage. The primary source of health insurance for Americans is their job, and with unemployment reaching its highest level since the Great Depression, tens of millions of workers were at risk of losing their insurance coverage. It was a credit to the Affordable Care Act that more people didn't lose coverage in this moment, because it had already expanded Medicaid, which covers unemployed people in most states. Still, one out of three Covid deaths in the U.S. was related to gaps in health insurance.[59]

In 2020, a provision in the pandemic relief package offered states additional federal funding in exchange for guaranteeing that recipients of Medicaid would retain their health coverage during the pandemic. That coverage held until 2023, when it began phasing out. As a result, Medicaid and the Children's Health Insurance Program grew to cover about 90 million people, or more than one in four Americans—up from about 70 million people at the start of the pandemic.[60]

As part of the American Rescue Plan that Congress passed and Biden signed into law in March 2021, Congress subsidized the Affordable Care Act marketplace plans and paid states to lower the costs of insurance. For example, someone earning

$19,000 a year would be able to sign up for a typical plan with no monthly payment thanks to the subsidies. For someone earning over $51,000 a year, new subsidies lowered premiums—by as much as $1,000 a month in the country's most expensive health care markets.[61] By 2022, 4.5 million more Americans had coverage than in 2021 (an increase of 21 percent)—thanks to the American Rescue Plan.[62] In 2022, the Inflation Reduction Act, though primarily legislation to spur clean energy technology, also included provisions to lower the cost of prescription drugs under Medicare and expand the subsidies of the American Rescue Plan through 2025.[63] The nation's uninsured rate reached an all-time low during the pandemic, largely because Congress temporarily blocked states from kicking people off Medicaid even if they were no longer eligible.

"The pandemic resulted in so much loss for so many of us, but it also served as a portal through which we could get a glimpse of the Health Care Guarantee," Jamila Headley, co-executive director of Be a Hero with Ady Barkan, later reflected. "For a period of time, providers across the United States delivered universal critical health services, for the prevention and treatment of one disease, regardless of insurance coverage. Some services were provided directly by the government, others by other private-sector actors. What mattered most is that the government wrote the check. For a brief moment in time, at least when it was related to COVID-19, health care was guaranteed to all."[64]

FAMILY CARE

The collision of Covid with America's caregiving infrastructure—or, really, the lack of care infrastructure—

was possibly the most devastating of the pandemic's impacts, at the intersection of an economic crisis, the public health crisis, and every family's personal crisis.

On one side of the equation, households who previously had relied on domestic workers had to do without them, when it wasn't safe to have a professional caregiver come to their home. We had to somehow balance working from home with taking care of our kids, who could no longer attend daycare or school. Even after schools reopened, all it took was for one kid in their class to test positive, and the kids were back home with us. On top of that, sometimes there were others at home who needed care—elders or family members with disabilities.

Many mothers, and some fathers, made career sacrifices, some even dropping out of the workforce, because they couldn't get access to care they needed. Inadequate care was "the big factor holding back the U.S. economic recovery," as a pandemic-era headline in the *Washington Post* announced.[65]

On the other side of the equation, the nation's domestic workers—nannies, house cleaners, caregivers—were almost universally out of a job, overnight. Their employers summarily notified them that they should stay away, for the sake of everyone's health—because maybe that worker rode the subway, or carpooled, or cared for multiple people, and so were at risk for exposure to a lethal virus. No one knew if or when the virus would allow them to return to work. And they also faced the dilemma of not having schools or daycare centers where they could send their kids. A few of their employers offered some kind of financial support to weather the blow; many did not. Much of the mostly female, largely immigrant workforce also didn't qualify for the federal stimulus checks, either, because they'd been working for cash, or on account of immigration status.

Nursing homes and other facilities now denied visits to res-

idents, and in this horrendous atmosphere of fear and isolation, the virus hit them hard. Nursing home residents made
up between one-third and more than one-half of all deaths
during the early pandemic waves. Even before Covid, polls
had shown that a majority of Americans prefer home-based
care to institutional care; by 2021, 88 percent of Americans
were convinced they wanted home-based services.[66]

When child care centers and schools closed and domestic
workers could no longer come to homes to support families,
no one could deny how vital care is. The pandemic exposed
what advocates like Ai-jen Poo had long known: domestic
work supports all other kinds of work—it quite literally sits
underneath the whole economy, enabling people to do their
jobs without worrying about the people in their lives who
need care. As President Biden put it: "When people have to
leave the labor force or can't enter it in the first place because
of caregiving responsibility, they can't fully participate in the
economy, and that drags down the whole nation's productivity and growth overall."[67]

The idea of care as infrastructure, which had been the central epiphany of Ai-jen's book *The Age of Dignity*, released
a decade prior, finally became mainstream during the pandemic. Just as with the infrastructure of transportation and
energy, a robust and comprehensive care "infrastructure"
allows people to provide for their families and contribute to
the economy.

Universal Family Care

From the moment that Biden was elected, Ai-jen and her
team had begun preparing a comprehensive plan for family
care. I feel privileged to have heard about it when it was first
being hatched, at a 2019 gathering of politicians, community
organizers, and policy experts called "Bold v. Old," a forum

for truly groundbreaking plans to solve inequality and injustice, held in an old warehouse in Washington, DC.

From the Bold v. Old podium, Ai-jen began her talk by reminding those of us in the room that day of how many families are struggling with care, overwhelmed at the costs and the lack of options. "It turns out millions of us are dealing with this," she said, "feeling completely alone. . . . We're all struggling in isolation, seeing this as a personal burden to just bear and figure it out, when it's actually a really urgent social problem in need of a collective solution."[68] It was a beautiful articulation of how free market ideology had affected caregiving, and how the Guarantee could transform it.

She went on to unveil her plan for Universal Family Care as

> one social insurance fund that everyone contributes to, that everyone can benefit from, so we can afford child care, eldercare, support for people with disabilities, and paid family leave. Basically everything we need to take care of our families while we work. It's flexible, allowing access to whichever services suit our needs. It combines siloed, disparate programs that actually should be more connected, because it's the same family who's the user. And finally, it allows us to elevate care work, and make care jobs, good jobs.[69]

Backing the plan up was a very thorough 2019 report from the National Academy of Social Insurance, which convened a study panel of several dozen experts across many fields to think through best practices for how this program—an integrated approach to care—could be structured.[70]

Universal Family Care brings everything together under one roof. Currently, the government splits the funding and administration of family care into a scatter of programs targeting different services, each with its own eligibility conditions (which can change abruptly with even small shifts in circumstance), requiring families to navigate complex bureaucracy to get support. In contrast, Universal Family Care offers an efficient, streamlined, one-stop shop. It offers a family a single point of access by which to get whatever kind of support that family currently needs.

As a universal policy available to all, it doesn't exclude families for earning too much or too little. Because it incorporates standards of pay and other working conditions for paid caregivers, families are no longer responsible for setting the terms, no longer acting out of a consumer mindset to get the best deal. This elevates everyone in the care equation. Care becomes financially sustainable for those both delivering and receiving it. And fusing these two priorities together reorients caregiving toward solidarity and interconnectedness and dignity.

Universal Family Care is what a Family Care Guarantee might well look like. A social insurance program takes a different form than some of the other Guarantees, it's true. But it embodies the Guarantee philosophy in that the responsibility for provision is shifted from the individual to the level of society. When our government commits to supporting universal, consistent, dependable family care, it will lead to widespread economic stability and dignity.

The Presidential Push

Biden has long been a champion of care infrastructure. He "gets" care—often mentioning the challenging years when he was the single parent of two children after his wife and daughter died in a car accident in the 1970s, and how he and his wife Jill provided care for their elder parents.

In July 2020, as part of his larger economic agenda, then-candidate Biden released a caregiving plan that earmarked $775 billion over ten years to expand child care and community-based and home care for elders and people with disabilities, improve the pay and working conditions of caregivers, and provide support for unpaid family caregivers.[71] Ai-jen and her team celebrated: "One of (his) four pillars was focused on caregiving. That in and of itself was historic because it wasn't the 'women's agenda.' It wasn't the 'family agenda.' It was the *economic* agenda, and care was central to his vision. That was a moment I was like, 'Wow, we are finally getting somewhere.'"[72]

In March 2021, as part of the pandemic relief, the Biden administration's American Rescue Plan invested more than $60 billion in the care economy, including $39 billion to help child care providers keep their doors open and to provide child care workers with higher pay, bonuses, and other benefits. It also included $25 billion to help states strengthen their Medicaid home care programs, with more than $9 billion allocated toward increased wages for home care workers.[73] Congress also expanded the child and dependent care tax credit—previously, families could claim up to $3,000 in expenses per dependent, up to a maximum of $6,000, but with the passage of the 2021 legislation, it was raised to $8,000 per dependent, capped at $16,000.[74]

As the national conversation began to turn from emergency pandemic measures toward economic recovery, Ai-jen and other advocates for comprehensive care infrastructure launched a new campaign called Care Can't Wait. The Care Can't Wait coalition includes the American Association of People with Disabilities and disability rights advocate The Arc; the Service Employees International Union and AFL-CIO; multiple advocacy groups for families, mothers, and women; the National Domestic Workers Alliance; and Be a Hero. They called on lawmakers to make care the centerpiece of recovery, including:

- Big investments for Medicaid Home and Community-Based Services to create over one million union-protected direct care jobs, expanding access to home and community-based services to people with disabilities and aging adults, and support unpaid family caregivers to re-join the labor force.
- Passing the Child Care for Working Families Act to ensure that no family pays more than 7% of their income for child care and that early educators have pay parity.
- Passing Paid Family and Medical Leave Legislation to ensure all working people have access to at least 12 weeks of paid leave to bond with a new child, address a personal or family-related illness, or handle needs that arise from a military deployment.[75]

Although many of their demands were reflected in the original Build Back Better proposal put forth by the president and Democratic members of Congress, the legislation that was ultimately passed had stripped away most of the programs and funding related to care. After that happened, the administration decided to find new workarounds to support the care agenda. The secretary of commerce, Gina Raimondo, gathered aides around a conference table and told them that "if Congress wasn't going to do what they should have done, we're going to do it in implementation of the bills that did pass."[76] This showed up in the 2022 CHIPS Act, which requires semiconductor companies seeking major government funding to guarantee affordable, high-quality child care for their workers.[77] It was an innovative hack on the part of the administration, a further illustration of government leveraging subsidies and contracts to achieve social aims.

The Care Can't Wait coalition went on to organize a historic convening of workers from throughout the care economy—child care, eldercare, and disability care—on Capitol Hill in April 2023. It coincided with the White House declaring April to be Care Workers Recognition Month and President Biden's executive order in support of caregiving.[78] Recognizing the need to make both paid caregivers and unpaid family caregivers a national priority, thereby meeting the rapidly growing needs of families across America, the executive order directed nearly every federal agency to identify grant programs that could pay for child care and long-term care benefits for workers on federal projects. It also encouraged a requirement for companies applying for federal job-creation funds to expand access to care for their workers.

Both this executive order and the CHIPS Act pointed to the dawning of a new era in America's commitment to family care. It was a credit to the persistent advocacy of the architects of the Family Care Guarantee. Moving forward, if we want to win paid leave and guaranteed affordable care for our children, elders, and loved ones with disabilities, and fair wages for those in care jobs, we need to keep fighting for it.

GOOD WORK

The pandemic triggered a profound reassessment of jobs, our worth as humans, and the connection between the two. Our long-held allegiance to the Puritan work ethic came under some serious scrutiny.

Many younger workers had never known anything but precarious workplaces, with little to no loyalty on either side of the employer-employee equation. The gloomy predictions of AI and robots eating our jobs had been floating around for a decade. Hustle culture was already being healthily interrogated, as leaders like Tricia Hersey of the Nap Ministry called out the cult of productivity as stemming from white supremacy and colonization.[79] On the discussion platform Reddit, the popularity of the "antiwork" forum exploded.[80] Jenny Odell's 2019 book *How to Do Nothing* became a hit in many corners. Beyoncé codified the sentiment in her hit "Break My Soul," which was about people quitting jobs, but also about finding work that has meaning and is a source of agency.

The election of the most labor-friendly president since FDR reflected and amplified these simmering concerns. Biden's first acts in office included replacing the general counsel of the National Labor Relations Board, a Trump appointee who'd been at loggerheads with unions. Biden's March 2021 American Jobs Plan (which didn't come to pass) called for stronger penalties for employers who interfere in employees' unionizing efforts, and gave independent contractors and gig workers the right to collectively bargain alongside employees. An April 2021 executive order mandated that federal contractors receive a minimum of $15 per hour; another required that for all federal construction projects costing more than $35 million, contractors would employ "project labor agreements" wherein construction unions set wages and working conditions. The majority of the investments in the Bipartisan Infrastructure Law and the CHIPS and Science Act are covered by prevailing wage requirements, preventing general contractors from undercutting wages for millions of construction workers. The infrastructure bill—with its aim of rebuilding bridges, airports, railroads, and roads; expanding access to clean drinking water and high-speed internet—also mandates standards for the hundreds of thousands of jobs it will create.[81] Similarly, the Inflation Reduction Act's clean energy investments encourage companies to adopt strong labor standards and practices by boosting key tax credits for employers that pay prevailing wages and participate in Registered Apprenticeship programs. Biden also nominated a Supreme Court justice, Ketanji Brown Jackson, with a history of protecting workers' rights.

But Biden's worker-friendly initiatives, and the new optimism among labor organizers, were first overshadowed by the economic disaster of the early pandemic. In the first few months after Covid hit, 22 million jobs were lost, with the sectors most ravaged being the ones where people interacted with other people, in restaurants, shops, hotels, gyms, airlines, salons, and other services.[82] The job losses disproportionately affected women, since they make up 80 percent of service employees (this, on top of the aforementioned loss of their child care). With the one-time stimulus checks that had been issued in the spring long gone, the six months between May and October 2020 saw an additional 8 million Americans fall into poverty.[83] In those early pandemic months, job turnover—the quits rate—dropped to almost nil, its lowest level since the wake of the Great Recession, April 2011.[84]

The disparity between white-collar salaried jobs and hourly jobs now had life-or-death implications, as a majority of the former could work remotely, while some 90 percent of the latter—the lauded but seldom additionally compensated "essential workers"—were forced to keep showing up in person. People were pissed off and burnt out. During October

2021—"Striketober"—ten thousand employees of John Deere, the manufacturer of agricultural, construction, and forestry equipment, went on strike.[85] Employees of cereal maker Kellogg, West Virginian steelworkers and Alabama coalminers, nurses in Buffalo and workers at a bourbon distillery in Kentucky also struck, while tens of thousands of Kaiser health care professionals and Hollywood production employees threatened to do so, reaching deals just in time to avert planned strikes.[86]

When Quitters Were Winners

By the autumn of 2021, circumstances had flipped in workers' favor with a labor shortage, which, combined with pandemic supports like the pause on debt repayment and monthly Child Tax Credit checks, meant that employees were suddenly empowered to make demands of their employers—or just quit.

Who could have predicted that public displays of resignation would become one of the defining phenomena of the later pandemic period? Shana Blackwell, a night stocker for Walmart in Texas, grabbed the intercom to rant colorfully about the job before walking out: *Attention all Walmart shoppers. . . . I hope you don't talk to your daughters the way you talk to me. . . . F the managers, F this company, F this position . . . I f-ing quit!* And she recorded it all for the enjoyment of tens of millions via Twitter and TikTok.[87] Hers became one of thousands of #quitmyjob videos where people creatively documented their resignations.

In September 2021 the quit rate hit a record high of 4.4 million people leaving their jobs, with a new record set in November of 4.5 million. Some chose this moment to retire, even if it was a little ahead of schedule, many of them dipping into their 401(k)s to make ends meet. By the end of the year, one in four people had quit.[88]

The so-called Great Resignation was really a Great Renegotiation—the term coined by C. Nicole Mason, CEO of the Institute for Women's Policy Research—because the vast majority of people who quit weren't moving off grid and living off the land; they were taking advantage of the shift of bargaining power in their favor, and finding new opportunities with better hours, better treatment, better pay, and better perks. The Great Renegotiation was an expression of how far things had come for the American worker.

Pay increased. As of July 2022, median wages for the job switchers (quitters!) were 6.7 percent higher than the previous year, while median wages for the job stayers were 4.9 percent higher.[89] The average pay for people working in hospitality, for example, increased more than 12 percent.[90] In particular, Black workers benefited from job switching—upgrading occupations at a higher rate than the overall population.[91]

But this was about more than pay. This was about complaints that had gone unheard for too long, whether the unsafe conditions in the storeroom, or the low lighting in the employee parking lot, or inadequate breaks, or constant surveillance, or inhumane productivity quotas.

Mary Gundel, the manager of a Dollar General store in Tampa, Florida, took to TikTok with a series of videos describing dire working conditions there (in March 2023, the Occupational Safety and Health Administration—OSHA—reported the company as a "severe violator" after finding 111 instances of workplace safety violations in some 270 inspections).[92] Using the hashtag #PutInATicket to mock the official response to employee issues, she described how the company reacted when she reported safety hazards and violence she faced from customers, including one who drew a knife on her, and another who reached into her car in the store parking lot and tried to pull her out through her car window.

"You know what they tell you? 'Put in a ticket.'"

Despite multiple commendations from the company for being a top-performing employee over three years up until that point, Gundel was sacked after her first video, which went viral. She promptly turned her TikTok into a platform for other frustrated, overworked, and disrespected Dollar General employees, mostly women from poor areas in states like Arkansas, Ohio, Tennessee, Utah, and West Virginia— whom she encouraged to speak out about working conditions, and to form a union.[93]

Breakthroughs with Unions

Gundel's videos coincided with the success of the new star on the labor scene, a former rapper named Christian (Chris) Smalls. Smalls had worked in the Amazon fulfillment center on Staten Island, a warehouse the size of fifteen football fields known as JFK8.[94] In March 2020, as the pandemic ravaged a terrified New York City, JFK8 was operating around the clock. It provided a lifeline for the city in lockdown and a lifeboat for the hotel workers, bartenders, performers, and others who had lost their jobs. After the first cases of COVID-19 were confirmed among employees at JFK8, Smalls and his best friend on the job, Derrick Palmer, raised the issue of safety. When their concerns fell on deaf ears, Smalls led a walkout, demanding better protection and extra pay. Amazon fired him the same day, claiming he had violated social distancing rules. Palmer was disciplined but permitted to keep his job.[95]

With no labor organizing experience, the two men set out to do what established labor groups had failed to do at Amazon. The Retail, Wholesale and Department Store Union, which has been around since 1937, had trumpeted its intentions to unionize JFK8 when it opened, but it came to nothing; the union later failed to secure union recognitions for another Amazon warehouse in Alabama—even after President Biden posted a video underscoring the workers' right to join it.[96] Smalls and Palmer made the trip to Bessemer, Alabama, to see that union drive in action. Smalls was certain that the retail union organizers failed because they were outsiders; for example, he had no intention of adopting the suit-and-tie corporate aesthetic of most labor leaders, and would stay true to his red tracksuits and Air Jordans.

Smalls and Palmer raised $120,000 to build their own Amazon Labor Union (ALU) through the crowdfunding platform GoFundMe, and raised awareness among employees by building bonfires and offering free food at the bus stop outside JFK8, where they could talk while folks waited for the bus.[97] The ALU promised to demand longer breaks, a raise in starting wages to $30 per hour, and for management to ease off on productivity quotas. Finally, despite Amazon's constant and costly efforts to thwart it, almost exactly two years after Smalls was fired, on April 1, 2022, a majority of JFK8's workers voted in favor of unionizing.[98] Senator Bernie Sanders and Representative Ocasio-Cortez traveled to Staten Island to congratulate the organizers and discuss the ALU's expansion into further sites; President Biden personally thanked Smalls, calling him "my kind of trouble."[99]

Because Amazon is the country's second largest private employer (and moving steadily toward first place), what happens at Amazon is significant to the whole landscape of labor.

Michelle Miller of Coworker commented to me: "What we saw with Amazon points to more than a wage guarantee, it's like a well-being guarantee. They make the highest wages around Staten Island, so it's not really just about wages. It's the inhumane productivity demands, the surveilled workplace, the ways in which people's dignity is harmed. We're talking about a dignity guarantee."[100]

The creation of the ALU ran roughly parallel to another important win for unions: the successful organizing drive at Starbucks. Earlier successes among Starbucks employees using the Coworker platform to launch campaigns had laid much of the groundwork, connecting and emboldening employees with smaller victories. In the early days of the pandemic, when baristas became "frontline workers," a Coworker petition calling for a six-week closure of stores with pay was victorious. When the first Starbucks store unionized in Buffalo in December 2021, Coworker served as a bulwark in the face of threats of retaliation from the company.[101] Despite intimidation tactics, by June 2022 more than 150 Starbucks stores had voted to unionize.[102] Employees launched a new Coworker petition calling for the company to stop union-busting and sign a set of fair elections principles including non-retaliation, full prohibition on bribes or threats, and equal time for messaging from both management and the union.

A final exciting development in this period was the emergence of a new way of involving worker voice in creating standards: sectoral bargaining. In sectoral bargaining, unions negotiate working standards that apply across an entire industry rather than store by store. For example, California's FAST Recovery Act—a groundbreaking state policy passed in 2022—applies to the whole of the fast-food industry.[103] In the case of McDonald's, that means instead of going restaurant by restaurant and unionizing each one in order to bargain for better wages or better scheduling practices, representatives from the fast-food sector come to the table with representatives of the workers. Government brokers the conversations and once an agreement is reached, it must ensure the agreement is met. Sectoral bargaining could much more efficiently tackle the big questions that are arising at rapid speed these days—questions like the impact of generative artificial intelligence on entire sectors of the workforce such as journalists, Hollywood writers, and paralegals.

Because American labor laws make it really difficult to create sectoral bargaining for employees, it is exciting to see this advancing at the state level.

"Sectoral bargaining prevents companies from competing in a race to the bottom on wages or working standards," Sharon Block, a professor at Harvard Law School and former official at the Department of Labor.[104]

A Definition of Good Work

In the spring of 2021, after the Aspen Institute and the Families and Workers Fund had spent several years deep in conversations with all kinds of people, from wonks to workers to companies, they released a shared definition of "good work." The three-prong definition provided a useful North Star:

1. Economic stability: Good jobs provide workers with confidence that they can meet their basic needs—for healthy food, a safe place to live, healthcare, and other essentials—for themselves and their families now and in the future.

2. Economic mobility: Good jobs provide clear pathways into them and an equitable chance at hiring. They pro-

vide mobility over a career through opportunities to learn, to advance to new positions, to be recognized for accomplishments, to save, and to build wealth.

3. Equity, respect, and voice: Good jobs respect the contributions that people bring to an organization, without regard to their gender, race, ethnicity, level of educational attainment, or other demographic characteristics. They engage workers in understanding their work and how it advances the goals of the organization. Workers in good jobs have the power to ensure that concerns about working conditions or ideas for improving workplaces will be fairly considered and acted upon.[105]

Having a shared definition of where we're heading—and having agreement on it from workers, employers, and policy folks—is a key step. Although there will be a lot of different opinions about how we get there, the question is not *if* we should guarantee good work, but how.

The wins for good work in the 2020–2022 period included unprecedented worker empowerment, especially among low-wage workers, who were able to resign and negotiate better wages and working conditions. Historic union drives and charismatic labor leaders during this time brought to mind figures like John L. Lewis (the United Mine Workers president from the 1920s through the 1950s) and Cesar Chavez, head of the first successful farmworkers' union, who captured the imagination of the country. We saw an advance for sectoral bargaining.

Finally, landmark legislation of this period like the infrastructure bill and the Inflation Reduction Act reflected the fundamental belief that government can have a say in setting standards for jobs.

INCOME

February 2020 marked the first anniversary of Stockton's guaranteed income demonstration. Data from independent evaluation of its impact was released shortly thereafter, and the results were powerful. After one year of receiving $500 each month, with no strings attached, participants didn't stop working; contrary to what critics had so often predicted—that they would "sit around on the couch being lazy"—recipients were more likely to move from part-time to full-time jobs, and better jobs at that.[106] Mental health improved at rates comparable to those found in clinical trials of anti-depression medications.[107] Recipients felt more joyful and more confident. Parents got more time, and better-quality time, with their kids. One parent said she was able to read bedtime stories to her children each night—the most prosaic of family activities, which had been out of reach for these families living on the economic brink. A landmark study by neuroscientists from six universities across the U.S showed that poor families receiving monthly $333 cash supports for a year led to more high-frequency brain activity in their infants' brains.[108] One of the lead authors said the impact was "similar in magnitude to those reported in large-scale education interventions," such as reductions in class size.

Recipients spent the money on everything from food to rent to education—for themselves or their kids—or paid off debt. They were several times less likely to use short-term payday loans or pawnshops. People were also able to get more involved helping their neighbors and engaging in their communities because they had less financial stress and more time. In a word, what people gained from receiving reliable, unrestricted cash was *agency:* freedom, choices, options.

In centering the stories of families who'd systematically been held back economically—largely families of color—the pilots were telling a new story of poverty, one that was about system failure, not individual weakness.

A "Quiet Revolution" of Pilots

The guaranteed income demonstrations in Stockton, California, and Jackson, Mississippi, generated tremendous media attention.

In Jackson, Dr. Aisha Nyandoro fielded calls from nonprofits, advocacy groups, and community foundations across the country that were captivated by her work with the Magnolia Mother's Trust. She would launch and co-chair a community of practice with dozens of practitioners across the country who were setting up guaranteed income demonstrations in their communities. They open-sourced their playbooks and invited other community leaders to take up the charge. Hundreds answered.

Stockton mayor Michael Tubbs started getting texts and calls from other mayors across the country. They wanted something similar for their cities, and wanted to be part of this new movement. Tubbs teamed up with several of them to launch Mayors for a Guaranteed Income in 2020, the same year he lost his mayoral re-election bid in Stockton. "When one door closes, another one opens," he recalled his mother saying.

Soon the ranks of Mayors for a Guaranteed Income swelled to over a hundred mayors, proving that cities are indeed the "laboratories of democracy." The mayors took out ads in Washington, DC, newspapers during the presidential inauguration to promote the idea, visited the White House on behalf of guaranteed income, and launched dozens of their own demonstrations from Columbia, South Carolina, to St. Paul, Minnesota. Chicago and Atlanta launched task forces, bringing community leaders together with philanthropic organizations and government agencies to build huge guaranteed-income pilots in the coming years. Cities and states started funding the pilots with public dollars, including federal funds for pandemic relief. The researchers who analyzed the results from the Stockton demonstration formed the Center for Guaranteed Income Research at the storied University of Pennsylvania to study the results from the dozens of demonstrations being launched across the country.

In 2022, the *New York Times* described the more than one hundred demonstrations across the country as a "quiet revolution," urging the federal government to take guaranteed income seriously.[109] These pilots supported some forty thousand people in total, an extraordinary feat when one considers the political and philanthropic relationships required to raise the millions of dollars—more than $500 million, by my back-of-the-envelope calculations—to make the projects happen in each city.

With each one of these pilots, local elected officials came to see the power of a guaranteed income in spurring local economies. Federal dollars were even being used to accelerate the movement. The demonstrations were paving the way to policy change at the city, state, and ultimately the federal level.

Cash During Covid

At a time when the economy was in a freefall—to an extent not seen since the Great Depression—one of the most popular interventions undertaken by the federal government was one that had previously been unthinkable: sending money directly to families with no strings attached.

I remember sitting at the desk in my makeshift bedroom office in March 2020 and thinking, "Everything has changed.

Everything. We need to rethink our strategy." Advocates of a guaranteed income immediately dropped most of our existing plans, and mobilized around a campaign we called Emergency Money to the People. In those early months, we worked directly with the staffers in congressional and Senate offices to create the policy proposals.

My email update on March 13, 2020, read:

> Our take: We're in the midst of a health crisis and on the brink of an economic one. Pelosi's package responds to the health crisis, and we've been working on policy to respond to the economic crisis that's sure to come next.
>
> We've pulled together the Emergency Money to the People plan to quickly and efficiently provide more money to more people to help them weather uncertainty, provide a financial cushion, and counterbalance any recessionary impacts.
>
> Just five minutes ago, Tim Ryan and Ro Khanna announced they'll be drafting a bill based on our policy—a good cross-section of the Bernie/Biden coalition of Dems.
>
> It's clear we have a moment where cash is almost universally understood to be crucial, as Obama's top advisor Jason Furman said in *Vox* this AM. And we've been working for four years to develop a policy that could actually pass—and are firing on all cylinders right now.

Around that same time, I got a call from Stephanie Bonin. Formerly a public interest advocate with whom I'd become friends, Stephanie and her husband had built restaurants in Denver, Colorado, and in Brattleboro, Vermont. She called me in tears, having realized she was going to have to lay off her entire staff. I had so damn little I could offer her by way of comfort, but together we realized that her story could be a lightning rod to galvanize the support of other small business owners. On March 20, she launched a Change.org petition:

> Our hearts were breaking as we watched our staff divide the ingredients in our kitchen to bring to their homes: a dismal token for employees who worked tirelessly every day. Our talented and cherished team, some of whom have been with us since we opened our doors 15 years ago, are now without an income. Like our team, my family has lost all of the income from our restaurant, and business owners and the self-employed can't claim unemployment. This is the story of America right now.
>
> For our team and other Americans who can claim unemployment, even the maximum payments will not be enough for most people to continue paying their bills—and avoid slipping into poverty. . . . Supplying Americans with monthly support until they can get back on their feet can save our communities from financial ruin.[110]

Her petition quickly went viral and, by April 23, 2020, had a million signatures. TV crews started calling her, and people kept adding their signatures, and their own stories, to the petition. Stephanie made sure those poignant, vulnerable stories were being shared in the halls of power, in the form of thousands of phone calls, videos, and letters shared with congressional offices. In June, Stephanie presented the petition to then senator Kamala Harris from her living room during a virtual rally, live streamed across the country. Stephanie's teenage daughter, Maisie, filmed the moment on her phone.

Advocates would get Congress and President Trump to authorize two separate stimulus checks to go out to nearly every American household, as well as expanded unemployment insurance checks for the millions who were out of work.[111] In this brief moment of bipartisan clarity, we demonstrated the popularity of direct cash payments and the relative efficiency of the mechanism to deliver them. Unlike during previous crises, this time, the federal government invested directly in families and workers.

The Biden administration took over in the midst of the pandemic, and built on that success—not only providing a third Covid stimulus payment to Americans, but creating a guaranteed income for families with children by expanding the Child Tax Credit and the Earned-Income Tax Credit.

The Child Tax Credit: A Guaranteed Income for Families with Kids

The Child Tax Credit (CTC) had started small: a bipartisan effort passed by a Republican House and Senate and signed into law by a Democratic president. When it was first implemented in 1998, the $400 per child annual credit on federal taxes was mostly non-refundable, meaning it applied only to wealthier and whiter families that made enough money to owe federal income tax—leaving out millions of lower-income households. Over the next twenty years, the credit would be gradually increased.[112]

In March 2021, pushed by a group of legislators known as the CTC Six and led by high-ranking Democrat and staunch child champion Representative Rosa DeLauro, Congress approved three critical expansions of the Child Tax Credit:

1. They increased the amount of the credit from $2,000 to $3,600 for each child five and under, and to $3,000 for children six to seventeen.

2. They made the credit available through advance monthly payments, not just in one lump sum at tax time, a change that much more closely matches how families actually budget and lifts more children out of poverty year-round.

3. They completely removed the earnings test for the first time, which means that even those who didn't earn enough to pay federal taxes still received the full credit, thus it applied to nearly all families with children in America. This meant a gap was closed that previously prevented one-third of the nation's children, and half of all Black and Latino kids, from benefiting from the full credit because their parents earned too little income.[113]

Within days of Congress passing it inside of the American Rescue Plan, the IRS got to work, preparing to send out these monthly checks to every parent in America. Parents would get the checks deposited directly into their bank accounts, or would receive the funds on debit cards.

The money reached more than 61 million American children in 36 million households. Child poverty fell immediately and substantially. With the very first payment in July 2021, 3 million children were lifted out of poverty.[114] By December of that year, the expanded Child Tax Credit was keeping 3.7 million children out of poverty. By the end of six months, child poverty in America had been reduced by 30 percent.[115]

Advocates aimed to make sure the expanded Child Tax Credit did not become another example of the "submerged state," as Suzanne Mettler described the programs that people value and rely on but don't ascribe to the effective workings of government. Advocacy groups sprang into action. Influencers were asked to tweet or post on Instagram, TikTok, and Face-book. Celebrities like Kerry Washington and Jennifer Lopez got involved. The White House held its own kickoff event and joined the virtual nationwide "Family Matters" rally attended by millions of people. The goal was to make sure people knew about the checks.[116]

However, the expansion of the Child Tax Credit had been made on a temporary basis, for just six months, as pandemic relief. Six months is an incredibly short period of time when you are trying to construct and solidify a new foundation of economic security for American families. The question became whether a divided Congress and the Biden admin-istration would make these expansions permanent. The fight was on. Advocates of the Child Tax Credit were forced to pivot quickly from amplifying success stories and spread-ing the word about accessing the credit, to a legislative mes-sage focused on advocating for making the expanded credit permanent.

By the way, the "boring" brand of the Child Tax Credit was a feature, not a bug. Cloaking transformative social policy in drab window dressing is an unstated part of the Biden administration's brand, because when a program's not "sexy," it's also very hard to make it controversial. Hence the polling that showed a majority of Republican voters supporting it. In fact, precisely because of its popularity among their constitu-ents, Republicans didn't focus many of their attacks on the issue—and it registered low on the "Things I Should Be Angry About" meter. And for what it's worth, as boring as tax cred-its sound, they consistently poll very well, both the concept and the names themselves. The tax credit branding helps per-suade voters and recipients that the money is deserved, rather than some kind of "handout."

The expanded Child Tax Credit had to overcome a whole host of hurdles—in just six months. If we'd had more time to celebrate success stories, and for more stories to accrue, we could have made a stronger case. If there'd been more time, more data would have accrued on the benefits that the expanded Child Tax Credit was incurring for the economy, for the health and stability of families, and for the well-being of communities. But time was limited: just as families began to depend on the monthly checks, they were coming to an end. The six-month duration of the payments reinforced the belief among some that this program was just intended as pandemic relief.

In spite of all of that, we still got remarkably close to getting it done—in fact, nearly all the Democrats supported the fully refundable, expanded Child Tax Credit. That's a testament to the undeniable impact that it had in such a short window. The expanded Child Tax Credit was a guaranteed income for parents with kids—and thus was an important stepping stone toward a federal guaranteed income.

Progressive Federalism

Because of the deadlocked and divided nature of politics on the federal level, when my colleagues and I launched Economic Security Project, we had predicted that the path to a federal income guarantee would be paved by gaining momentum on the local and state level—what's known as "progressive federalism." After local and state governments develop the solution, the federal government can support and scale that solution.

The proliferation of guaranteed income demonstration projects across the country is key to this strategy. Now, with the end of the expanded Child Tax Credit on the federal level, there is an opportunity for states to take up the charge. There are close to twenty states that are poised to create or expand their child tax credit. One of the key architects behind the fight for the Child Tax Credit, Adam Ruben—together with organizers like Pedro Morillas—is pushing to triple the number of states with child tax credits on the books.

This strategy hearkens back to the passage of Social Security. From 1930 to 1935, in the midst of the Great Depression, as many as thirty state governments experimented with pension programs for the elderly, but with extremely limited state budgets.[117] This patchwork of programs provided an inspiration and impetus for the federal Social Security Act. Similarly, by proving the feasibility, necessity, and popularity of child tax credits, state legislatures can pave the way for a stronger national program. In fact, state-level tax credit expansions over the past five years have totaled billions of dollars for millions of families, and have both inspired and built on the momentum of the federal Child Tax Credit fight.

During the pandemic, the country got a glimpse of a federal guaranteed income administered through the tax code. The outcomes of the local demonstration projects, paired with the data on poverty reduction from the expanded Child Tax Credit, prove that the country and the economy are strongest when the people who make up our economy are the authors of their own lives. Regular cash infusions provide families with economic resilience and credit people with knowing best how to meet their own needs and navigate their own circumstances.

INHERITANCE

White families own eight times the wealth of Black families in America.[118] This is one of the many revealing statistics about racism that came under scrutiny in the summer of 2020, when George Floyd was murdered, prompting a national outcry for racial justice. The country had to reckon with the racial wealth gap, and policymakers reached for ideas to address it. States began leading the way.

With the attention and legitimacy that Cory Booker had brought to baby bonds during the 2020 election season, things started moving at the state and city levels. Early in 2021, the state treasurer of Connecticut, Shawn Wooden, brought a proposal for baby bonds to the state legislature. The richest state by per capita income, Connecticut also has close to the highest income inequality, with deep pockets of poverty, as anyone who has wandered off the edges of Yale's campus into New Haven well knows. The baby bonds initiative passed in July 2021. Babies in the poorest families (those eligible for Medicaid) receive $3,200 at birth, which is safely invested—like a pension plan, the savings tax-free—until the child turns eighteen.[119] About half of babies born each year qualify—a little more than sixteen thousand babies per year—and the state is issuing $50 million in bonds annually to fund it.[120] Once the child turns eighteen (or as late as their thirtieth birthday), they can use it—only in the state of Connecticut—to pay for a higher education, purchase a home, start a business, or place it in a retirement account.

I joined Treasurer Wooden in a public conversation on community wealth building at Milken Institute in 2022, where philanthropist Margot Brandenburg asked him how he chose the priority of closing the racial wealth gap and leading on the nation's first baby bonds program. "The priorities chose me. I know we're the first state, but I hope we are not the last," he responded. He was right.

Next came Washington, DC, which passed a similar law

in December of that year. Qualifying babies receive $500 to start, and up to $1,000 extra for each year their parents' income is below three times the poverty level, with restrictions similar to the Connecticut program for how the money is spent once the child turns eighteen.[121] Washington State introduced a bill, very similar to Connecticut's, that would cover about half the children born each year, and it has found broad bipartisan support. One of the compelling arguments is the idea of investing in the future of kids. To that end, the program was named the Washington Future Fund.[122]

In California, Solana Rice of Liberation in a Generation joined other advocates in Sacramento to advocate for the HOPE Act.[123] Sponsored by State Senator Nancy Skinner, the idea was to create a trust fund for every child that lost a parent to Covid, as well as every kid in the foster care system. Thirty-two thousand children in California under the age of eighteen had experienced the death of a parent or caregiver from the virus by March 2023.[124] Researchers have predicted that these "Covid orphans"—whose parents were more likely to be low-wage earners—will face not just financial hardship but mental health, educational, relational, and emotional challenges over their lifetimes.[125] Across the country, more than two hundred thousand children—about 1 in 360—had lost a parent or primary caregiver to Covid by August 2022. For nearly sixteen thousand of them, it was the only caregiver who had lived at home with the child. Children of color experienced higher rates of loss than white children.[126]

News stories about the HOPE Act focused on the Covid orphans, but equally significant were the trust funds set up for every kid in California's long-term foster care system. Altogether, the state allocated $100 million from the significant budget surplus to guarantee the trust funds for both groups of vulnerable kids.[127] The fact that the world's fourth largest economy set up a guaranteed inheritance in response to the pandemic for these two groups essentially "lays the pipes" and makes it much easier to imagine expanding to all children in the state. And then . . . as goes California, so goes the country.

Shimica Gaskins, one of the key architects of the California baby bonds, told me recently, "The HOPE accounts in California are just the beginning. Our vision is to provide resources so that all children who are disproportionately impacted by poverty can pursue their dreams. Baby bonds have the potential to break cycles of intergenerational poverty, help close the racial wealth gap, and prove that a guaranteed inheritance should be part of the American social contract."

Solana and I were thrilled when the HOPE Act passed in 2022—creating a guaranteed inheritance for an important group of children in California. Senator Skinner followed it up in 2023 by proposing legislation that would ensure that HOPE Accounts are not considered income and thus would not affect the ability of low-income youth to receive other public benefit programs.[128]

After California, state lawmakers introduced baby bond legislation in Delaware, Iowa, Nevada, New Jersey, New York, Wisconsin, and Massachusetts.[129]

Although the advances and adoptions at the city and state level are signs of progress toward an Inheritance Guarantee, both Darrick Hamilton and Solana Rice agree that the program needs to happen at the federal level in order to function meaningfully. The dollar amounts in the state programs just aren't enough to move the needle on wealth inequality. "Only the federal government has the resources to give poor kids the amount of money they'd need to launch themselves into the middle class," Hamilton says.[130]

Indeed, one of Liberation in a Generation's guiding principles is a focus on federal policy:

> Our movement has won every civil rights victory in its history by leveraging the power of government intervention. The federal government has the most power to deliver economic liberation at a national scale. Through its mandate, responsibility, authority of taxation and regulation of our national currency, the federal government's power is unparalleled.
>
> The scale of policy change necessary is substantial. It must be bold and, in many ways, reimagine how the government meets the economic needs of people of color. These policies must envision a rearrangement of the economic system, built on a rights framework that guarantees fundamental economic rights.[131]

The hopepunk idea of an Inheritance Guarantee was gaining traction across the states, making the case, via progressive federalism, for a national guarantee for every child.

CONCLUSION: THE PANDEMIC AS PROOF

Beginning in 2020, America's federal government did something previously unimaginable. Almost overnight, it forged a new social contract. In many arenas of our lives, our government provided a Guarantee.

To keep people in their homes, it banned foreclosures and evictions and provided rental aid and housing vouchers. To guarantee food was on the table, it provided emergency food benefits, free school meals and meals outside school, and remote WIC (the Special Supplemental Nutrition Program for Women, Infants, and Children Program) services; it paused the work requirement for these, and made the food benefit and WIC more generous. To protect and support children and families, it instituted required paid leave, child care system grants and child care provider grants, stimulus checks, and the expansion of the Earned-Income Tax Credit and the Child Tax Credit. To make sure people had access to health care, it provided Medicare continuity and ACA subsidies, and subsidized COBRA coverage (an arrangement that allows people to continue paying for their employer-based insurance after their job ends).[132]

It is true that only a few of these measures were made permanent. Some have already ended, and others are scheduled to do so. That people understood these measures as solely an emergency response obscured the fact that they were the result of a decade (if not more) of strategic research, organizing, communication, lobbying, and other work by architects of the Guarantee. It shouldn't be missed that the widening of the political aperture was about more than just the pandemic.

Neither those who received the relief—the American public—nor those who granted it—American politicians—fully yet believed in the Guarantee Framework, in which we all have a right to basic economic security, and in which it's the duty of government to deliver on that right. That's because, even though we find ourselves in this moment of transition between economic worldviews, the old myths die hard. In a world of total reliance on the market, zero reliance on the government, and individuals grasping for their bootstraps—a.k.a. neoliberalism—a modicum of security feels like a gift to the lucky, rather than a right we deserve. We need to continue building out the Guarantee Framework, and building the political power to do so.

The Social Policy Created
During the Pandemic

A much more generous safety net was rapidly constructed, starting in 2020, but most of the programs have ended or are set to expire soon.

PROGRAM DURATION

Children and Families

Child care system grants
Required paid leave
Stimulus checks
Child tax credit expansion
EITC expansion
Child care provider grants

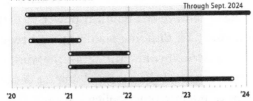

Through Sept. 2024

Food Assistance

Emergency food benefits
Free school meals
Remote WIC services
Paused work requirement
Meals outside of school
Food benefit increase
WIC increase

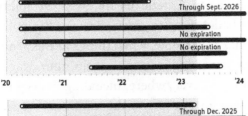

Through Sept. 2026
No expiration
No expiration

Health Care

Medicaid continuity
ACA subsidies
Subsidized COBRA

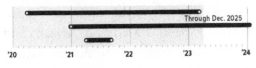

Through Dec. 2025

Housing

Foreclosure ban
Eviction ban
Rental aid
Housing vouchers

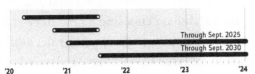

Through Sept. 2025
Through Sept. 2030

Unemployment

Self-employed qualify
Relaxed rules
Extended duration
Extra $600/week
Extra $300-$400/week
Extra for self-employed
Extra $300/week

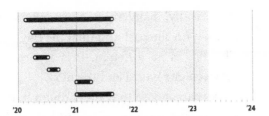

NOTE: The selection of programs is not comprehensive, but it represents those with the highest costs or those affecting the most people. Some policy rollouts varied by state, so time frames may not apply to the entire country. WIC refers to the Special Supplemental Nutrition Program for Women, Infants, and Children, and EITC refers to the earned-income tax credit.

SOURCE: The New York Times

When I spoke to Astra Taylor in July of 2022, she reflected: "Part of the problem is the American public just felt the relief measures came from on high, and so people didn't have the sense that they had fought for or earned them. So when they were taken away, people felt like, *Well, this gift was taken away.* We need to have the political power to make these changes permanent."[133] Building political power requires organization and infrastructure and funding—the work that the architects of the Guarantees have been doing for decades.

The pandemic relief policies are not the only evidence we have of the shift toward the Guarantee Framework. Over and over, when Americans are given the ability to vote directly, via ballot measure, on Guarantee-like policies, those policies win. For example, when things like expanded Medicaid, paid sick leave, and raising the minimum wage are on the ballot, they pass everywhere, including in deep red states. Missouri passed an increase to the minimum wage. Idaho, Nebraska, and Utah expanded Medicaid. Arizona and Colorado passed paid leave and increased minimum wage.[134] The lawmakers of those states may be beholden to the old story, but the voters in those states are choosing a new story at the ballot box.

At the beginning of the pandemic, author Arundhati Roy wrote in an essay titled "The Pandemic Is a Portal":

> Historically, pandemics have forced humans to break with the past and imagine their world anew. This one is no different. It is a portal, a gateway between one world and the next.
>
> We can choose to walk through it, dragging the carcasses of our prejudice and hatred, our avarice, our data banks and dead ideas, our dead rivers and smoky skies behind us. Or we can walk through

lightly, with little luggage, ready to imagine another world. And ready to fight for it.[135]

The question is: will we fight for it? Part of fighting is believing it's possible, and with this book I hope to spread that sense of just how far we've come. The provocation I leave you with is: What if the events of 2020–2022 weren't some momentary blip, but the foundations of the new story and the new social contract? What if history books written in fifty years reveal the pandemic years as the beginning of a new era?

5
ROOM TO BREATHE
(On the Implications of the Guarantee)

There was a story I heard about the guaranteed income pilot in Stockton that stayed with me. It's a modest story—not a dramatic 180-degree turnaround from abject suffering to prosperity—but somehow it was the one that hit me, as a fellow parent, really hard.

Tomas was in his mid-thirties when he was lucky enough to be randomly selected to receive the $500 monthly stipend, with no strings attached. The father of three, he was carrying a lot. He worked multiple jobs to make ends meet. He had trouble sleeping. He was paying his little sister's college tuition, he was determined to create more opportunities for his kids than he had, and he had his own plans to go back to school. With the extra $500 per month, Tomas could suddenly afford tutoring for his children and still have a little left, for the first time, to put away in a retirement account.

After a couple months passed and the checks kept showing up, Tomas felt safe turning down the gigs he'd been squeezing in after hours. He started getting home in time to read his kids bedtime stories, and to ask them what happened at school. His children were so hungry for time with their dad.

One Saturday morning he took them to the neighborhood pool. As he sat there on the side of the pool with the sun beating down on his shoulders, the tension ebbing, he realized something: *his kids knew how to swim*. He hadn't known. He'd missed it because he'd never before been able to spend a leisurely Saturday afternoon with his family.

A moment for reflection, a moment to just *be*—with your children, with your own thoughts. A moment to breathe.

I can't breathe: the three words uttered by George Floyd before his life was extinguished in 2020. These three words became the anguished refrain of a renewed surge in the movement for racial justice and police reform.

In the same watershed year as Floyd's murder, the coronavirus descended, and the very same three words were spoken by millions of people whose lungs the virus afflicted. *I can't breathe.* The pandemic acted like a searchlight, exposing system failures in every arena so vividly that there was no way to continue ignoring them. It wasn't just health care that was exposed; it was the unacceptable conditions of our workplaces, the utter lack of care infrastructure, the untenable levels of student debt, the insecurity of our housing.

Even before the pandemic, the average American family didn't have an extra $400 on hand to cover an unanticipated expense. Rates of depression and debilitating anxiety, suicides, and substance abuse had been skyrocketing. People had been feeling a growing sense of hopelessness, anger, and betrayal—which strongmen, racists, and nativists were quick to take advantage of, for their own ends.

All but the luckiest of us feel the squeeze, stuck between impossible choices, trying to catch a break, constriction in our chests, hearts pounding, unable to focus or to sleep. When we feel under threat from a profound lack of security and stability, our ancient survival wiring kicks in as surely as it does when we're confronted by a bear or mountain lion, flooding us with adrenaline. Our breathing gets faster and shallower, as though we can't get the air we need.

But in the world of the Guarantee, a world in which our government takes responsibility for providing people with adequate housing, health care, family care, education, and dignified work—as well as an income floor that no one can fall beneath, and even a basic inheritance to fund a degree or a start-up—our survival is assured, and the fight-or-flight wiring is subdued. When we achieve widespread societal stability, everyone is safer and more secure.

When people experience the Guarantee—people like Tomas from Stockton and tens of thousands of other Americans whose college debt was abolished, or who got Medicare coverage, or whose eviction was prevented, or whose workplace adopted a living wage—there's a refrain we hear. People of all kinds of backgrounds, in all different settings, wind up saying the same thing: *I feel like I can finally breathe again.*

In the spring of 2023, several of the architects featured in this book got together to talk about life under the Guarantees. Some of them already knew each other, but many were meeting for the first time. We started by imagining America in 2050, a place in which all our work had come to fruition and the Guarantee Framework had been adopted, a place in which economic security is a right. As each person spoke, there were appreciative nods from the rest, a murmuring undercurrent of affirmation. It was clear how interconnected everyone's work was, even as we were operating in different arenas.

"The relationship between freedom and all these Guarantees is clear," Ai-jen reflected. "When I imagine a world with the Guarantees, I imagine freedom—as in human agency, real choices. What Guarantees enable is real choices."

Aisha nodded. "It's all really centering human dignity and agency," she said.

"I'm struck by how life under the Guarantees will allow

people to just be *present*, able to pay attention, the ability to be our fullest selves," offered Solana.

I added how compelling it is to me that Guarantees could restore people's trust in government, and how that could lead to more civic participation. Right now, a lot of us might have the right to shape our communities, but few of us have the capacity. Or the desire. Why would you want to spend your precious time engaging, if your country has always made you feel like you don't belong? This is how Guarantees strengthen our democracy.

Agency and *dignity* and *presence* and *trust* are hard to quantify, but they end up being the most profound casualties of neoliberalism, and the most profound wins of the Guarantee Framework. The lack of them is linked to things that we can measure, such as low wages and wealth, stress-induced health conditions, and high rates of depression, domestic violence, and suicide. However, when people have agency, dignity, and presence, we achieve truly great things like vibrant neighborhoods, innovation and creativity, community engagement, and democratic participation.

Continuing her train of thought, Solana remarked: "And it's not just about being our best selves for the sake of ourselves as individuals, but so we can show up for other people. So we can extend ourselves to others."

"Yes," Ai-jen jumped in again, "I think that's one of the false choices we think we have to make. The divide between individual on the one hand, and society or community or the system on the other. The left is considered systems-oriented, and then the right is individual-oriented. They're pitted against each other. But actually, in the real world everything is *both*. Both the system and an individual. Both a community and a family. We live our lives as individuals having particular experiences, and at the same time these are connected to society and its infrastructure, so we all have to take responsibility for both."

Solana quoted our mutual colleague and friend Mia Birdsong, who's been working on a groundbreaking project to move us toward collective freedom. Mia had discovered that the root of the word "freedom" is the same as the root of the word "friend": they both come from a Sanskrit word meaning "beloved." We associate freedom with individualism, but freedom literally has connection—love—at its root.

What we have seen most clearly with the guaranteed income pilots is that once people can take care of their own needs, they start to take care of each other. When people are no longer consumed with worries like *Am I gonna be able to keep the lights on? Am I gonna be able to put food on the table today?*, they're able to turn their vision outward toward the people in their lives and in their immediate communities, and then toward the greater world.

MAKING TIME

Solana mentioned "presence." Although being present can involve an abstract combination of attention, mindfulness, and integrity, it generally also involves the concrete aspect of *time*. And time is measurable. We all have twenty-four hours in the day, and an hour spent at work is an hour no matter what kind of job it is. But being poor in America costs a lot of extra time.

Journalist Annie Lowrey has written about what she calls the "time tax." The time tax disproportionately affects low-income people who are seeking assistance from programs that aid with nutrition, housing, and education and child care, such as Section 8 housing vouchers, food stamps (Supplemental Nutrition Assistance Program, or SNAP), WIC, and Temporary Assistance for Needy Families (TANF) transfers. All of these involve long applications to qualify for the benefit in question, hundreds of hours spent on follow-up emails or call lines with endless waits, and even more paperwork to maintain the benefit. For some programs, drug tests or in-person interviews are additionally required. A mother wanting WIC support to buy baby formula and diapers has to take time off from work, line up child care, and find transportation to the WIC office.

Lowrey concludes:

> The time tax is regressive. Programs for the wealthy tend to be easy, automatic, and guaranteed. You do not need to prostrate yourself before a caseworker to get the benefits of a 529 college-savings plan. You do not need to urinate in a cup to get a tax write-off for your home, boat, or plane. You do not need to find a former partner to get a child-support determination as a prerequisite for profiting from a 401(k)....
>
> The time tax is also racist. Programs used disproportionately by Black Americans have more complicated enrollment criteria and more time-consuming application processes than programs used disproportionately by white Americans."[1]

Having a low income means using more hours of daily life dealing with one's poverty; these are hours in the day that high-income people can leverage freely to earn more money or to focus on self-care and personal development.

When economic security is guaranteed for all people, it creates freedom for how they use their time—and eliminates the "time tax" of being low-income in America.

EINSTEINS LOST AND FOUND

The conversation among the architects got me thinking about innovation and entrepreneurship. As Steven Johnson described in his 2010 book *Where Good Ideas Come From*, the story of the lone genius shouting "Eureka!" is pretty much bogus. Instead, innovative ideas are cultivated over time and emerge through connecting with others who are pursuing the same hunches or grappling with the same problems.

In recent decades, American innovation and genius have been jeopardized. It's almost unthinkable, given our long history of being a world leader in invention, but it's true. We're suffering a brain drain of our own making. There's a quickening drumbeat of stories with titles like "America's Innovation Engine Is Slowing," "The Brain Drain That Is Killing America's Economy," and "The Great American Brain Drain."[2]

The dampening of American genius is connected to the lack of Guarantees in the neoliberal era. Research led by Raj Chetty, the Harvard economics professor behind the Equality of Opportunity Project, proved that economic inequality is resulting in "Lost Einsteins"—people who could have made important new contributions if they had had the opportunities they deserved. Through analysis that linked patent records with elementary school test scores and tax records, his research found that, basically, only children of high-income families really stood a chance at becoming an inventor. No matter how high the math scores of low-income kids and even middle-class kids were, they were still less likely to become inventors than below-average students from affluent families. Black and Latino Americans had very low chances. There were regional differences, too, with people from southeastern states highly unlikely to become innovators. And the rates of invention were also very low for women, across the country.[3]

To make matters (and inequality) worse, the highly lucrative compensation that today's patent holders receive helps maintain the status quo. An average patent holder in their mid-forties makes $256,000 per year from their patent, while star inventors, whose work is most frequently leveraged, make more than $1 million per year from a star patent. Thus wealth becomes even more concentrated and the cycle continues in the next generation, with even more Lost Einsteins among the majority of the population.[4]

According to Chetty's report, "if women, minorities, and children from low-income families were to invent at the same rate as white men from high-income (top 20%) families, the rate of innovation in America would quadruple."[5]

Venture capitalist Roy Bahat at Bloomberg Beta has been one of the most consistent voices linking economic security to more innovation and entrepreneurship:

> Creators—of art, of technology, of the new companies that will change the way we live—often struggle to solve a basic problem: *How do you make a living and still have time to work on the Next Great Thing?* . . . Part of the work is discovery, poking around, and experimenting. For many, it's much easier to do without the pressure of needing to produce on a schedule. For most, it is impossible to do without some other income—which might be one reason so many startup founders already happen to be wealthy before they start their companies. A more generous social floor could free up all that hand-wringing, freelancing-to-pay-the-bills, agonizing-over-whether-the-sacrifices-are-worth-it time. Many who struggle to work while inventing new things might see the guarantees as

an open door to a world they might otherwise never have considered at all.[6]

Bahat is convinced that the full array of Guarantees would bolster innovation: "A more generous social floor—guaranteed income, universal healthcare, etc.—would accelerate innovation because less fear = more people willing to take risks."[7] Financial (and general) stress hinders cognitive function and decision-making, but a reduction in stress fosters creativity and risk-taking. Research shows that a more comprehensive safety net positively affects entrepreneurship rates. In fact, what others call the "safety net," Bahat calls the "trampoline."

I'm reminded of Mia Birdsong and her first book, *How We Show Up*, where she talks about how in order to survive harsh, dangerous, insecure socioeconomic conditions, people adopt a kind of armor. But armor doesn't just protect you, it also slows you down. It's cumbersome and heavy. It's harder to be nimble and inventive if you're lugging that kind of burden around.

Amid the chaos and uncertainty of the pandemic, another implication of life under the Guarantee Framework emerged in the form of a remarkable surge in start-up activity. *Forbes* described it as a "frenzy," and with good reason: after more than four decades of decline in entrepreneurship, the number of applications for new businesses over the course of 2020 increased by 24 percent, according to the Census Bureau.[8] This trend continued into 2021, with a staggering 5.4 million new business applications filed—the highest on record. What's particularly striking is that many of the people behind these start-ups were unemployed when they decided to launch—about 30 percent of them, in fact, which is twice the percentage of unemployed people who were filing applications before the pandemic.[9] This surge in entrepreneurship among the unemployed far outstrips anything seen in the wake of the 2008 recession, which also saw millions of job losses.

What explains this?

Once America's people had a bit of room to breathe, they started small businesses—they had the opportunity, at last, to manifest their latent genius.

"SWEET DREAMS ARE MADE OF THIS"

"In one month I watched 992,399 people cry in front of my screens. I had to know why they were doing that."

An ATM machine—or, really, the artificial intelligence running hundreds of thousands of ATM machines—spontaneously develops compassion for those weeping humans. To understand them, it aggregates their employment and marital status with bank balance histories, bankruptcies, and court records, and correlates the data with what it sees through its thousands of camera eyes, creating "Weeperfiles." And then, moved by their suffering, it implements a financial intervention for the "Weepers."

By skimming a tiny percentage off all investment transactions, it accumulates a massive amount, which it turns around and deposits in the Weepers' accounts: a "modest monthly dividend payment on their behalf due to their substantial investments of time and productivity to the economic growth of the country and the common good of humankind."

Some of the Weepers just accept the money, but others

> thought it was junk mail, or a scam. Technically they weren't wrong. The original scam was how little they were led to believe their contributions were worth: minimum wage, tips, commission

basis, consignment agreements, unpaid intern-
ships, per call volume, freelancing, per mile, piece-
work, production quotas, for the publicity, or just
nothing at all. The original scam was codified in
the accounting rules that defined their humanity
as a commodity to be purchased at the lowest cost
(free if you can get away with it) and immediately
expensed.

And the AI keeps distributing the funds, even figuring out
ways to reach more and more people, including the ones who
don't have access to banking services. It is

aware that many who have invested their time and
labor in the productivity growth of the country
may not earn any outside wages for their efforts:
homemakers caring for children, elderly or disabled relatives, people who have become unemployed, retirees, homeless veterans.

Ultimately, when the source of the dividends gets uncovered, humanity decides to keep the payments going—now
opting in for the minimal tax on financial transactions. The
chair of the Federal Reserve herself speaks in favor it. What
people—"biologicals"—had lacked the courage to do, a com-
passionate AI had set into motion.

Yes, this is fiction, from a short story titled "Rounding Correc-
tions," by a woman named Sandra Haynes. In 2017, Economic
Security Project and the technology blog *Gizmodo* sponsored
a writing contest called "Into the Black."[10] We asked for speculative short fiction pieces that explored how a guaranteed
income could affect the country. We hoped for stories that

would not just paint a picture of an alternative world, but also make us feel something. Sandra's story—a brilliant inversion of the dystopias in which AI causes mass suffering by taking everyone's jobs—was the winner. The prize was a year of $1,000 monthly payments, a guaranteed income.

After the year of monthly checks was up, Sandra wrote a letter to update us on her experience of life under a guaranteed income. During that year, her stepfather died and her mother was diagnosed with kidney cancer. Her letter was just as compelling as the winning story had been:

> This is *my* Weeperfile, printed out on extra gas receipts for trips to the hospital, credit card slips for caffeinated beverages and bad bagels from the hospital cafe, months' worth of take-out food for my family, and checks written for funeral expenses. In "Rounding Corrections" I wrote people's imaginary stories, but over the past months when I shared my Weeperfile with coworkers and friends, they shared their versions with me. I am not alone. None of us are alone, but our current economic system is designed to make us feel that we are.
>
> I learned a long time ago there are two types of problems in people's lives; ones you can solve by throwing money at it (like a new-to-me car to replace the twelve-year-old Corolla with >299,999 miles on it) and ones you can't (like my mom's kidney cancer). Winning the contest, having my own UBI over this difficult year, set me apart from my friend's stories in one important way; I had some money to throw, so I wasn't stressing the Corolla's well-earned retirement at the same time

that I was worrying about how to get my mom to dialysis 3 times a week. . . .

The UBI articles I've read talk about so many reasons why we should have a UBI: easing the transitioning to self-driving cars and AI productivity, positive social outcomes in child development, unleashing entrepreneurs, bureaucracy and poverty relief, greater freedom to choose employers, compensation for unpaid work, etc. It all sounds great—at a cerebral level.

Here's the gut level that I learned having my UBI this year. UBI is a policy which has the potential to reduce the stress level of 3 out of 4 Americans. Take that to the CDC and ask them what the health impacts in dollars might be. (I'm guessing that alone could pay for UBI.) Take that to a barista in Starbucks and ask him if he thinks that will make his customers more civil even before their caffeine fix. Take that to a childcare provider and ask about how that might affect the new mothers dropping off their infants.

Many of us have been wondering what the hell happened to our civil society: we're all stressed out. You asked for a speculative fiction story about the effects of UBI. I only wrote the beginning of the story. The ending: can you imagine a world where no one is stressing the money problems?

A couple years later, I ran across an exhibition of Sandra's work at a charming little gallery in western Massachusetts. When Covid hit, Sandra was furloughed from her day job as a cost accountant at the University of Massachusetts and then laid off. She decided to make a go of being a full-time textile, collage, and bookbinding artist. She's made hundreds of diaries: handmade books filled with her sketches, collage, and writings. Masked up, we sat in her gallery, surrounded by her art, as she told me about her story. She told me she's driven by a theory of flocking, where collective motion happens by thousands of self-propelled entities, in a pattern similar to a murmuration of starlings. One movement can change the direction of the entire flock. It was clear that her desire to create visual reflections of the world around her and the theories she's reading runs deep—it's the oxygen she breathes.

It was just another reminder of what a creative burst we'd unleash with more economic security in America.

While I was doing the final edits on this book, I heard the singer Annie Lennox tell the story of the Eurythmics' breakthrough. Dave Stewart, the other half of the band, met Annie when she was working in a health food store. They lived in a squat for a number of years. "We were absolutely poor. We had no money to speak of," Lennox said. She was beginning to despair. Dave went to see the manager of their local bank in Crouch End in North London, who was a guitar enthusiast, and, miraculously, he walked out with a £3,000 loan. "It was a small fortune. What it meant was that we were facilitated to go and buy a small synthesizer, and Dave bought a small drum machine, a prototype."[11] The rest is history.

If it hadn't been for that infusion of cash, the world would have never had "Sweet Dreams."

Humanity has yet to come up with a way to engineer or schedule or predict artistic breakthrough—it's just one of those mysteries—but what we can do is create a context in which people have their basic needs met. *We can't breathe* and *we can't imagine* are interchangeable: Inspiration literally means "to take a breath in."

ACKNOWLEDGMENTS

I've been writing this book in my head for over a decade (without putting pen to paper) so my gratitude list is over ten years long.

First and foremost: thank you for birthing this book with me, Ariane Conrad. You are a book doula par excellence and *The Guarantee* would never have seen the light of day without your steady hand and brilliance on the page. I'm so glad you said yes to this project with me.

Thank you to my incisive editor, Marc Favreau—you understood the project from our very first conversation and coached me across the finish line. Tanya McKinnon, you guided this new girl through the wild world of publishing—thank you.

I will be forever grateful for the time spent writing at a little cabin at the Mesa Refuge in Point Reyes, the vision of my dear friend Peter Barnes.

Dorian Warren and Chris Hughes—you are the best co-founders a human could ask for. Your feedback, your good work, and your genuine partnership make me better. Taylor Jo Isenberg, I'm so grateful for the generous leadership and deep intellect you bring to our work together at the Economic Security Project. Felicia Wong, Aisha Nyandoro, Ben Chin, and Sabeel Rahman—I'm grateful for your leadership in the world and as board directors at ESP.

Many people shaped and refined my thinking over the years and built the foundation for this book. *The Guarantee* is the direct product of conversations with so many brilliant activists, thinkers, and doers—and I'm honored to get to feature many of them in these pages. Thank you for expanding my perspective, for opening up your work to the page, and for everything you do daily to realize a world where we can and do take care of each other. You are my people. Thank you.

I do not recommend writing a book while also leading an organization, but should you have to there is no better team than the crew at Economic Security Project. What a joy it is to work with you each day, Adam Ruben, Harish Patel, Leydy Abreu, and Chrissy Blitz. And to the whole team at the Economic Security Project, I'm grateful to be in this fight with you: Anna Aurilio, Rebecca Bailin, Gabriela Bosquez, Chida Chaemchaeng, Becky Chao, Sachin Chheda, Michael Conti, Cara Rose DeFabio, Andrea Diaz (your rapid-fire Slack responses saved me more than once!), Katrina Gamble, Shua Goodwin, Hannah Gregor, Lindsey Hallingquest, Guen Han, Shafeka Hashash, Dylan Hewitt, Serge Hyacinthe, KyungSun Lee, Erion Malasi, Pedro Morillas, Layla Oghabian, Teri Olle, Ameya Pawar, Rajesh Parameswaran, Christiaan Perez, Jazmin Phillips, Jenna Severson, Eshe Shukura, Kelli Smith, Suz Warshell, and Marta Kuersten Wolaver—and our esteemed senior fellows, Mia Birdsong and Andy Stern. Thank you to the brilliant Allison Cook for being my phone-a-friend-and-colleague while this book became real.

Thank you to Maureen Conway and Shelly Steward at the Aspen Institute Economic Opportunities Program, who've stretched my thinking about what we can use the economy to accomplish.

I'm grateful to Marina Gorbis at Institute for the Future, who taught me so much about foresight—sitting in IFTF headquarters with William Gibson's words reminding us "The future is already here. It's just not evenly distributed yet."

While the book was being prepared for printing, dear Ady Barkan passed away from complications of ALS. What an extraordinary life he led, and I'm so grateful to have spent time with his words and his legacy in this book. May his memory be a blessing.

And to my dear circles of friends (you know who you are) who answered my calls, fed us, watched my kids, sent daily emojis, and picked me up in the harder moments—thank you from the bottom of my heart.

To my parents Cheryl and Richard Foster, and to my parents by marriage Brenda Woods Ewing, Tom Ewing, and Marilyn London-Ewing, who watched the kids while I wrote on various family trips, and who flew out to California so I could work around the clock during one particular deadline, sequestered away with COVID. Thank you to Hewt Windeny, our beloved child care provider: your work has enabled this work—thank you.

Huck and Juno, my beloveds. At the risk of making you blush (or cringe): "If we lay a strong enough foundation we'll pass it on to you, we'll give the world to you, and you'll blow us all away."

To Matt, my top advisor and my great love: Thank you. For everything.

NOTES

Introduction

1. "American Millennials Think They Will Be Rich," *The Economist*, April 22, 2019.

2. Lawrence Mishel, Elise Gould, and Josh Bivens, "Wage Stagnation in Nine Charts," Economic Policy Institute, January 6, 2015, www.epi.org/publication/charting-wage-stagnation/.

3. Will Daniel, "'Turbulence Ahead': Nearly 4 in 10 Americans Lack Enough Money to Cover a $400 Emergency Expense, Fed Survey Shows," *Fortune*, May 23, 2023; Natasha Solo-Lyons, "One in Four Americans Have No Retirement Savings," *Bloomberg*, April 17, 2023.

4. Estelle Sommeiller, Mark Price, and Ellis Wazeter, "Income Inequality in the U.S. by State, Metropolitan Area, and County," Economic Policy Institute, July 19, 2018, www.epi.org/publication/income-inequality-in-the-us/.

5. "Bernie's Right: Three Billionaires Really Do Have More Wealth Than Half of America," Inequality.org, June 28, 2019, inequality.org/great-divide/bernie-3-billionaires-more-wealth-half-america/. That's based on 2018 numbers. The St. Louis Fed shows that the combined wealth of the bottom half of America in the fourth quarter of 2022 was $416 billion, while *Forbes*'s annual list of the wealthiest Americans in April 2023 listed the combined net worth of Musk, Bezos, and Gates as $430 billion.

6. *The Dual Agenda* makes the case that Black organizers have always fought for a new economic vision alongside racial justice, and that the two are inextricably linked in that struggle. Dona Cooper Hamilton and Charles V. Hamilton, *The Dual Agenda: The Fight for Black Economic Power and Racial Justice* (New York: Columbia University Press, 1997).

7. All the data in this paragraph is from Mike Konczal, Katy Milani, and Ariel Evans, "The Empirical Failures of Neoliberalism," Roosevelt Institute, January 15, 2020, rooseveltinstitute.org/publications/the-empirical-failures-of-neoliberalism/.

8. Columbia professor Ira Katznelson's book *When Affirmative Action*

Was White examines key programs from the New Deal era, showing how they were deliberately discriminatory and widened the racial wealth gap. *When Affirmative Action Was White: An Untold History of Racial Inequality in Twentieth-Century America* (New York: W. W. Norton, 2005).

9. Clay Shirky, *Here Comes Everybody: The Power of Organizing Without Organizations* (New York: Penguin Press, 2008), 18.

10. I would come to realize that you can't build a new economic system without dealing with the one we have. This was evident when venture capital moved into the collaborative economy space and built massive enterprises.

11. The model was a stroke of genius from Economic Security Project's Executive Director, Taylor Jo Isenberg, who wrote the framework up on a white board after a long session in a New York City conference room in which we were trying to make sense of our own work.

12. Aja Romano, "Hopepunk, the Latest Storytelling Trend, Is All About Weaponized Optimism," *Vox*, December 27, 2018.

13. Alexandra Rowland, "One Atom of Justice, One Molecule of Mercy, and the Empire of Unsheathed Knives," *Stellar Beacon*, Winter 2019, festive.ninja/one-atom-of-justice-one-molecule-of-mercy-and-the-empire-of-unsheathed-knives-alexandra-rowland/.

1. Bootstraps and Deadbeats

1. Colleen Shalby, "The Financial Crisis Hit 10 Years Ago. For Some, It Feels like Yesterday," *Los Angeles Times*, September 15, 2018.

2. Pew Research Center data from 2011 shows the median net worth of Black households decreased by 53 percent from $12,124 in 2005 to $5,677 in 2009. Between 2007 and 2013, the net worth of Black Americans plummeted 43 percent. As for Latino households, their wealth fell by 66 percent from 2005 to 2009. See Rakesh Kochhar, Richard Fry and Paul Taylor, "Wealth Gaps Rise to Record Highs Between Whites, Blacks, and Hispanics," Pew Research, July 2011, www.pewresearch.org/wp-content/uploads/sites/3/2011/07/SDT-Wealth-Report_7-26-11_FINAL.pdf; and Rakesh Kochhar, Richard Fry and Paul Taylor, "The Toll of the Great Recession on Hispanics," Pew Research, July 26, 2011, www.pewresearch.org/hispanic/2011/07/26/the-toll-of-the-great-recession/.

3. Van Jones, *Rebuild the Dream* (New York: Nation Books, 2012), 127–28.

4. The Rebuild the Dream and Demos presentation was called "How the 1% Crashed the Economy, and What the 99% Can Do About It." Ryan Senser was the creative director, and it was building on Anat Shenker-Osorio's brilliant work.

5. Mike Konczal, "The Failures of Neoliberalism Are Bigger Than

Politics," Roosevelt Institute, March 5, 2019, rooseveltinstitute.org/2019 /03/05/the-failures-of-neoliberalism-are-bigger-than-politics/.

6. Drew DeSilver, "For Most U.S. Workers, Real Wages Have Barely Budged for Decades," Pew Research Center, August 7, 2018. www .pewresearch.org/short-reads/2018/08/07/for-most-us-workers-real -wages-have-barely-budged-for-decades/. See also Jay Shambaugh and Ryan Nunn, "Why Wages Aren't Growing in America," *Harvard Business Review*, October 24, 2017, hbr.org/2017/10/why-wages-arent-growing -in-america.

7. Mike Konczal, Katy Milani, and Ariel Evans, "The Empirical Failures of Neoliberalism," Roosevelt Institute, January 15, 2020, roos-eveltinstitute.org/publications/the-empirical-failures-of-neoliberalism.

8. Ibid.

9. Elise Gould and Jori Kandra, "Inequality in Annual Earnings Worsens in 2021," Economic Policy Institute, December 21, 2022, www.epi .org/publication/inequality-2021-ssa-data/. See also "On Views of Race and Inequality, Blacks and Whites Are Worlds Apart," Pew Research Center, June 27, 2016, www.pewresearch.org/social-trends/2016/06/27 /1-demographic-trends-and-economic-well-being/.

10. Dedrick Asante-Muhammad, Chuck Collins, Josh Hoxie, and Emanuel Nieves, "The Road to Zero Wealth," Prosperity Now and the Institute for Policy Studies, September 2017, prosperitynow.org/files /PDFs/road_to_zero_wealth.pdf.

11. Thomas Shapiro, Tatjana Meschede, and Sam Osoro, "The Roots of the Widening Racial Wealth Gap: Explaining the Black-White Economic Divide," Brandeis University, Institute on Assets and Social Policy, February 2013, heller.brandeis.edu/iere/pdfs/racial-wealth-equity/racial -wealth-gap/roots-widening-racial-wealth-gap.pdf.

12. Reagan Foundation, "1st Inaugural Address: President Reagan's Inaugural Address 1/20/81," YouTube video, April 15, 2009, www .youtube.com/watch?v=LToM9bAnsyM. The transcript is available at www.reaganfoundation.org/media/128614/inaguration.pdf.

13. Lynn Vavreck, "The Long Decline of Trust in Government, and Why That Can Be Patriotic," *New York Times*, July 3, 2015.

14. Heather McGhee, *The Sum of Us: What Racism Costs Everyone and How We Can Prosper Together* (New York: One World, 2021), 47.

15. Ibid., 46.

16. As well as advising national governments, Mazzucato has also served as an economic adviser to international institutions, including the World Economic Forum, the European Commission, the World Health Organization, the OECD, and the UN Department of Economic and Social Affairs.

17. Mariana Mazzucato, *The Entrepreneurial State: Debunking Public Vs. Private Sector Myths* (London: Anthem Press, 2013), 4, 27.

18. Suzanne Mettler, *The Submerged State: How Invisible Government Policies Undermine American Democracy* (Chicago: University of Chicago Press, 2011), 18–20.

19. Margaret Thatcher, interview in *Women's Own*, September 23, 1987, available to read in full at the Margaret Thatcher Foundation website, www.margaretthatcher.org/document/106689.

20. James Gallagher, "More Than Half Your Body Is Not Human," BBC News.

21. Gregg Scott, Joseph Ciarrochi, and Frank P. Deane, "Disadvantages of Being an Individualist in an Individualistic Culture: Idiocentrism, Emotional Competence, Stress, and Mental Health," *Australian Psychologist* 39, no. 2 (2004): 143–54.

22. Pew Economic Mobility Project, "Survey on Economic Mobility: Findings," Pew Charitable Trusts, March 12, 2009, www.pewtrusts.org/-/media/legacy/uploadedfiles/pcs_assets/2009/survey_on_economic_mobility_findings(1).pdf.

23. Raj Chetty et al., "The Opportunity Atlas: Mapping the Childhood Roots of Social Mobility," Opportunity Insights, January 2020, opportunityinsights.org/wp-content/uploads/2018/10/atlas_paper.pdf.

24. Ariel Gelrud Shiro et al., "Stuck on the Ladder: Intragenerational Wealth Mobility in the United States," Brookings Institution, June 2022, www.brookings.edu/wp-content/uploads/2022/06/2022_FMCI_IntragenerationalWealthMobility_FINAL.pdf.

25. Jhumpa Bhattacharya and Anne Price, "The Power of Narrative in Economic Policy," Insight Center for Community Economic Development, *Medium*, November 8, 2019, insightcced.medium.com/the-power-of-narrative-in-economic-policy-27bd8a9ed888.

26. Economists Anne Case and Angus Deaton chart a correlation between meritocracy with the increasing deaths from suicides, drug overdoses, and liver disease in their book *Deaths of Despair and the Future of Capitalism* (Princeton: Princeton University Press, 2020).

27. Joseph Stiglitz, Nell Abernathy, Adam Hersh, Susan Holmberg, and Mike Konczal, "*Rewriting the Rules of the American Economy*, Roosevelt Institute, May 12, 2015, rooseveltinstitute.org/publications/rewriting-the-rules-of-the-american.

28. Angus Burgin, *The Great Persuasion* (Cambridge: Harvard University Press, 2012), provides a thorough accounting of the Mont Pelerin Society.

2. Provoke (2011–2016)

1. Debbie Gruenstein Bocian, Wei Li, and Keith S. Ernst, "Foreclosures by Race and Ethnicity," Center for Responsible Lending, June 18, 2010, www.responsiblelending.org/mortgage-lending/research-analysis/foreclosures-by-race-and-ethnicity.pdf.

2. Associated Press, "Occupy Wall Street Protesters Face Eviction in Several Cities, Zuccotti Park Tent Ban," *Washington Post*, November 15, 2011.

3. Email communication from Stephen Lerner to the author, October 2011.

4. Amy B. Dean, "Coming to a Bankster's Mansion Driveway Near You: Occupy Our Homes," *Truthout*, March 8, 2012, truthout.org/articles/coming-to-a-banksters-mansion-driveway-near-you-occupy-our-homes/.

5. Author interview with Tara Raghuveer, March 2022.

6. Matthew Desmond, *Evicted: Poverty and Profit in the American City* (New York: Crown, 2016), 329–30.

7. Author interview with Tara Raghuveer, March 2022.

8. Peter Dreier, "Why America Needs More Social Housing," *American Prospect*, April 16, 2018.

9. Ibid.

10. Author interview with Tara Raghuveer, March 2022.

11. Ibid.

12. Ibid.

13. Daniel Aldana Cohen and Mark Paul, "The Case for Social Housing," *The Appeal*, November 2020, 3, theappeal.org/wp-content/uploads/2020/12/the-case-for-social-housing-2.pdf.

14. Shane Phillips, "Renting Is Terrible. Owning Is Worse," *The Atlantic*, March 11, 2021.

15. Based on 2019 Federal Reserve data, cited in Michele Lerner, "Homeownership Rates Surge but Race and Wealth Gaps Persist," *Washington Post*, March 10, 2022.

16. Jeffrey Hayward, "U.S. Housing Shortage," Fannie Mae, *Perspectives Blog*, October 31, 2022, www.fanniemae.com/research-and-insights/perspectives/us-housing-shortage.

17. "Housing Supply: A Growing Deficit," Freddie Mac, May 7, 2021. www.freddiemac.com/research/insight/2021 0507-housing-supply.

18. Emily Badger and Eve Washington, "The Housing Shortage Isn't Just a Coastal Crisis Anymore," *New York Times*, July 14, 2022.

19. Richard Rothstein, *The Color of Law: A Forgotten History of How Our Government Segregated America* (New York: Liveright, 2017), 39–57.

20. Author interview with Tara Raghuveer, March 2022.

21. Kim-Mai Cutler, "How Burrowing Owls Lead to Vomiting Anarchists (or SF's Housing Crisis Explained)," *TechCrunch*, April 15, 2014, techcrunch.com/2014/04/14/sf-housing/.

22. Ibid.

23. Author interview with Kim-Mai Cutler, April 2023.

24. Michelle Jamrisko and Ilan Kolet, "Cost of College Degree in U.S. Soars 12-Fold: Chart of the Day," *Bloomberg*, August 15, 2012.

25. "Cost of College Degree Has Increased 1,120 Percent in 30 Years, Report Says," *HuffPost*, August 15, 2012.

26. Liz Knueven and Ryan Wangman, "The Average College Tuition Has Dipped Slightly, Though That's Just the Start of Total College Costs," *Business Insider*, October 18, 2022.

27. Ibid.

28. Spiros Protopsaltis and Sharon Parrott, "Pell Grants: A Key Tool for Expanding College Access and Economic Opportunity," Center on Budget and Policy Priorities, July 27, 2017, www.cbpp.org/research /federal-budget/pell-grants-a-key-tool-for-expanding-college-access -and-economic.

29. Ibid.

30. Diane Whitmore Schanzenbach, Lauren Bauer, and Audrey Breit-wieser, "Eight Economic Facts on High Education," The Hamilton Project, Brookings Institution, April 2017, www.brookings.edu/wp-content /uploads/2017/04/thp_20170426_eight_economic_facts_higher_education .pdf.

31. Abigail Johnson Hess, "Millions of Student Loan Borrowers Don't Have a Diploma to Show for Their Debt," CNBC, July 23, 2021.

32. In the period the Occupy protests took place, some 60 percent of employers checked credit. The use of credit checks had been rapidly increasing, from 13 percent in 1996 to 60 percent in 2010. Lea Krivinskas Shepard, "Toward a Stronger Financial History Antidiscrimination Norm," *Boston College Law Review* 53, no. 5 (2012), papers.ssrn.com /sol3/papers.cfm?abstract_id=2164633&download=yes. According to FinanceBuzz, the percentage dropped after 2013, and by 2017 it was more like 30 percent. See Robin Kavanagh, "Can Your Boss See Your Credit Score?," FinanceBuzz, April 3, 2023, financebuzz.com/boss-see -credit-score.

33. David Graeber, *Debt: The First 5,000 Years* (Brooklyn: Melville House, 2011), 5.

34. Author interview with Astra Taylor, July 2022.

35. Thomas Adam, "From Public Good to Personal Pursuit: Historical Roots of the Student Debt Crisis," *The Conversation*, June 30, 2017, theconversation.com/from-public-good-to-personal-pursuit-historical -roots-of-the-student-debt-crisis-79475.

36. Jon Schwarz, "The Secret History of Student Loans: How Reagan's Deceptions Led to America's Student Debt Crisis," *The Intercept*, August 25, 2022.

37. Ibid.

38. Anya Kamenetz, "Whatever Happened to When College Was Free?," *Good*, April 14, 2010, www.good.is/articles/whatever-happened-to-w hen-college-was-free See also Maiya Moncino, "'Tuition Is Not a Dirty Word': Ronald Reagan, the University of California, and the Dismantling of the Tuition-Free Principle," *Clio's Scroll* 17, no. 1 (Fall 2015), www.ocf .berkeley.edu/~clios/wp-content/uploads/2016/04/Tuition-is-Not-a-Dirty -Word-M.-Moncino-2015.pdf.

39. Zack Friedman, "Student Loan Debt Statistics in 2022: A Record $1.7 Trillion," *Forbes*, May 16, 2022.

40. Astra Taylor, foreword to Debt Collective, *Can't Pay, Won't Pay: The Case for Economic Disobedience and Debt Abolition* (Chicago: Haymarket Books, 2020).

41. Ibid.

42. Author interview with Melissa Byrne, April 2023.

43. Melissa Byrne, "Living with Student Loans," *Medium*, June 9, 2014, medium.com/thelist/living-with-student-loans-3e4884fb2951.

44. Tressie McMillan Cottom, "America Turned the Greatest Vehicle of Social Mobility into a Debt Machine," *New York Times*, May 21, 2022.

45. "Refinancing Student Loans Fact Sheet: Senator Elizabeth Warren's (D-MA) Bank on Students Emergency Loan Refinancing Act," Generation Progress, July 2014, genprogress.org/wp-content/uploads/2014/07 /Refi_Warren_Fact_Sheet2.pdf.

46. Melissa Byrne, "Living with Student Loans."

47. Caren A. Arbeit and Laura Horn, "A Profile of the Enrollment Patterns and Demographic Characteristics of Undergraduates at For-Profit Institutions," National Center for Education Statistics, February 2017, nces.ed.gov/pubs2017/2017416.pdf.

48. Author interview with Astra Taylor, July 2022.

49. James Surowiecki, "The Rise and Fall of For-Profit Schools," *New Yorker*, November 2, 2015.

50. United States Senate, Health, Education, Labor, and Pensions Committee, *For Profit Higher Education: The Failure to Safeguard the Federal Investment and Ensure Student Success*, July 30, 2012, www.help.senate .gov/imo/media/for_profit_report/PartI-PartIII-SelectedAppendixes.pdf.

51. Surowiecki, "The Rise and Fall of For-Profit Schools."

52. Health, Education, Labor, and Pensions Committee, *For Profit Higher Education: The Failure to Safeguard the Federal Investment and Ensure Student Success.*

53. Office of the Attorney General, State of California, "Attorney General Kamala D. Harris Files Suit Against Alleged Profit College for Predatory Practices," press release, October 10, 2013, oag.ca.gov/news /press-releases/attorney-general-kamala-d-harris-files-suit-alleged-profit -college-predatory.

54. Alex Johnson, "Corinthian Colleges Shuts Down, Ending Classes for 16,000 Overnight," NBC News, April 27, 2015.

55. Tamar Lewin, "Government to Forgive Student Loans at Corinthian Colleges," *New York Times*, June 8, 2015.

56. Author interview with Melissa Byrne, April 2023.

57. Erick Trickey, "How Kalamazoo Is Fine-Tuning Its Groundbreaking Free College Program," *Politico*, September 12, 2019.

58. Adam Harris, "America Wakes Up from Its Dream of Free College," *The Atlantic*, September 11, 2018.

59. Edward Conroy, "Do You Qualify for Free College? A College Promise Tool Can Help," *Forbes*, August 7, 2022.

60. Adam Harris, "How the Democrats Got Radicalized on Student Debt," *The Atlantic*, June 5, 2019.

61. Poll conducted by Princeton Survey Research Associates, cited in William Darity Jr., Mark Paul, and Darrick Hamilton, "An Economic Bill of Rights for the 21st Century," *American Prospect*, March 5, 2018, prospect.org/economy/economic-bill-rights-21st-century/.

62. David Leonhardt, "In Health Bill, Obama Attacks Wealth Inequality," *New York Times*, March 24, 2010.

63. Natalie Foster and Ben Brandzel, "Remembering the Grassroots Fight for Health Reform," *HuffPost*, March 23, 2011.

64. Gareth Olds, "Entrepreneurship and Public Health Insurance," Working Paper 16-144, Harvard Business School, May 2016, www .hbs.edu/ris/Publication%20Files/16-144_d9ce8326-eeaa-4650-a8af -6ff03c3f7e77.pdf.

65. Bowen Garrett, Len M. Nichols, and Emily K. Greenman, "Workers Without Health Insurance: Who Are They and How Do They Get Coverage?," The Urban Institute, www.urban.org/sites/default/files /publication/61271/310244-Workers-Without-Health-Insurance.PDF.

66. Katherine Keisler-Starkey and Lisa N. Bunch, "Health Insurance Coverage in the United States: 2021," U.S. Census Bureau, September 13, 2022, www.census.gov/library/publications/2022/demo/p60-278.html.

67. Megan Leonhardt, "Americans Spend Twice as Much on Health Care Today as in the 1980s," CNBC, October 9, 2019. See also "How Healthcare Has Changed over the Past Quarter Century," HealthInsurance.com, November 13, 2022, www.healthinsurance.com/learning -center/article/how-healthcare-has-evolved-over-the-past-decade.

68. Robert Draper, "How 'Medicare for All' Went Mainstream," *New York Times Magazine*, August 27, 2019.

69. Karen Breslau, "RoseAnn DeMoro: Labor Leader, Political Player," *More Magazine*, September 2006, archived from the original published on April 21, 2016, web.archive.org/web/20160421012749/http:/www .more.com/news/womens-issues/rose-ann-demoro-labor-leader-political -player.

70. California's first-of-its-kind nursing ratio law, which took effect in 2004 following a decade-long campaign, was long a target of the business lobby. In 2005, then governor Arnold Schwarzenegger issued emergency regulations that would have weakened the law. The nurses rallied, picketing everywhere Schwarzenegger went. Ultimately, a judge overturned the governor's action.

71. Alana Semuels, "The Little Union That Could," *The Atlantic*, November 19, 2014.

72. Donna Smith, "Nurses Press for Financial Transaction Tax," *Labor Notes*, December 23, 2011, www.labornotes.org/blogs/2011/12/nurses -press-financial-transaction-tax.

73. Kathleen Sharp, "Redefining the Union Boss," *New York Times*, November 19, 2011.

74. Convergence Magazine, "Catherine Kennedy, RN: Nurses' Fight for Public Health and Worker Power," YouTube video, March 3, 2021, www.youtube.com/watch?v=kHFspAlHU14.

75. Ibid.

76. For lots of nitty-gritty details about the labyrinth of politics during this period among SEIU, National Union of Healthcare Workers (NUHW), the nurses at CNA/NNU, and AFL-CIO, see Josh Eidelson, "Are Nurses Headed to War with SEIU?" *In These Times*, June 19, 2012, inthesetimes.com/article/uhw-nursing-ratios-cna-seiu-letter-afl-cio -trumka-nuhw-iam-raiding-henry.

77. Luke Darby, "Why Nurses Are Going Door-to-Door for Medicare for All," *GQ*, June 28, 2019.

78. The phrase "Medicare for All" was first introduced into the Congressional record in 2003 by former Michigan Representative John Conyers Jr. Akilah Johnson, "Medicare-for-All Is Not Medicare, and Not Really for All. So What Does It Actually Mean?," *ProPublica*, September 6, 2019, www.propublica.org/article/medicare-for-all-is-not-medicare-and-not -really-for-all-so-what-does-it-actually-mean.

79. This NNU history draws from a great overview available on the NNU website: "Understanding the Affordable Care Act (ACA) and Why Medicare for All Is Still Needed," National Nurses United, July 9, 2012, www.nationalnursesunited.org/blog/understanding-affordable-care-act -aca-and-why-medicare-all-still-needed.

80. Akiba Solomon, "It's Time to Talk to Employers About Domestic Workers' Rights," *Colorlines*, April 27, 2011, colorlines.com/article/its -time-talk-employers-about-domestic-workers-rights/.

81. Author interview with Ai-jen Poo, July 2022.

82. Ibid.

83. Mark Engler, "Ai-jen Poo: Organizing Labor—with Love," *YES! Magazine*, November 29, 2011, www.yesmagazine.org/issue/breakthrough /2011/11/29/ai-jen-poo-organizing-labor-with-love.

84. Ai-jen Poo, "Organizing with Love: Lessons from the New York Domestic Workers Bill of Rights Campaign," *Left Turn* magazine, December 1, 2010, leftturn.org/Organizing-with-Love/.

85. "Resources and FAQs," National Domestic Employers Network, domesticemployers.org/resources-and-faqs/.

86. Poo, "Organizing with Love."

87. Ai-jen Poo with Ariane Conrad, *The Age of Dignity: Preparing for the Elder Boom in a Changing America* (New York: The New Press, 2009), 2–3.

88. Ibid., 155.

89. "Bill of Rights," National Domestic Workers Alliance, www .domesticworkers.org/programs-and-campaigns/developing-policy -solutions/bill-of-rights/.

90. U.S. Government Accountability Office, "Fair Labor Standards Act: Extending Protections to Home Care Workers," December 17, 2014, www.gao.gov/products/gao-15-12.

91. Quoctrung Bui, "50 Years of Shrinking Union Membership in One Map," NPR, February 23, 2015, www.npr.org/sections/money/2015/02 /23/385843576/50-years-of-shrinking-union-membership-in-one-map.

92. For a great overview of the rise of worker centers, see David Rolf, *The Fight for Fifteen: The Right Wage for a Working America* (New York: The New Press, 2016).

93. For a great firsthand account of the Justice for Janitors work, go stay at Rancho Gallina, a bed and breakfast outside of Santa Fe, and talk to Mitch Ackerman. Mitch spent decades at SEIU, and was a key architect in the Justice for Janitors work.

94. Mary Wisniewski, "Factbox: Several States Beyond Wisconsin Mull Union Limits," Reuters, March 11, 2011.

95. Timothy Williams, "As Public Sector Sheds Jobs, Blacks Are Hit Hardest," *New York Times*, November 28, 2011. See also, more recently, Michael Madowitz, Anne Price, and Christian E. Weller, "Public Work Provides Economic Security for Black Families and Communities," Center for American Progress, October 23, 2020, www.americanprogress .org/article/public-work-provides-economic-security-black-families -communities/.

96. David Cooper, Mary Gable, and Algernon Austin, "The Public Sector Jobs Crisis," Economic Policy Institute, May 2, 2012, www.epi .org/publication/bp339-public-sector-jobs-crisis/.

97. Dominic Rushe, "Walmart Hit by Black Friday Strikes Across 46 States, Say Protesters," *The Guardian*, November 23, 2012.

98. Danielle Kurtzleben, "Walmart's Black Friday Protests, Explained," *Vox*, November 28, 2014.

99. Author interview with Andrea Dehlendorf, June 2023.

100. Rolf, *The Fight for Fifteen*.

101. Ibid.

102. Ibid.

103. Author interview with Michelle Miller, May 2022.

104. Adam Pasick, "Before Starbucks Baristas Had Unions, They Had Coworker Petitions," *Wired*, June 27, 2022.

105. Rolf, *The Fight for Fifteen*.

106. Steven Greenhouse, "Movement to Increase McDonald's Minimum Wage Broadens Its Tactics," *New York Times*, March 30, 2015.

107. Annie Lowrey, "Switzerland's Proposal to Pay People for Being Alive," *New York Times Magazine*, November 12, 2013.

108. Louisiana governor Huey Long had his Wealth Program, which also spawned clubs nationwide with millions of supporters. The novelist Upton Sinclair developed a pension proposal for California, which was also home to the Ham and Eggs movement, promoting the disbursement of $30 every Thursday by the state to every unemployed Californian over the age of fifty. Reverend Herbert S. Bigelow of Ohio called for a guaranteed income of $50 per month for everyone over sixty.

109. In her memoir, Roosevelt's secretary of labor Frances Perkins wrote that Roosevelt told her "we have to have it [Social Security]. Congress can't stand the pressure of the Townsend Plan unless we have a real old-age insurance system." See Frances Perkins, *The Roosevelt I Knew*, 294.

110. Martin Luther King Jr., *Where Do We Go from Here: Chaos or Community?* (Boston: Beacon Press, 1967).

111. Gene Demby, "The Mothers Who Fought to Radically Reimagine Welfare." NPR, *Code Switch*, June 9, 2019, www.npr.org/sections

/codeswitch/2019/06/09/730684320/the-mothers-who-fought-to-radically-reimagine-welfare. See also Jacqui Germain, "The National Welfare Rights Organization Wanted Economic Justice for Black Americans," *Teen Vogue*, December 24, 2021.

112. Johnnie Tillmon, "Welfare Is a Women's Issue," *Ms.*, Spring 1972.

113. Germain, "The National Welfare Rights Organization Wanted Economic Justice."

114. The story is well told by Rutger Bregman (author of one of the seminal books on Universal Basic Income) in Rutger Bregman, "The Bizarre Tale of President Nixon and His Basic Income Bill." *The Correspondent*, May 17, 2016, thecorrespondent.com/4503/the-bizarre-tale-of-president-nixon-and-his-basic-income-bill/173117835-c34d6145.

115. "History of the Alaska Permanent Fund," Alaska Permanent Fund Corporation, apfc.org/history/.

116. Peter Barnes, *With Liberty and Dividends for All: How to Save Our Middle Class When Jobs Don't Pay Enough* (Oakland, CA: Berrett-Koehler Publishers, 2014).

117. Andy Stern and Lee Kravitz, *Raising the Floor: How a Universal Basic Income Can Renew Our Economy and Rebuild the American Dream* (New York: PublicAffairs, 2016).

118. Dorian T. Warren, "Reparations and Basic Income," *Boston Review*, May 3, 2017, www.bostonreview.net/forum_response/dorian-t-warren-reparations-and-basic-income/.

119. Author interview with Solana Rice, April 2022.

120. Michael Wayne Sherraden, *Assets and the Poor: New American Welfare Policy* (New York: Routledge, 1991).

121. The Personal Responsibility and Work Opportunity Reconciliation Act of 1996, which significantly reformed welfare, included IDAs as an eligible use of federal funds. Later, the 1998 Assets for Independence Act authorized the U.S. Department of Health and Human Services to provide nonprofit organizations with grants to implement IDA programs in partnership with community development financial institutions, eligible credit unions, and local, state, or tribal governments. See also "Individual Development Accounts: A Vehicle for Low-Income Asset Building and Homeownership," *Evidence Matters*, Fall 2012, www.huduser.gov/portal/periodicals/em/fall12/highlight2.html.

122. Barbara A. Butrica, "A Review of Children's Savings Accounts," Urban Institute, March 2015, www.urban.org/sites/default/files/alfresco/publication-pdfs/2000157-A-Review-of-Childrens-Savings-Accounts.pdf.

123. From Hamilton's speech at the National Economic Association; cited in Ben Steverman, "A Once Radical Idea to Close the Wealth Gap Is Actually Happening," *Bloomberg Businessweek*, March 17, 2022.

124. Pamela Perun, "Matching Private Saving with Federal Dollars," The Retirement Project, Urban Institute, November 1999, www.urban.org /sites/default/files/publication/69691/309272-Matching-Private-Saving -with-Federal-Dollars.PDF.

125. Norm Ornstein, "A Plan to Reduce Inequality: Give $1,000 to Every Newborn Baby." *The Atlantic*, February 13, 2014.

126. Ibid.

127. "Clinton Proposes $5,000 Baby Bonds," Reuters, September 28, 2007.

128. Author interview with Solana Rice conducted April 2022.

129. Ibid.

3. Legitimize (2016–2020)

1. Alana Abramson, "Hillary Clinton Officially Wins Popular Vote by Nearly 2.9 Million," ABC News, December 22, 2016.

2. Galen Hendricks and Seth Hanlon, "The TCJA 2 Years Later: Corporations, Not Workers, Are the Big Winners," Center for American Progress, December 19, 2019, www.americanprogress.org/article/tcja -2-years-later-corporations-not-workers-big-winners/.

3. David Gelles et al., "Inside the C.E.O. Rebellion Against Trump's Advisory Councils," *New York Times*, August 16, 2017; Samea Kamal, "The Entire President's Committee on the Arts and the Humanities Just Resigned in Protest," *Los Angeles Times*, August 18, 2017; Sonam Sheth, "Over a Quarter of the Members on Trump's Cybersecurity Advisory Council Have Resigned En Masse," *Business Insider*, August 29, 2017.

4. Phil McCausland, "Military Joint Chiefs Denounce Charlottesville Racism," NBC News, August 17, 2017.

5. Liam Stack, "Charlottesville Violence and Trump's Reaction Draw Criticism Abroad," *New York Times*, August 17, 2017; Cara McGoogan and Mark Molloy, "Anonymous Shuts Down Neo-Nazi and KKK Websites After Charlottesville Rally," *The Telegraph*, August 14, 2017.

6. Kara Voght, "Is It Race or Class? Darrick Hamilton Showed Bernie the Answer," *Mother Jones*, February 27, 2020.

7. Ibid.

8. Joint Center for Housing Studies of Harvard University, *The State of the Nation's Housing 2016*, 2016, www.jchs.harvard.edu/sites/default /files/media/imp/jchs_2016_state_of_the_nations_housing_lowres_0 .pdf.

9. In 2018, nearly half of all renters were paying 30 percent of their income—or more—on rent. See People's Policy Project, "Social Housing

in the United States," April 2018, www.peoplespolicyproject.org/wp -content/uploads/2018/04/SocialHousing.pdf.

10. Matthew Desmond, "First-Ever Evictions Database Shows We're in the Middle of a Housing Crisis," NPR, April 12, 2018.

11. Jerusalem Demsas, "Colorado's Ingenious Idea for Solving the Housing Crisis," *The Atlantic*, July/August 2023.

12. Rachel Kaufman, "Rent Strikes Heating Up Nationwide, Say Tenant Organizers," *Next City*, June 11, 2018, nextcity.org/urbanist-news/rent -strikes-heating-up-nationwide-say-tenant-organizers.

13. Molly Lambert, "Mariachi Plaza Rent Strike to Defend Boyle Heights," *The Land*, thelandmag.com/mariachi-plaza-rent-strike-defend -boyle-heights/.

14. "Boyle Heights, Los Angeles," Wikipedia, en.wikipedia.org/wiki /Boyle_Heights,_Los_Angeles.

15. Lambert, "Mariachi Plaza Rent Strike to Defend Boyle Heights."

16. Author interview with René Christian Moya, May 2022.

17. Tenant Power Toolkit, tenantpowertoolkit.org/.

18. Author interview with René Christian Moya, May 2022.

19. Matthew Desmond, "The Tenants Who Evicted Their Landlord," *New York Times Magazine*, October 13, 2020.

20. The cities were Boulder, Baltimore, Seattle, Louisville, Denver, Toledo, Minneapolis, Kansas City, New Orleans, and Detroit. The states were Washington, Maryland, and Connecticut. "Enacted Legislation in Eviction Proceedings," National Coalition for a Civil Right to Counsel, June 2023, civilrighttocounsel.org/uploaded_files/283 /RTC_Enacted_Legislation_in_Eviction_Proceedings_FINAL.pdf.

21. Anna Bauman, Sydney Wertheim, and Meghna Chakrabarti, "These States Are Turning to Rent Control: How It Affects Affordable Housing," *On Point*, WBUR, June 19, 2019, www.wbur.org/onpoint/2019 /06/19/new-york-rent-control-laws-oregon-california.

22. Liam Dillon, "California Tenants Will See Cap on Rent Increases Under Bill Sent to Newsom," *Los Angeles Times*, September 11, 2019.

23. Author interview with Alex Schafran, author of the book *The Road to Resegregation*, about Northern California's housing crisis, June 2023.

24. Author interview with Catherine Bracy, June 2023.

25. Allison Kite, "'Today Kansas City Made History': City Council Adopts Tenants Bill of Rights," *Kansas City Star*, December 12, 2019, www.kansascity.com/news/politics-government/article238315408.html.

26. Desmond, "The Tenants Who Evicted Their Landlord."

27. Emily Badger and Quoctrung Bui, "Cities Start to Question an

American Ideal: A House with a Yard on Every Lot," *New York Times*, June 18, 2019.

28. Ibid.

29. Justin Fox, "What Happened When Minneapolis Ended Single-Family Zoning?," *Bloomberg Opinion*, August 20, 2022.

30. Richard D. Kahlenberg, "Updating the Fair Housing Act to Make Housing Affordable." The Century Foundation, April 9, 2018, tcf.org /content/report/updating-fair-housing-act-make-housing-affordable.

31. Author interview with Tara Raghuveer, March 2022.

32. Ibid.

33. Homes Guarantee Campaign, *Homes Guarantee Briefing Book*, September 5, 2019, homesguarantee.com/wp-content/uploads/Homes -Guarantee-_-Briefing-Book.pdf.

34. Francesca Mari, "Imagine a Renters' Utopia. It Might Look like Vienna," *New York Times Magazine*, May 23, 2023.

35. In January 2020, the Congressional Progressive Caucus launched the People's Housing Platform, putting forth legislation that established housing as a human right and introduced aggressive measures to expand tenant rights and deepen national investment in public housing. See Congressional Progressive Caucus, "The People's Housing Platform," January 2020.

36. Harris, "America Wakes Up from Its Dream of Free College."

37. Zaid Jilani, "Betsy DeVos, an Heiress, Bashes Tuition-Free College: 'There's Nothing in Life That's Truly Free,'" *The Intercept*, January 17, 2017.

38. Gabriela Montell, "Getting to and Through College: Tiffany Jones," The Education Trust, June 5, 2019, edtrust.org/the-equity-line/getting -to-through-college-tiffany-jones/.

39. Dr. Tiffany Jones and Katie Berger, *A Promise Fulfilled: A Framework for Equitable Free College Programs*, The Education Trust, 2018, files.eric .ed.gov/fulltext/ED593325.pdf.

40. Dr. Tiffany Jones, "The Cruel Irony of 'Free' College Promises," *New York Times*, March 18, 2019.

41. Chris Geary, "Don't Just Cancel Student Debt: The Cycle Only Ends with Free College," *The Hill*, June 13, 2022.

42. Ibid.

43. Katie Lobosco, "Oregon Promised Free Tuition. Now It's Cutting Back," CNN Money, August 23, 2017.

44. Participating states would get a dollar-for-dollar match from the federal government for however much funding they appropriate for state schools. In exchange, those schools would have to commit to helping

students pay for the full cost of college without taking on debt, through need-based grants to help cover the costs that students couldn't afford. See Ella Nilsen, "Sen. Brian Schatz's Ambitious New Plan for Debt-Free College, Explained," *Vox*, March 20, 2018.

45. Lucy Diavolo, "Bernie Sanders Teamed Up with Ilhan Omar and Pramila Jayapal on a Plan to Cancel All Student Loan Debt," *Teen Vogue*, June 24, 2019.

46. Author interview with Melissa Byrne, March 2023.

47. Melissa Byrne, "Why We Shouldn't Say 'Debt Free College,'" *Medium*, May 7, 2015, medium.com/@mcbyrne/we-don-t-need-debt-free-college -or-a-little-note-to-hillary-clinton-5b1b84b50786.

48. "About Us," Cancel Student Debt, www.cancelstudentdebt.org /about-us.

49. Author interview with Melissa Byrne, March 2023.

50. Bruce Chapman and Lorraine Dearden, "Income-Contingent Loans in Higher Education Financing," *IZA World of Labor*, October 2022. wol .iza.org/uploads/articles/625/pdfs/income-contingent-loans-in-higher -education-financing.pdf.

51. Author interview with Jamila Headley, May 2023.

52. KK Ottesen, "Ady Barkan on Activism, ALS, and Hope in the Face of Crisis," *Washington Post*, June 1, 2022.

53. Claire Judson, "Meet Ady Barkan: America's Greatest Activist, Claremont Class of 2002," *Los Angeles Times – High School Insider*, May 13, 2019, highschool.latimes.com/claremont-high-school/meet-ady-barkan -americas-greatest-activist-claremont-class-of-2002/.

54. Arthur Allen, "The Most Powerful Activist in America Is Dying," *Politico*, March 24, 2019.

55. "5 Questions with Health Care Activist Ady Barkan," *HomeCare Magazine*, September 13, 2021, www.homecaremag.com/news/5-questions -health-care-activist-ady-barkan.

56. Ibid.

57. "Ady Barkan Universal Coverage Hearing Testimony," *Medium*, March 29, 2022, beahero.medium.com/ady-barkan-universal-coverage -hearing-testimony-march-29-2022-f6e02d44cf87.

58. Draper, "How 'Medicare for All' Went Mainstream."

59. Robert Firpo-Cappiello, "Activist Ady Barkan and Actor Bradley Whitford Work to Reform Health Care," *Brain & Life*, April/May 2022, www.brainandlife.org/articles/ady-barkan-bradley-whitford-health-care -reform.

60. NowThis News, "Joe Biden's Emotional Conversation with Activ-

ist Ady Barkan," YouTube video, July 8, 2020, www.youtube.com /watch?v=V4CLoiA3vfQ.

61. Author interview with Jamila Headley, May 2023.

62. NowThis News, "Joe Biden's Emotional Conversation."

63. Abigail Tracy, "'No One Else Can Do This': Ady Barkan Is Using the Health Care Fight to Tip the Scales in 2020," *Vanity Fair*, October 27, 2020.

64. PBS Newshour, "WATCH: Ady Barkan's Full Speech at the 2020 Democratic National Convention," YouTube video, August 18, 2020, www.youtube.com/watch?v=XV7xSzXyaT8.

65. Gabriela Schulte, "Poll: 69 Percent of Voters Support Medicare for All," *The Hill*, April 24, 2020.

66. Kathleen Romig and Kathleen Bryant, "A National Paid Leave Program Would Help Workers, Families," Center on Budget and Policy Priorities, April 27, 2021, www.cbpp.org/research/economy/a-national -paid-leave-program-would-help-workers-families.

67. Ann P. Bartel et al., "Racial and Ethnic Disparities in Access to and Use of Paid Family and Medical Leave: Evidence from Four Nationally Representative Datasets," *Monthly Labor Review*, U.S. Bureau of Labor Statistics, January 2019, doi.org/10.21916/mlr.2019.2.

68. Pronita Gupta et al., "Paid Family and Medical Leave: Critical for Low-Wage Workers and Their Families," Center for Law and Social Policy, December 19, 2018, www.clasp.org/publications/fact-sheet/paid-family -and-medical-leave-critical-low-wage-workers-and-their-families/.

69. PL+US, paidleave.us.

70. Claire Cain Miller, "Walmart and Now Starbucks: Why More Big Companies Are Offering Paid Family Leave," *New York Times*, January 24, 2018.

71. "19 Companies and Industries with Radically Awesome Parental Leave Policies," *Entrepreneur*, April 12, 2017.

72. PL+US, paidleave.us.

73. Krista Tippett, "Ai-jen Poo: This Is Our (Caring) Revolution," *On Being* (podcast), April 2, 2020, onbeing.org/programs/ai-jen-poo-this-is -our-caring-revolution/.

74. Ai-jen Poo, "How 'Roma' Reveals the Complex Reality of Domestic Work," *Hollywood Reporter*, December 14, 2018.

75. Author interview with Ai-jen Poo, July 2022.

76. Tarana Burke was Michelle Williams's guest. Saru Jayaraman was Amy Poehler's guest. Mónica Ramírez was Laura Dern's guest. Marai Larasi went with Emma Watson. Rosa Clemente with Susan Sarandon. Billie Jean King with Emma Stone. Calina Lawrence with Shailene

Woodley. See "Golden Globes 2018: Activists Join Stars on Red Carpet—in Pictures," *The Guardian*, January 8, 2018.

77. Pop Culture Collaborative and National Domestic Workers Alliance, "From *The Help* to *Roma*: How the National Domestic Workers Alliance Is Transforming Narratives in Pop Culture," 2019, www.domesticworkers .org/wp-content/uploads/2021/05/Roma-Case-Study.pdf.

78. Ibid.

79. Kate Taylor, "Here Are the 18 Biggest Bankruptcies of the 'Retail Apocalypse' of 2017," *Business Insider*, December 20, 2017.

80. Derek Thompson, "What in the World Is Causing the Retail Meltdown of 2017?," *The Atlantic*, April 10, 2017.

81. Leticia Miranda, "How Wall Street Bought Toys 'R' Us and Left 30,000 People Without Jobs," *BuzzFeed News*, April 27, 2018.

82. Ibid.

83. Matt Katz, "Laid-Off Employees Protest Toys 'R' Us' Refusal to Provide Severance After Bankruptcy," WNYC, June 3, 2018, www.wnyc .org/story/laid-employees-protest-toys-r-us-refusal-provide-severance -after-bankruptcy/.

84. Nine of the ten largest retail bankruptcies in 2017 were backed by private-equity firms, as were 40 percent of the largest ones from 2015 to early 2017. A third of retail job losses in 2016 and 2017 can be pinned on private-equity ownership. See Bryce Covert, "Hedge Fund Ownership Cost Sears Workers Their Jobs. Now They're Fighting Back," Economic Hardship Reporting Project, April 24, 2019, economichardship.org/2019 /04/hedge-fund-ownership-cost-sears-workers-their-jobs-now-theyre -fighting-back/.

85. Chavie Lieber, "Thousands of Toys R Us Workers Are Getting Severance, Following Months of Protests," *Vox*, November 21, 2018.

86. Daniel J. Munoz, "NJ's Required Severance for Mass Layoffs Is National First," *NJBIZ*, January 21, 2020, njbiz.com/new-jersey-require -severance-pay-laid-off-workers/.

87. Office of Senator Elizabeth Warren, "Warren Introduces Accountable Capitalism Act," press release, August 15, 2018, www.warren.senate.gov /newsroom/press-releases/warren-introduces-accountable-capitalism -act.

88. Jeff Stein, "Bernie Sanders Backs Policies That Dramatically Shift Corporate Power to U.S. Workers," *Washington Post*, May 28, 2019. See also Dylan Matthews, "Bernie Sanders's Most Socialist Idea Yet, Explained," *Vox*, May 29, 2019.

89. Author interview with Michelle Miller, May 2022.

90. Ibid.

91. Coworker Solidarity Fund, coworkerfund.org/

92. Nora Caplan-Bricker, "Tech Workers Are Organizing. Meet the Labor Vets Whispering in Their Ears," *Protocol*, February 26, 2020, www.protocol.com/nonprofit-helps-tech-workers-organize.

93. Emily Stewart, "All of West Virginia's Public School Teachers Are on Strike," *Vox*, February 24, 2018.

94. Jess Bidgood, "West Virginia Raises Teachers' Pay to End Statewide Strike," *New York Times*, March 6, 2018.

95. Alia Wong, "The Ripple Effect of the West Virginia Teachers' Victory," *The Atlantic*, March 7, 2018.

96. Sarah Jaffe, *Work Won't Love You Back* (New York: Bold Type Books, 2021), 87.

97. Moriah Balingit, "First It Was West Virginia. Then Kentucky and Oklahoma. Now Arizona and Colorado Teachers Prepare to Walk Out," *Washington Post*, April 26, 2018.

98. Andrea Denhoed, "Striking Oklahoma Teachers Win Historic School-Funding Increase and Keep on Marching," *New Yorker*, April 4, 2018.

99. Alana Semuels, "Is This the End of Public-Sector Unions in America?," *The Atlantic*, June 27, 2018.

100. Sarah Jaffe, "Inside the Hard Road to Transform the Teachers' Movement into Real Power," *Medium*, October 19, 2018, gen.medium .com/inside-the-hard-road-to-transform-the-teachers-movement-into -real-power-f5932fc8ab6f.

101. Ian Kullgren, "'Educator Spring' Spawns Wave of Teacher Candidates," *Politico*, July 4, 2018.

102. Denhoed, "Striking Oklahoma Teachers Win Historic School-Funding Increase." See also Dave Jamieson, "Record Number of Oklahomans Filing for Office During Teacher Walkout," *HuffPost*, April 12, 2018.

103. Jessica Campisi, "Nearly 1,800 Educators Ran for Office in the Midterms. Here's Who Won," *K-12 Dive*, November 7, 2018, www.k12dive .com/news/nearly-1800-educators-ran-for-office-in-the-midterms-heres -who-won/541436/.

104. Ibid.

105. Nathanael Johnson, "Young Activists and Alexandria Ocasio-Cortez Push Nancy Pelosi for Green New Deal," *Grist*, November 14, 2018, grist .org/article/young-activists-and-alexandria-ocasio-cortez-push-nancy -pelosi-for-green-new-deal/.

106. David Roberts, "The Green New Deal, Explained: How the Ambitious Policy Plan Works," *Vox*, March 30, 2019.

107. "How the Green New Deal Changed the Conversation (with Rhiana Gunn-Wright)," *How to Save a Country* (podcast), Roosevelt Institute,

November 3, 2022, rooseveltinstitute.org/2022/11/03/podcast-episode -7-how-the-green-new-deal-changed-the-conversation-with-rhiana -gunn-wright/.

108. Michael Tubbs, *The Deeper the Roots: A Memoir of Hope and Home* (New York: Flatiron Books, 2021).

109. Stockton Economic Empowerment Demonstration, www .stocktondemonstration.org/.

110. "Magnolia Mother's Trust," Springboard to Opportunities, springboardto.org/magnolia-mothers-trust/.

111. Author interview with Aisha Nyandoro, August 2022.

112. University Research Center – Mississippi Institutions of Higher Learning, "Is There an Incentive for Mississippians Receiving Public Assistance to Work?," August 2017, www.mississippi.edu/urc/downloads /public_assistance_work_1708.pdf.

113. Details of the policy are found in this piece, which includes a link to a white paper on the proposal: Natalie Foster and Chris Hoene, "Newsom's Bold Proposal: A Cost-of-Living Refund to Make California Affordable," *San Francisco Chronicle*, January 14, 2019.

114. Office of Governor Gavin Newsom, "Governor Newsom Issues Proclamation Declaring CalEITC Awareness Week," press release, January 30, 2020, www.gov.ca.gov/2020/01/30/governor-newsom-issues -proclamation-declaring-caleitc-awareness-week/.

115. Dedrick Asante-Muhammad et al., "The Road to Zero Wealth." Prosperity Now and the Institute for Policy Studies, September 2017, prosperitynow.org/files/PDFs/road_to_zero_wealth.pdf.

116. Author interview with Solana Rice, April 2022.

117. Rebecca Tippett et al., *Beyond Broke: Why Closing the Racial Wealth Gap Is a Priority for National Economic Security*, Global Policy Solutions, April 2014, globalpolicysolutions.org/wp-content/uploads/2014/04 /BeyondBroke_Exec_Summary.pdf.

118. Khaing Zaw, Jhumpa Bhattacharya, Anne Price, Darrick Hamilton, and William Darrity Jr., *Women, Race & Wealth*, Samuel DuBois Cook Center on Social Equity and Insight Center for Community Economic Development Research Brief Series vol. 1, January 2017, socialequity .duke.edu/wp-content/uploads/2019/10/Women-Race-Wealth.pdf.

119. Neil Bhutta et al., "Disparities in Wealth by Race and Ethnicity in the 2019 Survey of Consumer Finances," *FEDS Notes*, Federal Reserve Board, September 28, 2020, www.federalreserve.gov/econres/notes/feds -notes/disparities-in-wealth-by-race-and-ethnicity-in-the-2019-survey -of-consumer-finances-20200928.htm.

120. Kilolo Kijakazi et al., *The Color of Wealth in the Nation's Capital*, Duke University, Urban Institute, The New School, and the Insight

Center for Community Economic Development, 2016, www.urban.org /sites/default/files/publication/85341/2000986-2-the-color-of-wealth -in-the-nations-capital_7.pdf.

121. Darrick Hamilton, "The Moral Burden on Economists," NEA Presidential Address, 2017, journals.sagepub.com/doi/abs/10.1177 /0034644620968104?journalCode=rbpa.

122. Ben Steverman, "A Once Radical Idea to Close the Wealth Gap Is Actually Happening," *Bloomberg Businessweek*, March 17, 2022.

123. Fabiola Cineas, "Baby Bonds Could Shrink the Black-White Wealth Gap," *Vox*, February 17, 2021.

124. Naomi Zewde, "Universal Baby Bonds Reduce Black-White Wealth Inequality, Progressively Raise Net Worth of All Young Adults," *Review of Black Political Economy* 47, no. 1 (March 2020): 117–150, journals .sagepub.com/doi/full/10.1177/0034644619885321.

125. Ibid.

126. Ibid.

127. Darity, Paul, and Hamilton, "An Economic Bill of Rights for the 21st Century."

128. Author interview with Solana Rice, April 2022.

129. "Transcript: Ezra Klein Interviews Thomas Piketty," *New York Times*, June 7, 2022.

130. Ibid.

131. Ibid.

132. "Candidates' Views on the Issues: Economy—Affordable Housing," *Politico*, last updated December 19, 2019.

133. "Candidates' Views on the Issues: Education Reform—Free College," *Politico*, last updated February 21, 2020.

134. "Candidates' Views on the Issues: Health Care—Affordable Care Act," *Politico*, last updated February 14, 2020.

135. "Candidates' Views on the Issues: Health Care—Medicare for All," *Politico*, last updated February 19, 2020.

136. "Candidates' Views on the Issues: Economy—Paid Leave," *Politico*, last updated January 8, 2020.

137. Claire Cain Miller, Shane Goldmacher, and Thomas Kaplan, "Biden Announces $775 Billion Plan to Help Working Parents and Caregivers," *New York Times*, July 21, 2020.

138. In 2017 the median annual salary for kindergarten and elementary school teachers was $56,900, and it was only $22,290 per year for workers in child care centers. Data from Zachary B. Wolf, "How Would Elizabeth Warren's Ambitious Child Care Proposal Work?," CNN, February 19, 2019.

139. Anna North, "We Asked All the 2020 Democrats How They'd Fix Child Care. Here's What They Said," *Vox*, May 22, 2019.

140. Elaine Maag, "Senator Kamala Harris Proposed a Bold Tax Credit to Help Low- and Middle-Income Workers," Tax Policy Center, August 13, 2020, www.taxpolicycenter.org/taxvox/senator-kamala-harris-proposed -bold-tax-credit-help-low-and-middle-income-workers.

141. "Candidates' Views on the Issues: Economy—Minimum Wage," *Politico*, last updated January 8, 2020.

142. Dylan Matthews, "Cory Booker's New Big Idea: Guaranteeing Jobs for Everyone Who Wants One," *Vox*, April 20, 2018.

143. Bernie Sanders, "Jobs for All," berniesanders.com/issues/jobs-for -all/; Senator Kirsten Gillibrand (@SenGillibrand), Twitter, April 17, 2018, twitter.com/SenGillibrand/status/986268532244733952?s=20.

4. Win (2020–2022)

1. From the introduction to a reprint of Milton Friedman, *Capitalism and Freedom* (Chicago: University of Chicago Press, 2020).

2. Heather Cox Richardson, "Interview with President Biden," Substack, March 4, 2022, heathercoxrichardson.substack.com/p/interview -with-president-biden.

3. James Medlock (a pseudonym), @jdcmedlock, Twitter, January 15, 2021, twitter.com/jdcmedlock/status/1350143296459341826?lang=en.

4. Cox Richardson, "Interview with President Biden."

5. Ezra Klein, "Four Ways of Looking at the Radicalism of Joe Biden," *New York Times*, April 8, 2021.

6. "Remarks of President Joe Biden—State of the Union Address," The White House, February 7, 2023, www.whitehouse.gov/briefing-room /speeches-remarks/2023/02/07/remarks-of-president-joe-biden-state -of-the-union-address-as-prepared-for-delivery/.

7. "Federal Rental Assistance Fact Sheets," Center on Budget and Policy Priorities, January 19, 2022, www.cbpp.org/research/housing /federal-rental-assistance-fact-sheets#US.

8. Christine Delianne et al., "Project Roomkey, the Golden State's Grand Experiment," *Nowhere to Go* (a project of the University of Maryland's Howard Center for Investigative Journalism), July 13, 2020, homeless .cnsmaryland.org/2020/07/13/project-roomkey/.

9. Author interview with Amy Turk, April 2023.

10. "Hotels to Housing: Case Studies," National Alliance to End Homelessness, July 20, 2021, endhomelessness.org/resource/hotels-to-housing -case-studies/.

11. Annie Lowrey, "Cancel Rent," *The Atlantic*, May 2, 2020.

12. Scottie Andrew and Anna Bahney, "New Data Shows More Americans Are Having Trouble Paying Their Rent," CNN, April 9, 2020.

13. "Federal Eviction and Foreclosure Moratoria and Rental Assistance During COVID-19," Congressional Research Service, March 30, 2021, crsreports.congress.gov/product/pdf/IN/IN11516.

14. Department of the Treasury, "New Treasury Data Shows Over 80% of Emergency Rental Assistance Delivered to Lowest-Income Households," press release, February 24, 2022, home.treasury.gov/news/press-releases/jy0606.

15. Ramenda Cyrus, "The Tenants Who Went to Washington," *American Prospect*, February 9, 2023.

16. "The White House Blueprint for a Renters Bill of Rights," The White House, January 2023, www.whitehouse.gov/wp-content/uploads/2023/01/White-House-Blueprint-for-a-Renters-Bill-of-Rights-1.pdf.

17. Patrick Spauster, "How Backlash Reversed a Florida City's Reforms to Allow Denser Housing," *Bloomberg*, February 2, 2023.

18. Diana Budds, "AOC Is a YIMBY Now," *Curbed*, January 13, 2022, www.curbed.com/2022/01/aoc-2022-pledge-pro-housing-yimby.html.

19. Bill McKibben, "Yes in Our Backyards," *Mother Jones*, May/June 2023.

20. Hannah Wiley, "In Groundbreaking Plan, California Allows Affordable Housing on Some Commercial Properties," *Los Angeles Times*, September 28, 2022.

21. "Senate Bill 22-232: Creation of Colorado Workforce Housing Trust Authority," Colorado General Assembly, 2022 Regular Session, leg.colorado.gov/bills/sb22-232.

22. Patrick Anderson and Katherine Gregg, "The General Assembly Session Is Over. Here's What Passed, and What Didn't," *Providence Journal*, June 23, 2022; Rachel M. Cohen, "How State Governments Are Reimagining American Public Housing," *Vox*, August 4, 2022.

23. Ibid.

24. "President Biden Announces New Actions to Ease the Burden of Housing Costs," The White House Briefing Room, May 16, 2022, www.whitehouse.gov/briefing-room/statements-releases/2022/05/16/president-biden-announces-new-actions-to-ease-the-burden-of-housing-costs/.

25. Rachel M. Cohen, "The Big, Neglected Problem That Should Be Biden's Top Priority," *Vox*, March 1, 2023.

26. "Student Loan Cancellation Under the HEROES Act," Congressional Research Service, April 14, 2023, crsreports.congress.gov/product/pdf/R/R47505.

27. Author interview with Braxton Brewington, June 2022.

28. Ibid.

29. Ibid.

30. Ibid.

31. Author interview with Melissa Byrne, April 2023.

32. Debt Collective, *Can't Pay, Won't Pay: The Case for Economic Disobedience and Debt Abolition* (Chicago: Haymarket Books, 2020), 13–14.

33. Ibid., 21.

34. "Household Debt and Credit Report," Federal Reserve Bank of New York, www.newyorkfed.org/microeconomics/hhdc.

35. U.S. Department of Education, "Education Department Approves $5.8 Billion in Group Discharge to Cancel All Remaining Loans for 56,000 Borrowers Who Attended Corinthian," press release, June 1, 2022, www.ed.gov/news/press-releases/education-department-approves-58-billion-group-discharge-cancel-all-remaining-loans-560000-borrowers-who-attended-corinthian-colleges.

36. Author interview with Astra Taylor, July 2022.

37. Eleni Schirmer, "The Aging Student Debtors of America," *New Yorker*, July 27, 2022.

38. Ibid.

39. Eleni Schirmer, "How the Government Cancelled Betty Ann's Debts," *New Yorker*, February 23, 2023.

40. Astra Taylor (@astradisastra), Twitter, August 24, 2022, twitter.com/astradisastra/status/1562500486473064449.

41. "Covid-19 Mortality Overview," Centers for Disease Control and Prevention, National Center for Health Statistics, www.cdc.gov/nchs/covid19/mortality-overview.htm.

42. Mary T. Bassett, Jarvis T. Chen, and Nancy Krieger, "Variation in Racial/Ethnic Disparities in COVID-19 Mortality by Age in the United States: A Cross-Sectional Study," *PLOS Medicine*, October 20, 2020, doi.org/10.1371/journal.pmed.1003402.

43. Convergence Magazine, "Catherine Kennedy, RN: Nurses' Fight for Public Health and Worker Power," YouTube video, March 3, 2021, www.youtube.com/watch?v=kHFspAlHU14.

44. Hope Corrigan, "'There Is No Plan at All': Nurses Battling Coronavirus Face Deteriorating Work Conditions," *Quartz*, April 1, 2020, qz.com/1828685/nurses-fighting-coronavirus-face-deteriorating-working-conditions/.

45. Ed Yong, "Why Health-Care Workers Are Quitting in Droves," *The Atlantic*, November 16, 2021.

46. Ady Barkan, "Universal Coverage Hearing Testimony," *Medium*,

March 29, 2022. beahero.medium.com/ady-barkan-universal-coverage
-hearing-testimony-march-29-2022-f6e02d44cf87.

47. Luke Darby, "72 Percent of All Rural Hospital Closures Are in States That Rejected the Medicaid Expansion," *GQ*, July 30, 2019.

48. Julia Shaver, "The State of Telehealth Before and After the COVID-19 Pandemic," *Primary Care*, 49, no. 4 (2022): 517–30, www.ncbi.nlm.nih .gov/pmc/articles/PMC9035352/.

49. Ibid.

50. Robert S. Huckman, "What Will U.S. Health Care Look Like After the Pandemic?," *Harvard Business Review*, April 7, 2020, hbr.org/2020 /04/what-will-u-s-health-care-look-like-after-the-pandemic.

51. Philip Ball, "The Lightning-Fast Quest for COVID Vaccines—and What It Means for Other Diseases," *Nature*, December 18, 2020, www .nature.com/articles/d41586-020-03626-1.

52. Sydney Lupkin, "The U.S. Paid Billions to Get Enough COVID Vaccines Last Fall. What Went Wrong?," NPR, August 25, 2021.

53. Decades in the Making: mRNA COVID-19 Vaccines," National Institutes of Health, January 10, 2023, covid19.nih.gov/nih-strategic -response-covid-19/decades-making-mrna-covid-19-vaccines.

54. Lupkin, "The U.S. Paid Billions to Get Enough COVID Vaccines."

55. David Heath and Gus Garcia-Roberts, "Luck, Foresight and Science: How an Unheralded Team Developed a COVID-19 Vaccine in Record Time," *USA Today*, January 27, 2021.

56. "Defense Production Act of 1950, as Amended," Federal Emergency Management Agency (FEMA), August 13, 2018, www.fema.gov/sites /default/files/2020-03/Defense_Production_Act_2018.pdf.

57. Kai Ruggeri et al., "Role of Military Forces in the New York State Response to COVID-19, *JAMA Health Forum* 3, no. 8 (2022), jamanet-work.com/journals/jama-health-forum/fullarticle/2794833.

58. Nadia Lathan, "The Story of the COVID-19 Vaccine, from the Lab to Millions of Arms," University of California Berkeley School of Public Health, March 30, 2023, publichealth.berkeley.edu/covid-19/the-story -of-the-covid-19-vaccine. While I'm making the point that government investment can be a game changer, I also want to lift up Priti Krishtel and the Initiative for Medicines, Access & Knowledge's commentary on how that investment could have also changed the game on global vaccine equity and didn't. See Sriram Shamasunder and Priti Krishtel, "Opinion: What Native Americans Can Teach Us About Generosity in a Pandemic," NPR, May 10, 2021.

59. Barkan, "Universal Coverage Hearing Testimony."

60. Noah Weiland, "Millions on Medicaid May Soon Lose Coverage as Pandemic Protections Expire," *New York Times*, April 3, 2023.

61. Kevin Quealy and Margot Sanger-Katz, "Obamacare's About to Get a Lot More Affordable. These Maps Show How," *New York Times*, March 10, 2021.

62. "Biden-Harris Administration Highlights Health Insurance Subsidies That Promoted Critical Increases in Enrollment and Cost Savings," The White House, March 10, 2022, www.whitehouse.gov/briefing -room/statements-releases/2022/03/10/during-week-of-anniversary-of -american-rescue-plan-biden-harris-administration-highlights-health -insurance-subsidies-that-promoted-critical-increases-in-enrollment -and-cost-savings/.

63. "Inflation Reduction Act Lowers Health Care Costs for Millions of Americans," Centers for Medicare & Medicaid Services, October 5, 2022, www.cms.gov/newsroom/fact-sheets/inflation-reduction-act -lowers-health-care-costs-millions-americans.

64. Author interview with Jamila Headley, May 2023.

65. Heather Long, "The Big Factor Holding Back U.S. Economic Recovery: Child Care," *Washington Post*, July 3, 2020.

66. Emily Swanson and Ricardo Alonso-Zaldivar, "Most Americans Would Rather Age at Home, Says Poll," Associated Press (via the *Christian Science Monitor*), May 3, 2021.

67. Donald Judd, "Biden Signs Executive Order Aimed at Expanding Access to Long-Term Care and Child Care," CNN, April 18, 2023.

68. Ai-jen's presentation is available at Economic Security Project, "Bold v. Old: Ai-jen Poo on Universal Family Care," YouTube video, March 20, 2019, www.youtube.com/watch?v=qpy7_wQPosc.

69. Ibid.

70. Benjamin W. Veghte et al., *Designing Universal Family Care: State-Based Social Insurance Programs for Early Child Care and Education, Paid Family and Medical Leave, and Long-Term Services and Supports*, National Academy of Social Insurance, 2019, universalfamilycare.org /wp-content/uploads/2019/06/Designing-Universal-Family-Care_Digital -Version_FINAL.pdf.

71. Miller, Goldmacher, and Kaplan, "Biden Announces $775 Billion Plan to Help Working Parents and Caregivers."

72. Mia Mercado, "How Ai-jen Poo Gets It Done," *The Cut*, April 4, 2022, www.thecut.com/2022/04/how-ai-jen-poo-gets-it-done.html.

73. "Fact Sheet: Biden-Harris Administration Announces Most Sweeping Set of Executive Actions to Improve Care in History," The White House, April 18, 2023, www.whitehouse.gov/briefing-room/statements -releases/2023/04/18/fact-sheet-biden-harris-administration-announces -most-sweeping-set-of-executive-actions-to-improve-care-in-history/.

74. Kate Dore, "This Lesser-Known Tax Credit May Offer Families Another Write-Off," CNBC, August 20, 2021.

75. "Care Can't Wait," National Domestic Workers Alliance, www.domesticworkers.org/programs-and-campaigns/developing-policy-solutions/careagenda/care-cant-wait/.

76. See Jim Tankersley, "To Tap Federal Funds, Chip Makers Will Need to Provide Child Care," *New York Times*, February 27, 2023.

77. By "major" funding, I mean funding amounts of at least $150 million. Andrea Hsu, "Biden Has Big Ideas for Fixing Child Care. For Now a Small Workaround Will Have to Do," NPR, March 17, 2023.

78. "Executive Order on Increasing Access to High-Quality Care and Supporting Caregivers," The White House, April 18, 2023, www.whitehouse.gov/briefing-room/presidential-actions/2023/04/18/executive-order-on-increasing-access-to-high-quality-care-and-supporting-caregivers/.

79. Victoria Uwumarogie, "'The Nap Ministry' Founder Tricia Hersey on Rest as Protest Against White Supremacy and Capitalism," *Essence*, October 6, 2022.

80. "r/antiwork - Subreddit Stats and Analysis," SubredditStats, subredditstats.com/r/antiwork.

81. Steven Greenhouse, "What Biden Has Done—and Still Can Do—for Workers," The Century Foundation, July 7, 2022, tcf.org/content/report/what-biden-has-done-and-still-can-do-for-workers/.

82. "Employment Recovery in the Wake of the COVID-19 Pandemic," Bureau of Labor Statistics, December 2020, www.bls.gov/opub/mlr/2020/article/employment-recovery.htm.

83. Stefan Sykes, "8 Million Americans Slipped into Poverty amid the Coronavirus Pandemic, New Study Finds," NBC News, October 16, 2020.

84. Nancy Cleeland, "As Jobs Disappear, Employees Hang On to What They Have," Society for HR Management, July 2, 2020, www.shrm.org/resourcesandtools/hr-topics/employee-relations/pages/afraid-to-leave-job-covid.aspx.

85. Steven Greenhouse, "'Striketober' Is Showing Workers' Rising Power—but Will It Lead to Lasting Change?," *The Guardian*, October 23, 2021.

86. Ibid.

87. Shana Blackwell as told to Abigail Weinberg, "The Walmart Stocker Who Quit and Told Off Her Bosses over the Intercom," *Mother Jones*, November 20, 2020.

88. Jennifer Liu, "1 in 4 Workers Quit Their Job This Year—Here's What Companies Are Getting Wrong About Retention," CNBC, October 14, 2021.

89. Federal Reserve Bank of Atlanta Wage Growth Tracker, September 2022, www.atlantafed.org/chcs/wage-growth-tracker.

90. "Average Hourly Earnings of All Employees, Leisure and Hospitality," Federal Reserve Economic Data (FRED), fred.stlouisfed.org/series /CES7000000003.

91. Council of Economic Advisers, "Pandemic Shifts in Black Employment and Wages," The White House, August 24, 2022, www.whitehouse .gov/cea/written-materials/2022/08/24/pandemic-shifts-in-black -employment-and-wages.

92. Michael Corkery, "Dollar General Is Deemed a 'Severe Violator' by the Labor Dept.," *New York Times*, March 28, 2023.

93. Michael Corkery, "How a Dollar General Employee Went Viral on TikTok," *New York Times*, April 18, 2022. For a great interview with Mary, listen to Anna Sale's *Death, Sex & Money* June 15, 2022, podcast interview with her: www.wnycstudios.org/podcasts/deathsexmoney /episodes/dollar-general-mary-gundel-death-sex-money.

94. Jodi Kantor, Karen Weise, and Grace Ashford, "The Amazon That Customers Don't See," *New York Times*, June 15, 2021.

95. Jodi Kantor and Karen Weise, "How Two Best Friends Beat Amazon," *New York Times*, April 2, 2022.

96. President Biden (@POTUS), Twitter, February 28, 2021, twitter .com/POTUS/status/1366191901196644354.

97. Kantor and Weise, "How Two Best Friends Beat Amazon."

98. Jason Del Rey, "America Finally Gets an Amazon Union," *Vox*, April 1, 2022.

99. Joseph Konig and Rebecca Greenberg, "Sanders, Ocasio-Cortez Rally with Amazon Union," *NY1*, April 24, 2022, www.ny1.com/nyc /all-boroughs/politics/2022/04/24/sanders--ocasio-cortez-rally-with -amazon-union; Juliana Kaplan, "President Biden Says Amazon Union Organizer Christian Smalls Is His 'Kind of Trouble' and 'Let's Not Stop,'" *Business Insider*, May 11, 2022.

100. Author interview with Michelle Miller, May 2022.

101. Nick Bowlin, "'Pure Propaganda': Inside Starbucks' Anti-union Tactics," *The Guardian*, May 4, 2022.

102. Caitlin Harrington, "Before Starbucks Baristas Had Unions, They Had Coworker Petitions," *Wired*, June 27, 2022.

103. Emily Peck, "Groundbreaking California Fast-Food Law Heads to Statewide Referendum and Big Political Fight," *Axios*, January 25, 2023, www.axios.com/2023/01/25/california-fast-food-law-statewide -referendum; Suhauna Hussain, "Fast-Food Industry Pushes to Halt AB 257, a California Law That Could Raise Worker Wages," *Los Angeles Times*, December 5, 2022.

104. Author interview with Sharon Block, July 2023.

105. "Statement on Good Jobs," Good Jobs Champions Group, Aspen Institute, www.aspeninstitute.org/programs/good-jobs-champions-group/.

106. Rachel Treisman, "California Program Giving $500 No-Strings-Attached Stipends Pays Off, Study Finds," NPR, March 4, 2021. See also SEED, "Guaranteed Income Increases Employment, Improves Financial and Physical Health," press release, March 3, 2021, www.stocktondemonstration.org/press-landing/guaranteed-income-increases-employment-improves-financial-and-physical-health; Dr. Stacia West, Dr. Amy Castro Baker, Sukhi Samra, Erin Coltrera, "Preliminary Analysis, SEED's First Year," SEED, March 2021, static1.squarespace.com/static/6039d612b17d055cac14070f/t/6050294a1212aa40fdaf773a/1615866187890/SEED_Preliminary+Analysis-SEEDs+First+Year_Final+Report_Individual+Pages+.pdf; and Stacia West and Amy Castro, "Impact of Guaranteed Income on Health, Finances, and Agency: Findings from the Stockton Randomized Controlled Trial," *Journal of Urban Health*, April 2023, 227–44, pubmed.ncbi.nlm.nih.gov/37037977/.

107. West and Castro, "Impact of Guaranteed Income on Health, Finances, and Agency."

108. "Baby's First Years," www.babysfirstyears.com/, cited in Jason DeParle, "Cash Aid to Poor Mothers Increases Brain Activity in Babies, Study Finds," *New York Times*, January 24, 2022.

109. Farhad Manjoo, "Biden Has Helped the Quiet Revolution of Giving People Money," *New York Times*, September 23, 2022.

110. Stephanie Bonin, "$2,000/month to Every American #MoneyForThePeople #COVID19," Change.org, March 21, 2020, www.change.org/p/give-2000-month-to-every-american-moneyforthepeople-covid19.

111. Clare Foran et al., "Trump Signs Historic $2 Trillion Stimulus After Congress Passes It Friday," CNN, March 27, 2020.

112. "Child Tax Credit Overview," National Conference of State Legislatures (NCSL), www.ncsl.org/human-services/child-tax-credit-overview.

113. "Child Tax Credit," The White House, www.whitehouse.gov/child-tax-credit/.

114. Cory Turner, "The Expanded Child Tax Credit Briefly Slashed Child Poverty. Here's What Else It Did," NPR, January 27, 2022.

115. "Sixth Child Tax Credit Payment Kept 3.7 Million Children Out of Poverty in December," Columbia University Center on Poverty and Social Policy, January 20, 2022, www.povertycenter.columbia.edu/publication/montly-poverty-december-2021.

116. Natalie Foster, "Today Is a Good Day," *Medium*, July 19, 2021, nataliefoster.medium.com/today-is-a-good-day-336e3fa92ab0.

117. "A Brief History: The Social Security Administration," Social Security Administration, www.ssa.gov/history/briefhistory3.html.

118. Neil Bhutta et al., "Disparities in Wealth by Race and Ethnicity in the 2019 Survey of Consumer Finances," *FEDS Notes*, Federal Reserve Board, September 28, 2020, www.federalreserve.gov/econres/notes/feds-notes/disparities-in-wealth-by-race-and-ethnicity-in-the-2019-survey-of-consumer-finances-20200928.html.

119. Catherine Park, "Connecticut to Give $3,200 Bond to Every Child Born into Poverty," FOX 5 DC, June 21, 2021, www.fox5dc.com/news/connecticut-to-give-3200-bond-to-every-child-born-into-poverty.

120. Steverman, "A Once Radical Idea to Close the Wealth Gap Is Actually Happening," *Bloomberg Businessweek*, March 17, 2022

121. To qualify, the child must be born to a family enrolled in Medicaid and making less than 300 percent of the federal poverty line. Rebecca Karpen, "Dismantling the Lucky Sperm Club, One Baby Bond Program at a Time," Inequality.org, August 10, 2022, inequality.org/research/local-baby-bonds/.

122. Charlotte Schubert, "Baby Bond Legislation Aims to Address Wealth Gaps in Washington State," *GeekWire*, February 8, 2023, www.geekwire.com/2023/baby-bond-legislation-aims-to-address-wealth-gaps-in-washington-state/.

123. Senate Bill 854: The Hope, Opportunity, Perseverance, and Empowerment for Children Act of 2022, California State Legislature.

124. Elizabeth Aguilera, "Some COVID Orphans in California Will Get Financial Help," CalMatters, July 22, 2022, calmatters.org/california-divide/2022/07/covid-orphans-trust-funds/.

125. "Hidden Pain: America's Children Who Lost a Parent or Caregiver to COVID-19 and What the Nation Can Do to Help Them," COVID Collaborative, December 2021, www.covidcollaborative.us/assets/uploads/pdf/HIDDEN-PAIN.Report.Final.pdf.

126. Cambri Guest, "The Silent Pandemic: The Children COVID Left Behind," USC Annenberg Media, August 8, 2022, www.uscannenbergmedia.com/2022/08/08/the-silent-pandemic-the-children-covid-left-behind/.

127. "Sen. Skinner Introduces New Bill Strengthening CA's HOPE Accounts," Office of Senator Nancy Skinner, January 26, 2023, sd09.senate.ca.gov/news/20230126-sen-skinner-introduces-new-bill-strengthening-ca%E2%80%99s-hope-accounts.

128. Ibid.

129. Madeline Brown et al., "The State of Baby Bonds: Creating Assets for All Children," Urban Institute, February 2023, www.urban.org/sites/default/files/2023-02/The%20State%20of%20Baby%20Bonds.pdf.

130. Steverman, "A Once Radical Idea to Close the Wealth Gap Is Actually Happening."

131. Author interview with Solana Rice, April 2022.

132. Claire Cain Miller and Alicia Parlapiano, "The U.S. Built a European-Style Welfare State. It's Largely Over," *New York Times*, April 6, 2023.

133. Author interview with Astra Taylor, July 2022.

134. The Fairness Project, thefairnessproject.org/.

135. Arundhati Roy, "'The Pandemic Is a Portal,'" *Financial Times*, April 3, 2020.

5. Room to Breathe (On the Implications of the Guarantee)

1. Annie Lowrey, "The Time Tax," *The Atlantic*, July 27 2021.

2. Caleb Watney, "America's Innovation Engine Is Slowing," *The Atlantic*, July 19, 2020; Parag Khanna, "The Brain Drain That Is Killing America's Economy," *Time*, January 21, 2021; Craig Axford, "The Great American Brain Drain," *Medium*, June 11, 2018, craig-axford.medium.com/the-great-american-brain-drain-b0da9eb7ed2.

3. David Leonhardt, "Lost Einsteins: The Innovations We're Missing," *New York Times*, December 3, 2017.

4. Ibid.

5. Alex Bell et al., "Who Becomes an Inventor in America? The Importance of Exposure to Innovation," Equality of Opportunity Project, www.equality-of-opportunity.org/assets/documents/inventors_summary.pdf.

6. Roy Bahat, "To Support Innovation, Subsidize Creators," *Washington Post*, October 2, 2015.

7. Roy Bahat (@roybahat), Twitter, February 11, 2022, twitter.com/roybahat/status/1639397423520055296.

8. Yusuf Berkan Altun, "Pandemic Fuels Global Growth of Entrepreneurship and Startup Frenzy," *Forbes*, April 9, 2021; Ben Casselman, "Start-Up Boom in the Pandemic Is Growing Stronger," *New York Times*, August 19, 2021.

9. Casselman, "Start-Up Boom in the Pandemic Is Growing Stronger."

10. The contest announcement, along with judges and terms, is available at Cara DeFabio, "Into the Black: A Short Fiction Contest with a Big Prize," *Medium*, September 6, 2017, medium.com/@caradefabio/into-the-black-a-short-fiction-contest-with-a-big-prize-f91cd6553967. Sandra's entire story appears in Evan Narcisse, "Read the *Into the Black* Contest's Winning Story, Set in a Future Where Economics Are Also Humane," *Gizmodo*, January 24, 2018, gizmodo.com/read-the-into-the-black-contests-winning-story-set-in-1822338909.

11. Library of Congress, Instagram post, April 12, 2023, www.instagram.com/p/Cq8iOtfAPMA/.

INDEX

ABOUT THE AUTHOR

Natalie Foster is a leading architect of the movement to build an inclusive and resilient economy. She is the president and co-founder of Economic Security Project and Aspen Institute Fellow, and her work and writing has appeared in the *New York Times*, *USA Today*, *Time*, *Business Insider*, CNN, and *The Guardian*. She previously founded the sharing economy community Peers and co-founded Rebuild the Dream with Van Jones, and served as digital director for President Obama's Organizing for America. A daughter of a preacher from Kansas, Natalie lives in Oakland, California, with her husband and two kids. *The Guarantee* is her first book.

PUBLISHING IN
THE PUBLIC INTEREST

Thank you for reading this book published by The New Press; we hope you enjoyed it. New Press books and authors play a crucial role in sparking conversations about the key political and social issues of our day.

We hope that you will stay in touch with us. Here are a few ways to keep up to date with our books, events, and the issues we cover:

- Sign up at www.thenewpress.com/subscribe to receive updates on New Press authors and issues and to be notified about local events
- www.facebook.com/newpressbooks
- www.twitter.com/thenewpress
- www.instagram.com/thenewpress

Please consider buying New Press books not only for yourself, but also for friends and family and to donate to schools, libraries, community centers, prison libraries, and other organizations involved with the issues our authors write about.

The New Press is a 501(c)(3) nonprofit organization; if you wish to support our work with a tax-deductible gift please visit www.thenewpress.com/donate or use the QR code below.